GW00643036

THE DUBLIN REVIEW READER

The Dublin Review Reader

EDITED BY BRENDAN BARRINGTON

For Anna
with thanks & love

Brian

Dublin Review Books

Dublin Review Books
P.O. Box 7948, Dublin 1, Ireland

www.thedublinreview.com

Set in Swift Light. Printed by Betaprint, Dublin.

ISBN 978-0-9556580-0-6

Contents

Editor's note 1

A Dublin journal
ANDREW O'HAGAN 5

Adventures with old things
ANGELA BOURKE 30

Yeats and the lights of Dublin
DEREK MAHON 39

Crossing the Delaware
CHRISTINA HUNT MAHONY 53

Shalom à la crème
IAN SANSOM 61

This is what libraries are for
CIARAN CARSON 75

Good works for the locals
MAURICE WALSH 88

Contents

Five, four, three, two, one
ANNE ENRIGHT 97

Lost time accidents
BRIAN DILLON 108

The shadow line
AMIT CHAUDHURI 129

Boarders
LIA MILLS 141

The red and the green
ROY FOSTER 151

Fables of home
GEORGE SZIRTES 159

If a guy doesn't think this is fun …
MOLLY MCCLOSKEY 175

The view from street level
CATRIONA CROWE 187

Sixth sense, seventh heaven
SEAMUS HEANEY 201

Writing against the writing on the wall
GLENN PATTERSON 212

'She's live, she's modern …'
ANN MARIE HOURIHANE 228

Barcelona, 1975
COLM TÓIBÍN 244

These derelict fields
SELINA GUINNESS 255

The poor old horse
JOHN BANVILLE 275

Letter from Ground Zero
PATRICK MCGRATH 285

On translating Joseph Roth
MICHAEL HOFMANN 295

Sabbath
KATHLEEN JAMIE 307

A hundred acres, a few ditches, some mist
VONA GROARKE 321

Ballistics
TIM ROBINSON 332

Notes on contributors 339

Editor's note

This gathering of pieces from *The Dublin Review* marks no anniversary or other milestone, drawing as it does from twenty-six issues published over six and a half years. Nor does it signal an ending: we continue to produce the magazine quarterly. It arises instead from a sense that we have published some enduring work and that this work bears collecting, and reading, and re-reading.

The story of the magazine's genesis is straightforward. It seemed to me an odd state of affairs, in the late 1990s, that there was no general literary periodical in Ireland publishing short fiction and substantial non-fiction pieces – essays, reportage, criticism, travel writing, memoir – by first-rate writers. The Arts Council of Ireland evidently felt the same way, providing a generous grant without which *The Dublin Review* would not have come into existence.

In its earliest days the magazine operated from a sturdy wooden table positioned between two tall windows in my ground-floor flat in Mountjoy Square. My ambitions were high and yet modest: I wanted to produce a world-class literary magazine, but I knew that it would succeed only if it did not overreach itself. I didn't rule out the possibility of the magazine getting better over time, but I knew that it should not under any circumstances get bigger. It has of course evolved – we stopped publishing poems; we are doing more reportage, and less criticism, than we used to; and there have probably been other changes of which I am not even conscious – but it is much the same beast, physically and editorially, as that which first appeared in December 2000.

A number of people noticed that the first issue contained no editorial statement. This was a calculated silence: manifestos and mission statements are by their nature overblown and instantly falsifiable, two things I was determined that *Dublin Review* pieces must never be. In any case it seemed, and still seems, to me that the work ought to be capable of speaking for itself. But if forced to articulate a governing idea behind the magazine, I might offer this: that the essay in its various guises is every bit as much an art form as the short story or the poem, and ought to be treated as such.

I hope this *Reader* stands as evidence in favour of that proposition. Although we have always published short stories, some of which have been among the strongest pieces to appear in the magazine, the present book comprises non-fiction only, and this is partly a way of saying that non-fiction is what defines *The Dublin Review*. An anthology that included a proportional selection of our best fiction would not, I believe, contain any more narrative variety, invention or virtuosity than the book you hold in your hands. The only other firm rule was that I would select no more than one piece by any single writer. I tried to favour essays that have not subsequently appeared elsewhere in book form, but it would have been perverse to be dogmatic about this, so there are two or three exceptions. Once I started selecting in earnest I realized I'd left it too long: this fattish book omits a number of strong pieces by fine writers whose absence I regret.

As the publisher, editor and sole proprietor of *The Dublin Review*, I sometimes feel like the unelected dictator of a country with a population of one. In fact, even on the narrowest definition the population is two: the magazine has been blessed with a succession of brilliant assistants, firstly Jessie Magee, then Marie Glancy, and now Angelina Lynch. When, in the spring of 2001, piles of paper threatened to crush every other form of life in my flat, I rented a cheap room in a residential house not far from the National Maternity Hospital, with french doors opening onto a paved yard that is haunted by feral cats and in danger, as I write, of being overrun by invasive weeds from next door. Because of the smallness of this room Angelina, like her predecessors, works here only when

Editor's note

I am elsewhere – a state of affairs that runs contrary to the romantic notion that a literary magazine ought to emanate from a clamorous office full of old sofas and unpaid assistants and hangers-on, drinking and debating. But Dublin at the tail-end of its boom period is not a romantic city, and we've got a magazine to produce.

The Dublin Review relies upon an informal network of advisers who generously contribute their ideas and share their contacts; without them it would be a smaller, narrower, duller thing. I will not attempt to list them, but they know who they are and I hope they know how grateful I am. Amongst other encouragers and facilitators, Robert Towers deserves a particular acknowledgment. The writers and readers, of course, are the most important people in the equation, but it feels peculiar to thank them in a general way for doing what it is, after all, that they do. I thank writers every day for accepting commissions, for delivering pieces and revisions, for their patience with me, and for their abundant talent and hard work; but I'm sure that all they really want is to be edited and published well, and paid reasonably and on time.

Thanks, finally, to the Arts Council of Ireland for its continuing support.

BB

A Dublin journal

ANDREW O'HAGAN

3 OCTOBER 2002, LONDON

There's something to be said for places like Simpson's in the Strand. When you ask for cigarettes they bring you a packet without any of them already smoked, or stolen, or held back, as happens with those terrible machines that demand the right money. In Simpson's they bring them on a silver plate, and the waiter smiles darkly, as if you had just ordered the head of John the Baptist. At the dinner to mark Norman Mailer's appearance as Hemingway at the Gielgud Theatre, they put me next to George Plimpton, elegant WASP, honourable putter-away of Johnnie Walker Red, editor of the *Paris Review*.

ME: 'I was just listening to the radio, just heard Clinton's speech to the Labour Party Conference. I wish it was Bush talking.'

PLIMPTON: 'So do I. Oh God, so do I.'

ME: 'He's a friend of yours, isn't he?'

PLIMPTON: 'Clinton? Well, I've met him.'

ME: 'In Martha's Vineyard.'

PLIMPTON: 'Indeed. At William Styron's place. Carlos Fuentes was there and Garcia Marquez. We thought things were getting a big bogged down in policy questions and so on, so I asked everyone at the table to say what their favourite book was. Styron said *Tom Sawyer*. Marquez said *Don Quixote*. And Clinton said *The Sound and the Fury*. Then he began to quote gigantic passages from it, and, you know, Faulkner's not an easy person to quote from memory.'

Mailer came over. We had worked together in February, and he asked me what I thought of the Hemingway stuff.

5

ME: 'I guess you understand him. It was sad to see how much he loved Fitzgerald and how much he disliked himself, and it makes you wonder, you know, can talent ever save talent?'

MAILER: 'Never. It's more a case of can you stop talent from savaging other talent to death. What you doing?'

ME: 'I'm going to Dublin for three months, to be a visiting fellow at Trinity College.'

MAILER: 'Beckett. Joyce. Sean O'Casey.'

ME: 'You once wrote a piece about Beckett saying he must be hopeless because any poet who promoted impotence was no good.'

MAILER: 'Yeah. God. That's right.'

ME: 'You hadn't seen the play. You hadn't seen *Waiting for Godot*. Why didn't you go and see the play?'

MAILER: 'I was young and arrogant. Young and stupid. I'm going on a long flight to Los Angeles tomorrow.'

ME: 'How old are you, Norman?'

MAILER: 'Eighty-one.'

ME: 'Jesus Christ.'

MAILER: 'Yes. Beckett. Promoter of impotence.'

6 OCTOBER 2002, DUBLIN

Holy Catholic Ireland. Just as I stoop to kiss the tarmac, I remember how much Fidel Castro admires the Pope. Once, when working as an editor at *George* magazine, my friend Inigo Thomas accompanied John F. Kennedy Jr on a secret trip to meet Castro. In a room in some palace in Havana, a room fringed with revolutionary-seeming leaves, they sat down to dinner, which started with a half grapefruit each topped with a cherry. Before embarking on a five-hour Shandean monologue, Castro told the American contingent how much he admired the Pope. 'He's very good,' Castro said. 'You know he gets up at 4 o'clock in the morning? That's why I like the Pope. He's an early riser.'

'Let your senses guide you,' says a large ad for Bailey's Irish Cream in Dublin Airport. For some reason, Irish advertisements don't only tell you what to buy, they tell you how to live. 'Don't give out if you don't,' says an advert telling people to vote in the referendum.

Trinity College is the kind of campus that Columbia could never hope to be: beautiful grey stone, trees a hundred years older than their planters, lamps that stand over the cobbled stones like a thought maintained. My rooms overlook the greens on either side; the large Georgian windows catch the shadows of the trees at night, and in the morning everything is clear, the Irish light, the leaves falling onto the stones.

The students arrived today in their thousands. Looking at them, I think of my old granny and her thoughts of the Ireland her family barely remembered, and her telling me constantly that it was all in front of me. It's all in front of them, I say to myself at the window, watching their smiles, their free-floating embarrassments, but the statues are there too, and the old buildings, and I realize how much it's all behind us as well.

7 OCTOBER 2002

At the National Bible Society Bookshop in Dawson Street, they have a large bible in the window, open at Romans 10:11: God's Mercy on Israel. 'It is the same way now: there is a small number left of those whom God has chosen.' Also in the window is Padre Pio, *In His Own Words*, and an instantly fascinating book written by Brother Victor Antoine, *Soups from a Monastery Kitchen*. Though it was a thoroughly Protestant outfit, I asked inside the shop if they had anything on the guy who was canonized yesterday in Rome, the new saint. Not a chance, so I bought the monk's soup book, and wondered halfway down the street if Nigella Lawson could improve on this small epiphany, The Immaculate Conception Winter Broth with Chard.

My rooms need a touch of Girl, so I go to Habitat and buy a red checked tablecloth, four candleholders, a dozen candles, and a glass vase, later to be filled with ten remorseless lilies from Molly Blooms. By the time I get back to Trinity I've also got six tumblers and a good bottle of whisky. I move the furniture around, remove the net curtains, borrow some paintings, which I never find time to hang, and there you have it, in no time at all, a set of rooms that would bring a spot of colour to the cheeks of Herbert Beerbohm Tree.

8 OCTOBER 2002

The rain is coming down so hard it is making the car alarms go off. Under my window, running long-armed over the cobbles, are a couple of giant gorillas, each clutching a sheaf of white leaflets in its rubbery paw. Hmmph. Rag week. Looking onto the green, I realize that no one except university lecturers and rock promoters ever sees this number of young people together. Here they all come, the youth of today, so self-conscious with their cigarettes and haircuts. Taking in the statues, I remember the words of J.P. Mahaffy, Trinity's former provost, who hated *Ulysses* with a vengeance. 'It was a mistake', he said, 'to establish a separate university for the aborigines of this island, for the cornerboys who spit into the Liffey.'

In the evening, Colm Tóibín meets me at the front gate. We go to the launch of a book at Liberty Hall; the book is about the brilliant Argentinean journalist Rodolfo Walsh. The man who wrote the book comes into the room wearing a red PLO-style scarf – one of those items one used to wear to annoy the priesthood. He passes a sign that says 'Yes, we want bread, but we want roses too.' I realize all of a sudden that I'm enjoying an evening with the Irish Left. The author, Michael McCaughan, is also wearing a too-small, velvet, pinstripe suit with baseball boots coming out the bottom; the suit is like something from the closet of the late Bunny Rogers.

TÓIBÍN: 'He's just wearing that scarf to annoy me, now.'

MCCAUGHAN: 'Hello, Colm.'

The author starts, quite unwittingly, unconsciously, without a word, and very slowly, to draw the scarf off his neck and stuff it into his pocket.

TÓIBÍN: 'Mmmm. The suit.'

MCCAUGHAN: 'Would you believe it? Second hand.'

TÓIBÍN: 'Yes. The nouveaux poor.'

Outside, for the first time, I see the autumn nights arriving. The glass towers over in the financial district are cold-looking, and the cranes around them are still busy, moving against the sky. The evening's props tell you everything you need to know about the party's personnel: South American drinking cups abound, as do knapsacks, Fair Isle jumpers, moustaches, children in full school uniform, and the pleasingly Leftish spectacle of every other person wearing small spectacles.

'Buenas noches!' shouts Mr McCaughan.

One of the schoolchildren sits on his father's knee drinking from a glass of red wine. Colm Tóibín has the task of introducing the book. He starts by saying it would be foolish to think, as people once did, of Argentina as a paradise, a European city in South America. He looks straight at the Lefties in their baseball boots, and speaks, in the context of the disintegration of Rodolfo Walsh's work, of 'the solitude, distance, and separateness that a writer needs'. I don't think the gathering quite understands him; they don't appear to believe in separateness, and distance is not what they care about. They don't want to be alone; they want togetherness, like this, the kind of togetherness that celebrates itself.

Out on the street I meet Ciarán Cuffe, the Green TD for Dún Laoghaire. 'Jeezo, that was a right '70s flashback that!' he says. When I tell him I'm working at Trinity, he starts talking about the College's unecological ambitions into Pearse Street, and asks if I could stop them buying up buildings and putting up walls and destroying the city. 'I just talk to young postgraduates about verbs and adjectives,' I wanted to say, but he was gone in a flash of environmental-friendliness.

A new play at the Peacock, *Done Up Like a Kipper* by Mark Harmon. As soon as I see the set – a suburban living-room – I begin to wonder if there will ever be a Scottish or Irish play not set in a living-room, a kitchen, or a pub. The theatre needs a new world of interiors: whatever happened to workplaces, where people spend most of their days, or bedrooms, where they lie all night? Orange-faced, working-class women talking over the kitchen table, things going badly, husbands-wise, things looking better, vodka-wise, and the production splutters almost as soon as it starts. Truth is the play is about six to ten drafts short of being ready, and the Abbey should know better than to expose a young writer to this kind of chaos.

Two women who review plays for the radio – calling themselves The Muppets, after the moany old men in the box – come into the foyer and start gossiping about the actors. The daughter in the play is supposed to bring in a black boyfriend; problem is the guy playing the black fella is not black, only a bit dark. The Muppets say they had a black actor but he disappeared to London to take part in the new series of the talent show *Popstars: The Rivals*. The Irish playwright Loughlin Deegan was standing nearby as The Muppets talked. 'Well,' he said, 'I know that actor playing the boyfriend and he's usually much darker than that.'

12 OCTOBER 2002

At 9.25 this morning, a strange, intergalactic noise was coming from Government Buildings on Merrion Street. Five clear notes, like those understood by the aliens in *Close Encounters of the Third Kind*. Nobody about the place, so I poked my face through the railings and thought: 'We are your friends.' A couple of Canadian tourists came past. 'What the hell is that?' said one of them.

'It's the Irish parliament,' I said. 'They bring a message from another world.'

Catriona Crowe, who works at the National Archives, is helping to set up a new women's refuge in County Longford. I go with her and the architect Denis Looby to see the proposed site and to have lunch with the women. The new centre is in the grounds of a ready-to-open facility for drugs rehabilitation; Coolamber House it is called, and the women gather on the landing. They are open-natured and used to one another's company. They wear pink cardigans and patterned jeans; they smoke heartily and laugh easily. What they seem to share more than anything is an unfussy understanding of what life can be like in modern Ireland, especially those parts made complex by poverty, violence, and addiction.

The cottage is dilapidated. An empty pink tin of Coconut Creams lay in the cupboard, bleached with the dampness, and the wallpaper was hanging in strips, and there were holes in the floor, but Denis, the architect, thought it could be renovated and parts could be rebuilt for about € 100,000. Some of the women – Cathleen O'Neill, Joan Byrne – are from the SAOL Project in Dublin, a group that works with women who have suffered from drug abuse or domestic violence. As I talk to the women, a line comes into my head: 'Masculinity is a nightmare from which Ireland is trying to awake.'

Catriona Crowe comes over as I stand by a fence, looking into the dumb eyes of an old ewe. 'Many of the women who come here will never have had a holiday in their lives,' she said. 'They'll be safe here now, miles from anywhere; you can't do better than that.'

I hear Denis saying a row of Scots pines should be got rid of. 'They're very depressing,' he said. 'Sure, you wouldn't want to be looking into those dark trees all day, so you wouldn't?'

Coolamber itself is a large Georgian house with outbuildings renovated for workshops. 'It costs € 100,000 to keep a man in prison for a year,' said one of them. 'A place like this – where long-term users can begin to prepare for a proper life – is much cheaper than that. All we'll ask is that the clients be over eighteen and off the drugs.'

In one of the rooms there's a mound of toothpaste boxes. I find myself wondering about the many mouths, the cleaning of teeth in the morning, the sense of an ending, and a fresh start. I think of the way the people might talk in this place, once it gets going: I see them looking over the fields, minty-mouthed, all decay set aside. 'Why are there pinboards beside all the beds?' I asked Cathleen.

'Often the thoughts you have last thing at night are the ones that matter. I have my deepest thoughts then.'

'I'm still waiting for a deep thought,' I said.

'I'm having insights,' Cathleen said, 'insights about why I'm not a good person.' I wanted to tell her she was a good person, but it was difficult to say, and she just smiled.

In the Gaiety for the last night of Tom Murphy's *Conversations on a Homecoming*. Sitting there, looking up the tiers, you can see, even now, that Irish theatre bears a deep and traditional relation to the political landscape and plays a part in the creation of a national consciousness. It is not in any way like the London theatre: here, and the other night too, at *Sive*, John B. Keane's play, you feel the audience is engaged in a conversation with some aspect of their own conscience, and that the words and events onstage pour over the people and through them into their own past, or perhaps into the past of the country itself. London theatregoers watch what is happening onstage as if it were happening behind glass. Maybe that is why television stars are currently so popular in the West End.

Evidence for the social interestingness of the Dublin theatre audience can be gleaned from watching them watching one another; there is drama in the stalls, opera in the dress circle, as people wave down to each other, whispering, gesturing, walking quickly down the aisles to say hello. Never in the London theatre does anyone wave to anyone, or recognize the events, onstage or off, as things that are happening in a social way. Maybe that's tourism, but I think it's more than tourism: it's culture, and the lack of it. If that's good news for Ireland, it's the last of such for tonight: Murphy's play tells as many difficult truths as you can tell in two hours.

In the green room afterwards, Tom Murphy stood with a pint. He had only just come back from New York, where *Bailegangaire* is being produced, and he seemed relieved to be among people he could talk to. Murphy stands something like a man who is standing his ground. He is quite compact, and he spreads his weight pretty evenly between his feet; he's proud of his chest in that way that some men are, and proud of his arms too, and he looks to me like he wouldn't go down in a hurry.

We talk about the origin of a line in the play, where the main character looks over the audience and says 'ugliness, ugliness, ugliness'.

MURPHY: 'It was a west of Ireland politician. He was to give a speech to the great and the good. He'd had a drink. A few drinks. He stood like that. [Murphy crosses his legs like someone desperate for a pee.] He looked over the audience and said "ugliness, ugliness,

ugliness" and that was all he said. He was going on later that he felt humiliated and I said I thought it was just the greatest eloquence.'

14 OCTOBER 2002

Monday drinks in my rooms at Trinity. First of a series to resist the Dublin dark, the frost, the fireworks. 'The old style,' says Anthony Cronin. 'People haven't been doing this in Dublin since the 1950s.' The table has thirty new wine glasses and a dozen bottles of Chateau Musar. Before anyone arrives, I look out through the shutters: can't believe how quiet Trinity is in the evening, an island of thoughts, most of them past thinking about now. The leaves are still coming off the trees; I think of the party, and the leaves coming down, and, inevitably, of the women taking coats at the opening of 'The Dead'.

I tell Anthony Cronin there's nothing better in all the world than the description in *Dead as Doornails* of Brendan Behan and him knocking around Paris without two ha'pennies to rub together. I remember them trying to sleep by the Seine, and of Cronin taking his shoes off to get comfortable, and someone stealing them in the night. The next day he finds some small shoes; he describes hilariously, unfussily, tear-makingly, the strange locomotion involved in walking in shoes that are so small you've had to crush the heels: pressing down and forward at the same time as you make your way.

CRONIN: 'There was worse.'

ME: 'It's a particular skill, that. Being able to write well about your friends.'

CRONIN: 'You know the Scottish poet Stanley Graham?'

ME: 'W.S. Graham. "The Nightfishing".'

CRONIN: 'Right. Well, he used to be asked to write a radio poem now and then for the Third Programme. Half the time he was in no fit state to write the thing. We used to sit in his flat. The producer would be waiting for the poem. Stanley was in the habit of breaking the plastic tube off those nasal inhalers: inside them was a strip ...'

ME: 'Soaked in Benzedrine. Jack Kerouac and all that mob were always at them.'

CRONIN: 'Stanley would heat the strips in front of the fire – all of them hanging just so – and would lick them one after the other. Of course he would be completely out of his head. The producer would say, "Now. We have to get a line down." I would say: "The light-reflecting brown water of the Clyde flows past in the night" or some such rubbish, and then Stanley would nod and the producer would write it down. Then it was another strip of the thing – giving it a lick.'

16 OCTOBER 2002

In the Long Room at Trinity, Professor Terence Brown shows me the bust of Jonathan Swift. 'It's the only distinguished one here,' he says. 'There's something very lifelike in the face. Very distinguished.' We look up at the arched ceiling and the beautiful beams. 'You know what John McGahern said about this place?' Brown says. 'He said this is the most beautiful room in Ireland.'

Later, in the Davis Theatre, Professor Nicholas Grene is introducing Merlin Holland, who will talk about the afterlife of his grandfather Oscar Wilde. 'Today is Oscar's birthday,' says Grene. 'He would have been 148 today had he lived. No one in this audience needs convincing about the importance of Wilde's Irishness. We don't need to be territorial about Wilde; we are willing to share him with the England where he made his reputation.'

Merlin Holland has the shape you imagine Wilde might have had. Big-shouldered, and broad, with thick fingers, thick lips, and a sweet lilac shirt and tie, very apt.

HOLLAND: 'My grandfather cast a rainbow of forbidden colours over the age of Victorian hypocrisy.'

I notice Holland – an elegant speaker – only ever stammers or trips when he mentions Lord Alfred Douglas.

HOLLAND: 'Someone claimed to have got drunk with Oscar in Paris on cherry wine, which seems unlikely, and that my grandfather did not touch him for 100 francs, which seems even more unlikely.'

There are many old ladies in the audience. They nod wisely and keenly when Holland uses the word 'queer'.

HOLLAND: 'Upton Sinclair, with impeccable socialist venom, said that Wilde was "the spoiled darling of the putrescence leisure class".'

There was a question about Wilde converting to Catholicism on his deathbed.

HOLLAND: 'Yes. He was quite delirious. Some have thought that when he waved his hand, as if to give assent, he was actually saying "get that priest away from me".'

Holland remembers an incident in Hyde Park, when he was very young, where a group of nannies took their children away from the Holland children in case they would be 'contaminated'. As he says this, I think of the incident happening in Kensington Park Gardens, where the children play, under the statue of Peter Pan.

But the biggest laugh comes with news of a letter sent to Holland's father by Rebecca West at the time of the first publication of Wilde's letters. 'It's a hateful thing to have to face,' she wrote, 'and your father cannot have written those letters expecting they would be read publicly. P.S. A friend of mine is a zoologist and she says giraffes are always at it and it's amazing to see.'

Later, in Bruno's, a cold restaurant in Kildare Street, Merlin Holland does something quite strange. He lays a place at the table for Oscar Wilde. It's not done overtly, or pretentiously, not much, but half-smilingly. 'Sherry started this early on,' Holland says. 'Whenever they had dinner. A place for Oscar.'

I ask him what he thought of the biography of Lord Alfred Douglas published last year.

HOLLAND: 'Shockingly edited. It was as if the book had just been shoved in without being read. A lot of hype – you know, the author is very young, an undergraduate …'

ME: 'Slightly enamoured of his subject.'

HOLLAND: 'Yes. And some people were slightly enamoured with him, the author – his publishers I mean. Enough said about that. I would really like a cigarette but I don't know.'

TERENCE BROWN: 'Go on. You know what your grandfather said about temptation.'

22 OCTOBER 2002

The high-rise flats at Inchicore are due to be pulled down, and something will be lost to the people there. 'You're going to have a special treat,' says Cathleen O'Neill. 'It's about the threat to an entire culture and it's about displacement in Dublin.' When I asked her to show me the condemned flats in St Michael's Estate, Cathleen had seemed pleased to make it happen, and drove me there in her car.

'Will You Go, Lassie, Go' is playing on the tape deck. Cathleen explains that Kehoe Square had been an army barracks before the British left, and was later turned into housing for those Dublin-dwellers who had trouble paying their rent. Then in the 1960s the old barracks were torn down and the new high-rises were put up. Like many in Glasgow or Manchester, the tower blocks quickly went bad, and people living on St Michael's Estate were surrounded by poverty. 'It became the place where many of the women we have worked with would have come to get their drugs,' said Cathleen.

Cathleen believes in progressive feminism, in 'empowering women', and she has a strong community development ethos, which would appear to grow out of her own experience and her sense of a commitment to working-class life in Ireland. 'Robert Emmet was hung, drawn and quartered there,' she says as we pass a church in Thomas Street. 'His memorial is on the ground for the dogs to pee on.' When we reach the high flats you see a long cloth hanging down the length of one of the blocks; it features the mostly-smiling faces of everybody who's ever lived on the estate.

Rita Fagan comes fizzing towards us. She's famous for a show called *Once Is Too Much*, about domestic violence. 'Hello hello,' she says, 'come in here. You be nice to him now, he's an illuminary.' She takes us into one of the ground-floor flats – most of the people had already gone from their homes – and Rita had turned the flat into an art gallery, a mini-Hayward, where work made by the St Michael's residents stood in pristine rooms. 'The exhibition is about memory,' said Rita. 'It's the hidden Ireland.' She pointed to a painting. 'And unlike the estate, this painting will last,' she said.

The most striking things to be found in the rooms are the 'Memory Chairs', where women have used photographs of their loved ones (some of them dead from cancer, asthma, and drugs) and fashioned patterns out of them around a chair, using bits of mirror and net curtain and domestic bric-à-brac. 'Love labour is what women do all the time in their lives,' said Cathleen, 'and it is not counted in the gross domestic product.' We stop in front of a wall of photographs, mainly young people going from the estate on summer bus trips years ago, and Rita begins pointing out young faces.

'Dead,' she says. 'Dead. Dead. Dead.'

'But it's about giving people their story back,' says Cathleen.

'Exactly,' says Rita. 'I can see my story in this, is what many of the women who come here say to me.'

I spoke to some of the old-age pensioners who had gathered that afternoon for a writing class. The elderly ladies spoke and laughed among themselves and someone pointed out that the ladies have the old Dublin way of speaking. 'I'm not very artistic, by any means,' says the first one.

'Where are you going to live now?' I asked.

'I'm getting a bungalow,' she said, 'if I'm not in St James's first. First I'd one bad leg and now it's two.'

'I know your face,' said a second old lady to Cathleen. 'Were you on the telly?'

'I was.'

'That was it, Joan. She was on the telly.'

'I'm still embarrassed by it,' said Cathleen.

'Why should you be?' said the second lady, hobbling over to the table and picking up a writing pad. 'It's your gift. You've got it.'

23 OCTOBER 2002

You learn a lot about the condition of Ireland from listening to the radio. On Anna Livia FM, there's a man called Gary talking about strange formations on his living-room wall. 'There's another face starting to appear within the face!' he says. It turns out there are 'cold feelings' in Gary's house, and he recently lost his dog. Just about that time, he says, a patch of Artex on his living room wall started to look like the face of Jesus. 'I couldn't believe it,' he says. 'There's definitely a face within the face,' he says. 'People come in and say, "Sure, you must've done it yourself," and I say, "If I could do the likes of that then I'd be doing it for a living. That's the paranormal, that is."'

Other listeners are moved by Gary's story. 'There's spiders coming out o' me hair,' says one. 'Little brownie-black fellas. I once knew a girl who had a mouse come out of her perm.'

25 OCTOBER 2002

Walking over O'Connell Bridge I'm stopped by a woman holding a baby. 'Please give,' she says.

'Where are you from?'

'Please give me,' she says.

Beggars are much keener to be ignored or humiliated than they are to be questioned. I found this out years ago when I spent several months hanging around with beggars. I remember a night-shelter next to the Tropical Diseases Hospital in Camden Town, where many of the men were Irish or Scottish, waiting out the night over their vast bowls of pea soup. All the intricacies of coins collected and drink procured could be discussed, but when you asked a person where he came from, how he got here, a sad, protective cloud of silence would gather about him, and he'd only shake his head.

'Are you Romanian?' I said to the woman on O'Connell Bridge.

'Little money for baby,' she said.

'I will give you money,' I replied. 'I will certainly give you this' – I took out a note – 'but can I only ask you about yourself?'

'This,' she said.

'Here it is,' I said. 'Will you speak with me for one minute? Did you come here from Romania?'

'The baby needs food,' she said. 'From Romania, yes.'

'Where do you live now?'

'We are living out here with family.'

'Your own family?'

'With family, yes. Here with family.'

'Do you live in a house?'

'In a house.'

Then she took the note, made a gesture with her hand, and made quickly off. I guess the woman was nervous about discussing her circumstances because they were quite possibly illegal. The Liffey looked dull as it flowed and when I turned round the woman had disappeared into the crowd, once again among the unknowables.

28 OCTOBER 2002

My friends Horatia Lawson from the BBC and the actress Maria McErlane arrive with no other project in mind but to spice up my Monday drinks party. They waltz through the gates of Trinity in excellent dark glasses, Jackie Onassis and Anita Ekberg: high-heeled, lipstuck, coiffed, wide-eyed, ruby-cheeked and ready to go.

They were having some trouble with the cobblestones. 'What's wrong with them round here?', Maria says. 'Have they never heard of tarmacadam?' After a series of tall gins at the Morrison, they come to the rooms and tickle the students with feather boas. 'All part of the literary education,' I say to Vivienne Guinness, who immediately and good-naturedly asks them to supper.

Maria used to co-host a show with Graham Norton. That means she understands the modern Irish temperament very well, according to her, and she remains resolutely un-shy when it comes to conversing with the students. 'Do you like commas and semi-colons,' she asks one, 'or do you prefer gigantic cocks?'

'Come now,' I say, 'let's stick to the influence of Ibsen on James Joyce's notion of the human.'

The student sips some of Berry Brothers' Good Ordinary Claret, and offers a single word to his friendly agitator. 'Both.'

In the snug at Kehoe's there's a painter who reckons the girls might be a little bit English.

'Show us your nipples,' says one of them.

Later, of course, the painter wants to take one of them home. 'It's only charitable,' she says, before hopping into a cab. Next morning she rings to say she's having to do the walk of shame in her Chanel heels. 'But listen. He lives with his mum. Can you imagine the sweetness? Is it like this in Dublin all the time?'

5 NOVEMBER 2002

Up in my room in the Oscar Wilde Centre, a man telephones the department to see if I'll not speak to him about 'the world of writing'. His name is Ian Steepe. I arrange to meet him in the bar of the Shelbourne Hotel, where the world of writing, according to the hotel's biographer Elizabeth Bowen, is always at least an hour behind the next bottle of champagne.

Mr Steepe is a scholar, and a gentleman too, but for the first few minutes of our meeting I couldn't stop looking at his mouth. Nancy Docherty, my paternal grandmother, found a whole new life when she improved the shape of her mouth; I mean, she got teeth, and they were the least Glasgow-like teeth ever worn. They were what the professionals call Number Ones: all the flashbulbs in Hollywood appeared to go off every time she smiled. She lived in a block of high flats and the planes used to be guided in to land at Glasgow Airport by the sight of her laughing out on the drying-roof. Ian Steepe didn't have Number Ones, but they were One-ish, and I thought of my lovely grandmother every time he smiled, which, pleasantly, was more often than the usual denizens of the Shelbourne Bar.

It's amazing how much a stranger might contain. Mr Steepe is a retired English teacher; his last port of call was Drogheda Grammar School in County Louth, and he loves his subject in the old-fashioned way, that's to say he reads a lot, and likes the often very dubious company of writers. You imagine a love of words going all the way back through Steepe's family: to the Germans from the Palatinate region who ended up in Munster, the Protestant small farmers and artisans, the newly-belonging, whom he speaks about carefully, as if it were indeed a responsibility of the living to regenerate the dead. As I look at him across the table I feel somehow that Ian Steepe is a rather noble kind of Irishman – an old man speaking, a self-realizer. And then his own past finds new air over his pint of Guinness.

'Michael Longley and I taught in adjoining classrooms at the Royal Belfast Academical Institute,' he says, 'and he and Derek Mahon attended there as schoolboys.'

'Do you run?' Mr Steepe is very healthy looking.

'Hockey,' he said. 'I was an Irish international for eleven years, 1961 to '72, then the national coach for the men's team for a few years, then, from 1981 to '88, coach for the women's team. I've coached in Zimbabwe and Ghana and Oman.'

He drinks the last pint slowly, and just as slowly I read through a vast folder he brought with him, full of holograph pages written by novelists and poets, a collection Mr Steepe has been making for ten years. I looked at dozens of writer's hands. I think it was Margaret Atwood who wrote like a snail. Paul Muldoon's was harmonious.

'Has anybody ever refused you?' I asked.

'Oh now,' he said. 'Let me think. Yes indeed. Salman Rushdie.'

To Iveagh House, the Department of Foreign Affairs, for the launch of the new volume of diplomatic papers, 1926–32. The room was full of doddery guys with white hair and old ladies who needed chairs. Out of the sea of watery eyes comes this bright young thing: you know the type, thirty-five-ish, bad skin, chardonnay rush. 'Are you Andrew O'Hagan?' he says.

'Yes,' I say.

'I used to run a literary magazine at Oxford. You ran a free ad for us.'

'Oh good. We tried to like small magazines.'

The Bright Young Thing mentions a friend of his. 'I was talking to him today,' he says. 'Like everybody else in Scotland he's going off his head about what you wrote in that essay about Scotland being addicted to injury.'

'Oh well.'

'No. It's the second time. That last time you did it he wrote a big attack on you. Did you see it?'

'Well, I don't see everything.'

'A really gigantic attack. Do you want me to send it to you?'

'No thanks.'

'He was worried after writing it that he'd never get to write for the *London Review*.'

'Well, that's silly. I didn't see it, but agreeing with me is not a qualification for being published in the *London Review*.'

'Well, he was panicking. Then they asked him to do something recently, a review of some shit book about Blackwoods.'

'It's a good subject.'

'He thought you must have suggested him.'

'I did.'

'For the piece? Christ. You haven't read the thing he wrote about you.'

'He's an interesting writer.'

'Is that Colm Tóibín standing next to you?'

'Yes.'

'Can I send you a copy of my book? It's very good. It's about Scotland and Ireland.'

He hands me his card, which Colm Tóibín – talking to a young diplomat – takes out of my hand.

TÓIBÍN: 'YOU ARE ... YOU FUCKING BASTARD!'

BRIGHT YOUNG THING: 'I'd like to speak to you. I know I've been horrible about your work.'

TÓIBÍN: 'This fucker thinks I should reconcile myself to the meaning of my own liberalism. Do you know what that means? It means I should join the IRA.'

BRIGHT YOUNG THING: 'Is that what I'm saying?'

TÓIBÍN: 'He writes this shite about me all the time. When are you going to stop?'

BRIGHT YOUNG THING: 'There's a chapter about you in my book. People say it's the best chapter in the whole book.'

TÓIBÍN: 'What these people do – like him. It's a very interesting technique. They lump you in with the dregs, and they hope that their mediocrity will rub off on you. Then they compare you as a

group to another group, a group of geniuses, Declan Kiberd and
Seamus Deane. It's a nasty, shitey business, and that's HIM!'

12 NOVEMBER 2002

Supper with Bernard O'Donoghue, a nice man and a good poet with
patience and intelligence to burn. He tells a funny story about a
novelist we both know, a man he taught at Oxford. 'I think he was
the most gifted student I ever had,' says O'Donoghue. 'I once made
reference to a passage from *Dombey & Son*. He leaned in very quietly,
very carefully, and said, "*Hard Times*, I think". And of course he was
right. Amazingly untidy, though. The man once lost a girlfriend
because of that. She said it was the last straw when she discovered
a half-eaten sandwich inside one of his socks.'

13 NOVEMBER 2002

Up early to go in a car to *Kenny Live*. It must be one of the chief
advantages of small-nationhood: you can feel everyone is listening
to the same radio show in the morning, and Britain has no national
equivalent to *Kenny Live*. Next to it the *Today* programme on Radio 4
can seem sepulchral.

Pat Kenny is Ireland's Tom Brokaw – so handsome he's almost
ugly, and similarly tuned in to the average appetites and pieties of
his own people. I was interviewed by him once before, a few years
ago on the television, and even there his technique seemed odd:
what he says with his mouth is quite intimate and cosy, but his eyes
are elsewhere, nowhere near yours, and if you fail to trust his
speech you can feel harried by his attentiveness to the clock. What
I most remember from our last encounter was him asking me to
explain something about Western culture's fascination with serial
killers, then, as the camera came to me, combing his hair repeatedly and very daintily with his fingers.

I only really want to say one thing about Scotland. That is that it
can not be the modern country it wants to be until it stops blaming
England for everything; it is not courageous, not manly, not intelligent, not faithful, not progressive, to rely on an ancient narrative of

injury to explain your current woes. It is the behaviour of a small culture, and Scotland is not a small culture, just a small country in which the national will is enslaved by its negative options. Fools among the Irish intelligentsia lean back in their pews to tell us that we should have followed their example and ditched England in 1920; that is a dense-minded view that little understands Scotland's experience within the British Union, its experience as an imperialist force, a colonizer, a world warrior, and a commercial entity *par excellence*. It is not the occupied territory the Scots Nats call it, nor has it, as a Protestant country, ever had (despite all our good songs) anything other than a footnote-able amount of the Home Rule spirit so pleasant to the Irish mind and heart, and liked by the Scottish ear alone.

Pat Kenny is tolerant enough of all this. Then he asks me what I think of the idea of a super-league that would include the English and Scottish football teams. Now, this allows me to tell you exactly what it means to be Scottish. Despite everything I've said, and despite not even liking football, at the sound of this question the Dr Jekyll of small patriotism rises unrestrained in my breast: I don't want a super-league, I want small divisional teams like Forfar and Brechin and Queen of the South not to fall by the wayside; I want equal rights for small towns in the Highlands; I want recognition for the small man; I want equality. I want our Scottish rights! I want FREEDOM!

By the time I reach the car my face has taken on the obligatory Mel Gibson aspect, imaginary blue wode and non-imaginary nationalistic fury blazing defiantly in the eyes of reason.

'That was good craic,' says the driver.

14 NOVEMBER 2002

Dublin doesn't really work, you know, as a city. If you want to be far-fetched it's like Calcutta – full of nice British buildings, with too many people for its size, too many cars, and a rather steep inner-city distinction between the newly rich and the old-fashioned poor. For what the tourist brochures like to call a twenty-first-century city, it has a mad shortage of cash machines, taxis, and wine shops, though no shortage of Ryanair Generation winos out on stag nights. The food in the restaurants isn't nice and it costs too much. There are queues everywhere, for cash, for drinks, for Marks & Spencer.

The glory is the Georgian squares, the talk of books, the neon signs, the poetic force of the drama, the jokes, the soda bread, and a general fair-play attitude that makes everybody seem accountable and nobody secluded from what is best and worst in the Irish day. Unlike Edinburgh, whose present-day middle class is unintellectual, the Dublin middle class are old-fashionedly attentive to their own political and literary culture: they read the *Irish Times* and fill the Abbey; the novelists appear on the radio discussing moral crises; the work of abstract painters goes on sale, and, in any event, the artists are given money and shelter by the government from the roughs of the marketplace. I'm too short to start arguing with the likes of James Joyce, so it may be true that Irish art is a cracked mirror held up by a servant, yet a mirror is at least a mirror, and not a pitiless void, and an outsider in Dublin may feel that all is not entirely lost when it comes to workaday relations between money and thoughts.

The artists this week were scared the government was about to remove their tax exemption, but it didn't happen. What's the point in pissing off the nation's premier big-mouths in order to accrue an extra two or three million euro a year? A London literary agent tells me all his Irish clients were phoning last week in a tremendous panic.

After the deluge, comes the deluge: rain is general all over Ireland. I walk to Lower Abbey Street in a treacly downpour to be interviewed on Eamon Dunphy's radio show. The neon is picking out the puddles at four o'clock in the afternoon.

I like Dunphy. He has the face he deserves at fifty-two. Into the room he comes like a punch-drunk Glasgow boxer – three parts Jimmy Breslin, two parts Ken Buchanan – and he's busy in the way good journalists ought always to be busy, keeping the spinning plates of the news diary and his lifelong obsessions turning on high sticks. Sitting in front of the microphone Dunphy is one of the last of the valiant smokers. He makes good points and he likes conversation; it's noticeable that he doesn't waste any of his famous ire on a friendly target. He's a populist, I suppose, but before long we're talking about Patrick Kavanagh and Brendan Behan, and he smirks when I say it's a myth about people not reading the way they used to. 'I know,' he says, 'I've sold over 500,000 copies of the Roy Keane book in hardback.'

15 NOVEMBER 2002

As part of my work at Trinity, at the behest of the British Council (who sponsor the International Creative Writing Fellowship), I've organized a Day of Scottish Literature and Talk. The arrivers all arrive at different times in Dublin today, with different enthusiasms, and different needs. Karl Miller's remain the funniest: 'We had a rather nervous time in the air,' he says, 'and a train to the place that leads to the air, which Robin Robertson appears to have brought into being.'

My girlfriend India arrives to inspect my rooms at Trinity. 'Oh darling, how sweet,' she says, 'and all your little books set out,' before immediately reserving a suite at the Fitzwilliam Hotel. Colm Tóibín throws a party to open the Scottish literary day; the guests eat curry and pass before the long windows. Karl Miller and Anthony Cronin are the two oldest people in the room. The first was literary editor of the *Spectator* while the second did the job at *Time and Tide*; that was in the late '50s, and they had never met, though Karl Fergus Connor Miller wondered if the Irishman across from him wasn't once known to be a ferocious hand at the drink. They are brought together, more than 140 years between them, senses of nationhood, literary friendships, governments, and a hill of marked galleys behind them, and they shake hands, standing together to talk about novels, seeming like two old knights with different accounts of the Crusades.

16 NOVEMBER 2002

There are about a hundred people at the Scottish event at Trinity, which is pleasing. Apart from my own students, the audience are people with shopping bags; I assume they are, like everybody in Ireland, listeners to *Kenny Live*.

ROBIN ROBERTSON: 'Most of these poems are about death and sex, or near-death experiences, and near-sex experiences.'

Alan Spence reads about undertakers, and Janice Galloway from her novel about Clara Schumann. Karl Miller speaks about Scots Bards and Scots Reviewers, the great period of Scottish self-inquiry. The audience seems to love it, and so do I, but I wonder if Scotland might not seem from all this talk of the dead to be a land of the passed and passing away. The day ends with the kind of debate that can only lead to further debate, and the security guards are frowning from the doors, and soon the entire group, Scots, Irish writers, Trinity clan, the lot, step over to St Andrew's Street for the evening, and prove that conviviality is the natural partner to Caledonian pessimism.

18 NOVEMBER 2002

I was telling a journalist in Neary's pub about my day on Saturday, and he puts me in my place by telling me about Bono's day on Saturday. 'First thing. Breakfast in his house with the US Secretary of Health and his three aides. Then he goes to a gallery at lunchtime to paint a big frieze for charity, works all the way to nine o'clock at night with hardly a break. Then he has his dinner and talks about another big project with a guy. Walks home and writes a song before going to bed at one o'clock. Then he gets up first thing to catch a flight to New York.'

1 DECEMBER 2002

You wonder how much of Dublin has been lost to the renovations. I walk past Sweny's chemist, the one that features in *Ulysses*, and notice they have heritage-style lemon soap in the window, to tickle the literary tourists no doubt, but everything around the shop and beyond suggests Dublin is a city much fiddled with and hammered, as if certain modern uglinesses have moral precedence over guilty old beauty every time.

Walking over the squares you see that nearly every one of the spectacular houses is now an office. Looking at the upper floors, I wonder what single people do now to live, and if they are still hanging in there and paying the exorbitant rents. The thought gives way to a stanza of Derek Mahon's poem 'Axel's Castle':

> Beyond
> the back-lit tree-tops of Fitzwilliam Square
> a high window is showing one studious light,
> somebody sitting late at a desk like me.
> There are some die-hards still on the upper floors,
> a Byzantine privacy in mews and lane,
> but mostly now the famous Georgian doors
> will house a junk-film outfit or an advertising agency.

10 DECEMBER 2002

Off to the National Archives in Bishop Street to look at the files from 1972 that will be released on the 1st of January.

The accredited people in the reading room are all interested in what the new papers might say about Bloody Sunday. It is harrowing, all over again, to read, for instance, Lord Brockway's original affidavit. He writes as someone who was present at the scene. Brockway is a good reporter, and he doesn't mince his words. 'When we reached Free Derry Corner there was a lorry for the speakers and a crowd around it of about 2,000,' he writes. 'It was a quiet and orderly crowd, except that a few girls in front were singing "We Shall Overcome", and a rather more militant song in denunciation of British troops. There was no evidence of disorderly indignation, however, and the people were as serious and quiet as they had been at the beginning of the march in The Creggan.'

I decide to leave off Bloody Sunday, and instead study some papers relating to the ashes of Charles Stewart Parnell.

Iris Leslie was living at 16A Palmeira Court in Hove, and the date of her initial letter was 23 September 1971. Her letter was addressed to the Irish Ambassador in London.

Your Excellency,
As you are no doubt aware my husband Sir Shane Leslie passed from this life on August 13 last. I am most anxious that the Parnell relics which ... were entrusted to Sir Shane should now be passed to the Irish nation. May I suggest that they be deposited in the safe keeping of your Embassy and transferred to Dublin at some date. Sir Shane did discuss the matter with Mr De Valera a few years ago but no immediate decision was taken as to where they could best be placed hence the fact that they are still here. There are photographs, miniatures, locks of hair, rings etc. and a set of silver gifts to Parnell's grandson when a child ... I will not be staying in Hove much longer and am most anxious to get this settled, and the relics placed in the right hands.

I love the notion of Parnell's ashes and those locks of hair sitting in Palmeira Court. Further on in the correspondence, a member of the family says that 'the contents of this box were treasured for nearly 30 years by Kitty O'Shea – from October 1891 to February 1921 ... It was Mrs Parnell's wish ... that one day these Parnell relics would find a lasting resting place in Ireland.'

Walking towards St Stephen's Green, the wind was cold. The autumn was truly over, the greys of a real winter lay ahead, but for today the sky was clear over the city of Dublin, and I walked ahead smiling at the thought of Parnell's ashes and the thought of my own great-grandfather, a Glasgow man with a memory of Ireland, making his way up the road with a song about the blushing Miss Kitty.

(Spring 2003)

Adventures with old things

ANGELA BOURKE

There used to be a dump just outside Dingle, but not any more. A couple of years ago it closed, and wheelie bins appeared outside every house on the small roads of Corca Dhuibhne. Last week, out there among the fuchsia and the sheep, I found myself responsible for disposing of a fridge: nearly twenty years old, its motor was dead, its body rusting.

The little house is bare and spare. There is no linen press, no cupboard under the stairs, no shed or garage: no place to look for an old rug or blanket to help me get the fridge into the back of the car without damaging the car or hurting myself. There is just one old towel, a thick white one with holes in it – from a hotel, probably – that we found on the sand dunes at Muiríoch a few years ago. It keeps the rain from coming under the door when the wind blows unkindly, and it mops things up when puddles are inevitable. I waltzed the fridge across the floor and along the little path that runs in front of the house, and the old towel padded the edge of the hatchback as I heaved the fridge up and in. It wasn't easy reversing down the narrow path between jagged stone walls with this white bulk between me and the back window, but I managed, and was on the road. After days of warm sunshine, it was raining steadily.

A phone call to the County Council had established that the nearest dump was the North Kerry Landfill, seven miles beyond Tralee, but they'd also said I could take the fridge to the new Transfer Station at Milltown, near Castlemaine. Setting out, I didn't know which one to go to. There's not much difference in the distance; Milltown would mean a beautiful road along the coast, and one I don't take often, but the way to Tralee is beautiful too, and I could do some shopping. I headed for Tralee.

At Camp village, on the far side of the mountains, it was still raining and I thought about lunch. It would be just my luck to arrive at the landfill hungry and find it closed until two, with no food in sight. I imagined a bowl of seafood chowder at Ashe's, but I didn't manage to conjure it up quite fast enough, and missed turning right in time to park in front of the pub. I took the turn alongside it. I thought it led to a car-park, but I was delighted to find that it was a real road, and that a house a little way along was called Caherconree.

I had always wanted to see exactly where *Cathair Con Roí* was: the iron-age stronghold of the legendary Cú Roí mac Dáire, with whose wife Bláthnat Cú Chulainn once carried on a dalliance. I knew it could be reached from Camp, and in fact it's signposted at a sharp bend further down the main road, but I'm usually just beginning or coming to the end of the long journey from Dublin, so I've never turned off before. Camp is *An Com*: the hollow on the hillside cut out by the Finglas river – *An Fhionnghlaise*, the white stream (Bláthnat poured milk into it once, far above, as a signal to Cú Chulainn) – and the road near the bridge there demands all my concentration. It's lush, too, because of the river, with more trees and thicker hedges than in many parts of this landscape, and there is a high railway bridge, now disused, so it's not easy to see what lies beyond the road.

The car began to climb, nosing up between mossy stone walls, with soft damp leaves almost meeting overhead, and I forgot about lunch. I knew by now that this road would go somewhere. It crossed the Dingle Way and came out at last onto an open bare mountainside. Up there, past all houses and all trees, with other mountains rolling away on either side and the wooded valley far behind me, I realized I didn't know where I was. A sign pointed to Aughils, a name I vaguely recalled, but that was all. I hadn't brought a decent map, much less Steve MacDonogh's indispensable book *The Dingle Peninsula*, and though my hiking boots were in the back of the car along with a large umbrella, the holey white towel and the fridge, I had no socks. Lack of preparation added to the adventure, but I did wonder if I'd arouse suspicion as I went: strangers must often drive along these roads, after all, looking furtively for places to dump cargo like mine.

I imagined that the road would loop back towards Tralee eventually, but I thought I must have missed a turn-off for Cathair Con Roí – if indeed I'd been on the right road to start with. But nobody was expecting me; I had petrol, some money and a phone (no signal up there, of course), and after a winter in Dublin and a spring when the hills were out of bounds because of foot-and-mouth disease, this was freedom. Of course I remembered Tony Hawks, who wrote a book about hitch-hiking with a fridge, but it seemed pathetic to let fear of being derivative deter me from adventure.

After miles without meeting a person or a car, I suddenly saw two men in long black raincoats, walking on the road. They smiled benignly as I waved – priests on holiday, perhaps? – so maybe I hadn't missed Cathair Con Roí after all. Another hundred yards and there it was, or there I thought it was. The road became suddenly much steeper and rougher, and a large sign with new white lettering on dark green informed me in elegant, clear Irish:

Ar bharr an tsléibhe seo tá Dún Chúroí Mhic Dáire, a bhí ina rí ar Iarmhumhan de réir an tSeanchais le linn Aois na Craoibhe Rua, is é sin le rá i rith na hIarann Aoise Moiche. Toisc a chumhacht draíochta, luaitear é in ana-chuid de laochscéalta na hÉireann agus tá a ainm luaite i measc na ndéithe i mbéaloideas na Breataine Bige.

(At the top of this mountain is the fort of Cú Roí mac Dáire, legendary king of west Munster during the Red Branch era, otherwise known as the Early Iron Age. With his magic powers, he features in many of the Irish hero-tales, and his name is found in Welsh folklore among those of the gods.)

That's my translation. The English version on the sign assumed the reader would know that the *cathair* itself was still some distance away, and referred simply to 'this fort'. One word was left out altogether, and another – Cú Roí's own name – was misspelled as Cúror. The poetic justice of this gave me a grim satisfaction out in that lonely place, where probably no English-speaker has ever lived.

A *cathair* in a place like this is not a city, as the word suggests; this is an older usage of the Irish word, and means a stone-built enclosure, roughly circular, or a reinforced hilltop. They always command stunning views, and prompt amazed respect for the strategic intelligence of the people who built them, their engineering knowhow and physical strength. That the later generations who have told intriguing stories about them over the centuries must have experienced a similar humbling amazement was a thought that consoled me as I stood there on the mountain beside my car. With the fridge still on board, a white metal box inside a blue metal box, it seemed a deeply ridiculous symbol of the way we live now. I felt myself flabby, pale and pathetic: a mollusc outside her shell.

But everything was green and grey, and lit into vividly shaded contrasts as the rain stopped, the mist suddenly cleared, and the sun came out. Among the short grass, the mosses and the lichens at my feet, looking at first like violets, were some small purple flowers, each growing out of a rosette of fleshy yellowish leaves. They were *Leith uisce*, the Large-flowered butterwort, *Pinguicula grandiflora*, which lures insects into its clutches with a sweet sticky substance and then digests them. It is common in Cork and Kerry, but nowhere else in these islands, and its flowers are large only by comparison with those of the common butterwort, which is, predictably, common. *Leith uisce* is also the name of the liver fluke that affects sheep, and Nicholas Williams in *Díolaim Luibheanna* suggests that the plant has borrowed it because it was widely believed to be a source of that infection. The bilingual *Flora Chorca Dhuibhne* adds that this plant is also known as the Kerry violet, and a colour photograph of it adorns the back cover of that beautiful book.

High up to my left, as I read the notice and admired the delicate and voracious butterwort and the stupendous view, was a spiky pinnacle of rock. Later I read on the Ordnance Survey Discovery map, sheet 71, that this peak is *An Géarán*: 'the sharp one' (Gearhane in

English). It is 792 metres above the sea. Cathair Con Roí was ahead and to my right, its summit a mere 683 metres above sea level, had I only known; but I didn't climb up, although the way was marked with red and white poles. Instead I walked up the next, steepest part of the road, to the crumbling black-and-yellow crash barrier I could see above me, just to assure myself that the road would continue past the bend. Puffing to the top, I saw the sea come clearly into view behind me.

Another few minutes walking, and there was the sea in front of me as well. I determined to drive on, and to come back and walk the hill another day, with good company and proper footwear – and without any large kitchen appliances. David Herman's *Hill Walker's Kerry* says it will take three hours to cover the six kilometres from the sign up to the top and back. The wall of the Cathair is still there, he says, over 100 metres long and four thick, and I want to reread the old stories before I go, about how Cú Roí could make his stronghold revolve so that its entrance could not be found after sunset, and about how Cú Chulainn climbed up there to cuckold him. In *Fled Bricrend*, the story of Bricriu's Feast, told in the thousand-year-old *Lebor na hUidre*, the 'Book of the Dun Cow', Cú Roí was the fearsome giant who invited the greatest champion to cut his head off, on condition that Cú Roí could come back the following night and behead him in return. Several heroes were happy to do the beheading, but only Cú Chulainn was man enough to turn up and lay his own neck bare on the second night. When the decapitated Cú Roí came back intact, Cú Chulainn was allowed to keep his own head and earned the *curadmír* – the tastiest morsel or 'champion's portion' – in recognition of his heroism. Cú Roí was pretty impressive, but altogether a rougher customer than the deft and sexy young hero of the *Ulaid*, and his weapons were cruder than the sword and spear Cú Chulainn used. Cathair Con Roí is what is called a promontory fort: one of only two inland examples on this peninsula, where so many headlands are defended on the landward side by thick stone walls. The *Archaeological Survey of the Dingle Peninsula* would have been another good book to have in the car.

My road pottered steadily downhill as I drove on, wondering where in Tralee Bay those sandy shallows were that I could see before me. The road ran between trees again, and walls, and houses, until at last I reached the main road and, much to my chagrin, came face-to-face with signs pointing left towards Castlemaine and right towards Inch. Instead of tending eastwards as I'd thought, my winding road had crossed the Dingle peninsula, cutting through the western end of the Sliabh Mis mountains in an almost straight line from north to south. *Sliabh Mis*, 'Mis's mountain', is called after the king's daughter who went mad and ran naked into the hills after drinking her father's blood when he was killed in battle – but that is another story, and another day's exploring. Today, whatever I might have decided earlier about heading for Tralee, the fridge and I were clearly going to Milltown.

Inch is the extravagant expanse of sand, *Trá Inse* – 'the peninsula-beach' – where Sarah Miles, clearly possessing the same fine sense of direction I'd been showing today, walked and walked in *Ryan's Daughter* and managed to arrive in Dunquin. The road from there to Castlemaine, the R561, runs dead straight along the coast, blipping slightly inland at Aughils, where *Bóthar na gCloch*, the stony road, had delivered me, and veering southeast at Boolteens to continue even straighter. Boolteens is *Na Buailtíní*, 'the milking-places', or 'the summer pastures', from the time when young people used to take the cows to higher ground for the summer, away from ripening crops, like Heidi in the Alps. Rattling along this road, with buttercups knee-high on either side, I spotted a sign on the left saying 'Restaurant', then 'Vegetarian' and 'Organic garden'. There were cobalt-blue windowboxes, yellow flowers, blue flowers, climbers: I recognized the cheerful nodding purple heads of the potato-vine bred at the Botanic Gardens in Dublin, *Solanum crispum* 'Glasnevin', and then it was all behind me. The fridge was still in the back of the car, and we had Things to Do. On the way back, perhaps – if I still hadn't eaten, and if I did come back that way – but considering how the journey had gone so far, nothing could be certain.

Through Castlemaine, and heading out for Milltown, my eyes

were peeled for County Council signs. At the T-junction where the N70 and the R561 part company stood a homemade sign for 'Mass Rock', and another that read 'Museum 4km'. Much as I love small museums, Museum 4km was in the wrong direction, and so I ploughed on, south into Milltown and out the other side, until a sign on the left pointed towards the Recycling and Waste Transfer Station, and on I drove, and on, between fields of gentlest green and hedgerows bursting with blossoming honeysuckle, that my father always called wild woodbine. Its picture was on his cigarette packet, and its smell was wonderful: the message being, presumably, Inhale! In Irish they call honeysuckle *Míl na nGabhar*, goats' honey.

The Transfer Station appeared, and a very fine place it was – clean and orderly, with a weighbridge leading to a mysterious tower, and receptacles for glass and plastic, waste oil and batteries. It was presided over by a polite man who helped me take the fridge out of the back of the car and line it up on a concrete base with others of its kind. There were cookers and fridges and washing machines and microwaves, standing demurely in the sunshine with a dignity that made me want to stay and hear their histories. The man in charge explained to me that they would all be squeezed before being dumped, and I thought about the way the language we use every day is not the same from place to place. In parts of America a sack is a little bag, and a bag is big; in Ireland it's the other way around. In Dublin you can only squeeze something (or someone) smaller than yourself, and usually something soft: an orange, perhaps, or a soft toy, or someone's hand; but in Kerry you can squeeze a screw with a screwdriver to tighten it, and you can squeeze a fridge to crush it. I would have liked to stay longer, to learn more about this different world, but I didn't think the Waste Transfer Station was a place where I could reasonably linger.

Back to Milltown, where I posted a letter and bought a newspaper. Sooner or later I would have to eat, and I hadn't brought a book to take the bare look off me. Back towards Castlemaine, and fridge-less, I decided to visit Museum 4km. Two-and-a-half miles wasn't far out of my way, after all, and I wasn't *that* hungry. Another straight road, and some very fast traffic: this was the R561 again, on its way to and from Farranfore airport. A sign on the roadside informed me that I would soon reach the Shamrock Bygones Museum, and sure enough, I did: a house on the right, with a car parked in front carrying a roof sign, and a large placard that said, 'Museum Open: It's Bigger than It Looks'.

The owner spotted me, and came to open the door, asking me for £2 only when I inquired how much he charged. 'There are over 4,000 items,' he told me, showing how the original space had been extended back and back. There were coins, china, utensils of all kinds, cigarette cards and cigarette packets in frames, and other memorabilia arranged on shelves and in cases around us, and as we walked around he told me the history of some of them, like the telegram sent in 1912 by 'Bridgie' to let relatives in Kerry know that a passenger on the *Titanic* had been saved.

In the next room were hundreds and hundreds of Dinky and Corgi cars and other toys: tiny and brilliantly coloured, though many of them had obviously survived long hours of robust play. A Victorian pram had a body made of wood. Prams were built deep, he told me, so that they could be used as playpens, where a child could stand upright. Radios and ancient tape-recorders were on shelves along the wall; farm tools and machinery took up the middle of the floor. There was a machine for grading potatoes, another for grooming horses, and one for shearing sheep. Beside spades and turf-slanes was a set of shepherd's crooks, designed to grab a sheep or lamb by the leg or around the neck; two of them had an extra curly loop at the top to hold a hanging lantern. There was a sheep-bell like the ones I've seen in the mountains of Italy and Switzerland, made of a single piece of metal folded over. It's Irish, though, the owner told me, and dates from the time when the big landlords employed shepherds to work in these mountains and the flock followed a leader. Farther down was a little red Austin Seven from 1935, a large car in toy-like miniature, restored to running order by this man's sons; then I saw a much larger Austin Ten, and a Ford Capri. There were bicycles of all vintages, at least one jukebox, children's tricycles, dolls in costume, and metal wall signs advertising tobacco, cigarettes and sweets. A bookcase held the two-gallon cans in which the early motorists bought petrol (at the chemist's). There were even a couple of the tall brown square gallon cans for paraffin; I used to carry one just like them as a child, when I was sent to Cobbe's hardware shop to buy paraffin for the heater. The brand name was on each different-coloured petrol tin, and the price was on some: three shillings.

If this museum were in America, it would be famous. Busloads of tourists would come to look again at things that used to be familiar. If this family were in America, and had lovingly assembled, repaired and displayed such a wealth of everyday treasures, articles would have been written about them, and films made. I thanked the owner, and wrote my appreciation in his visitors' book, but I didn't learn his name.

(Autumn 2001)

Yeats and the lights of Dublin

DEREK MAHON

J.W. ('Basher') Boyle taught us English at Belfast 'Inst'. Dr Boyle was a Dublin Protestant and a graduate of Trinity, where, in the thirties, he knew the likes of Conor Cruise O'Brien and Owen Sheehy Skeffington. Inst, founded in 1791, was and is a large city-centre grammar school best known for its old boys' rugby club, Instonians, which always provided at least one or two names in the Irish international XV. The school, though Unionist in ethos (the principal was always an Englishman), had a vaguely liberal tradition, and numbered among its former pupils the poets Ferguson and Allingham. More recent old boys included one Charles Monteith, a director of Faber & Faber and a friend of Eliot. We knew about that because there were several books by Eliot in the school library signed 'for the boys of Inst' by the author himself; and the publishers' address, then 24 Russell Square, London WC1, in those rich, 'linen-bound' editions, left an authoritative imprint on those of us who took a precocious interest in such things.

'Basher' Boyle was so called not because he was physically violent but because, though of gentlemanly appearance, he had the large frame and concave features of one who could fight his corner. (He should really have been nicknamed Orson, since he bore a striking resemblance to middle-period Orson Welles.) He was put in charge of our Upper Sixth scholarship class where the syllabus covered a number of canonical texts from Shakespeare to modern times including *King Lear*, *Tom Jones* and *Heart of Darkness*. It also included a volume of verse entitled *The Tower*; and so it was that we embarked for the first time, during the school year 1959–60, on a serious reading of Yeats. Boyle had an insider's knowledge of Dublin personality, folklore and anecdote, and his idea of teaching five hundred years of English Literature was to race through Shakespeare and the rest in the first term and spend the remaining two terms on a close study of Yeats. No doubt I exaggerate, but that's how it seems in retrospect. Not only had he known O'Brien (soon to be in the news because of the 1961 Congo crisis); he had met the septuagenarian Maud Gonne. He had never actually met Yeats but had occasionally seen him, and other giants of that time, in the streets of Dublin; so when he read aloud the lines –

> I have met them at close of day
> Coming with vivid faces
> From counter or desk among grey
> Eighteenth-century houses

– a magically recent world sprang to life: the streets of Dublin, a hundred miles down the road! Our own Belfast streets were Victorian and gloomy; but the Georgian streets of Dublin, glimpsed on our early travels, housed, we knew, a different and more glamorous spirit. Enchanted, we didn't confine ourselves to *The Tower* but ranged freely over the *Collected Poems* in the old buff-coloured Macmillan (London) edition. I can still recall the excitement we felt as we turned to page 217 and the sonorous *ottava rima* of 'Sailing to Byzantium', a sublime gift from the gods far transcending what contemporary poetry we knew then – except for pop songs, of course.

The contemporary poetry we knew at Inst in January 1960 was of three kinds: the Illustrious, the Local and the New English. (Of Clarke and Kavanagh, the Dublin poets, we as yet knew nothing.) The illustrious were Eliot, Graves, and above all Dylan Thomas, whom we strove to imitate. The locals were MacNeice, Rodgers and Hewitt; and the New English, notably Larkin and Davie, were the ones we sometimes saw mentioned in the book pages of the London *Observer* – which, as young sophisticates, we knew we had to read or at least be seen with. MacNeice and Rodgers, far off in London, seemed local no more. Hewitt ran an art gallery in Coventry but was known to spend his summers in a cottage at Cushendall, Co. Antrim, which made him seem more neighbourly. A regionalist, he spoke of the 'identity crisis' of that now familiar creature, the Ulster writer, and had written, in the magazine *Lagan* in 1945, that 'the Ulster writer must be a rooted man [*sic*], must carry the native tang of his idiom like the native dust on his sleeve; otherwise he is an airy internationalist, thistledown, a twig in the stream'. We came to like and respect John Hewitt when we made his acquaintance later; but in those days, without knowing him, we thought of him as rather programmatic and authoritarian, even his admirable radical-ism rather methodical. To us airy twigs the real question was: what's happening in London, where they do the *Observer*? And the curious answer was that some of what was happening there was really happening, or had just happened, in Ireland.

Larkin, for example, was a former librarian at Queen's University; and Donald Davie had recently taught at Trinity. Somehow there came into our possession, at least for a time, Davie's volume *A Winter Talent* (1957), which we took as illustrative of the state of English poetry, and perhaps we weren't far wrong. It con-tained, among other modest achievements, 'Samuel Beckett's Dublin', 'The Mushroom Gatherers', 'The Fountain', 'Hearing Russian Spoken' and 'Rejoinder to a Critic'. There was at the time in England a circle who called themselves, or allowed themselves to be called, the 'Movement'; sometimes, adopting the title of Robert Conquest's anthology of Movement verse, they were known as the New Lines poets. Larkin was one, Davie was another; and 'Rejoinder to a Critic' is not only a typical but even, in its prohibitive con-straint, an emblematic Movement poem; indeed, it's virtually a Movement manifesto. A critic of the time, perhaps someone nostal-gic for the glorious excesses of Dylan Thomas, had rebuked Davie for a lack of feeling, no doubt suggesting his poems were arid and academic. As if to prove it, Davie responded with a poem notable for strict form, argumentativeness, direct quotations from Coleridge and Donne, self-deprecating irony and an almost complete absence

of imagery – except for the atomic mushroom cloud, a picture presented with the clinical detachment of a physicist in a lecture room:

> Love's radio-active fall-out on a large
> Expanse around the point it bursts above.

Davie, himself a Navy man during the Second World War, clearly
felt implicated in the destruction of Hiroshima and Nagasaki, and
there is something of Adorno here in the suggestion that, after the
atrocities of the period, there could be no more 'poetry' (a theory
contemporaneously refuted by Paul Celan, and indeed Dylan
Thomas); or, at least, that one should 'appear concerned only to
make it scan'. This and the last line, 'How dare we now be anything
but numb?', were often quoted in those years, and these prescriptions contributed significantly to the rather glum rationalism
(Whiggery, Yeats would have called it) of Movement aesthetics;
while their pedagogical tone and lack of interest in imagery were
reflected also in more bohemian circles like the long-ago London
'Group', to which I'll return.

Irony is a feature attributed to liberal Ulster Protestants generally, the tone having been set by MacNeice, as if to absolve us of
responsibility for our reprehensible heritage: one might write a love
poem, or a plea for the wretched of the earth, and someone would
say, 'Oh, he's a liberal Ulster Protestant, he's being ironical.' No one
could describe Yeats as ironical (sarcastic sometimes, never ironical);
indeed, it was always part of his public persona, and his appeal to
satirical spectators like George Moore, that he was, if anything, too
much in earnest. It has been said that he had no sense of humour;
to which the answer is that he wasn't interested in humour but in
passion and in wit, a different thing. Humour he would have considered beneath him, or rather a waste of time (one of his
Middleton relations he calls 'a humorous, unambitious man'). He
had, though, like his brother Jack, a sense of fun, of the festive –
and, of course, the grotesque. Also, I'm afraid, a deplorable taste in
puns. Mrs French in 'The Tower', for example, whose manservant

presents her with a pair of ears in 'a little covered dish', is later described as 'gifted with so fine an ear'. The question of wit, humour, irony and the like may seem unimportant, but it is really quite central. Gramsci, in the prison notebooks, called irony 'a disease of the interregnum', which makes it sound peculiarly excruciating. While the world got on with the business of history, specifically the mutation of societies, irony remained and perhaps remains a resource for rueful liberals and nostalgic humanists, many addicted to the backward gaze. Yeats looked back too, of course – to the eighteenth century, to Byzantium – but in order to understand the present and anticipate the future; for, despite his patrician airs and flirtation with fascism, he remains to this day a revolutionary figure, a proto-hippie, eco-feminist and prophet of the new world disorder: 'The arts lie dreaming of what is to come'. Nor was he 'patriarchal'; the women in his life were, like himself, active, disputatious and independent.

John Boyle's extramural activites involved him with left-wing politics and an interesting if shamefully middle-class cultural experiment off the elitist Malone Road, where Mary O'Malley, a Dublin woman, and her psychiatrist husband Pearse, ran an amateur back-garden outfit called the Lyric Theatre. The Lyric is now one of Belfast's most venerable institutions, but in those days it subsisted on the energy and enthusiasm of a few, of whom Boyle was one. He sat on the board, as did John Hewitt and Austin Clarke. The Lyric specialized in the Yeatsian repertoire and brought out a quarterly magazine, *Threshold*, which published, among other things, work by Clarke and Rodgers, Hewitt and Montague. Yeats's attitude to the North, specifically to the Protestant North, had been unappreciative. He visited often enough – first as a boy, for there were relations in Co. Down; later with the Abbey touring company; and later still to broadcast for the regional BBC. Politeness confined his frankest comments to the correspondence with Lady Gregory, to whom he remarked at the time of partition: 'I have long been of opinion that, if such disagreeable people shut the door, we should turn the key in the lock before they change their mind.'

We got our scholarships, drank a bottle of Guinness with John Boyle in the Crown Liquor Saloon, and went down to Trinity – not a place, according to Yeats, that produced 'artistic minds', though his own father was only one obvious exception. I'm sure the lectures were all very good, but we didn't go to lectures much except to hear Alec Reid, an endearingly helpless Englishman of Irish antecedents who, like Boyle with pre-Yeatsian English literature, took an oblique stance vis-à-vis the curriculum. He was that legendary figure, the inspiring teacher who stimulates the imagination; and he often conducted informal tutorials in O'Neill's Bar and Lounge, Suffolk Street. Trinity lecturers didn't publish much in those days, not the older ones anyway; perhaps it was thought a bit pushy. The gentle R.B.D. French, for example, confined himself to a tasteful monograph on Wodehouse and contributed brief comic sketches annually to the Trinity Week undergraduate revue. Alec would go on to write a short but insightful study of Beckett's plays entitled *All I Can Manage, More than I Could*; but at the time of which I speak he was the author only of some theatre reviews in the *Irish Times* and a single poem which he recited sonorously to us in its entirety during our first lecture:

> Remembering the eagle's high adventure
> And eager to resume the ethereal search,
> I sit in a suburban drawing-room,
> A clever parrot on a polished perch.

This memorable quatrain (note the subtle variation of 'e' sounds) first appeared on the first page of the first number of Trinity's literary magazine *Icarus*, founded by Alec ten years before in 1950; and that simple, unadorned phrase, 'a suburban drawing-room', opens up a whole era – for I remember Alec's drawing-room in Ballybrack, where he and his wife Beatrice sometimes had us out for 'tea' (bottles of stout), and very nice it was too for a Belfast scholarship boy then kipping, unsupervised, in a back room of the unrenovated Brazen Head: unrenovated, it seemed, since Swiftian times. Dublin was full of drawing-rooms in those days, all of them in Edwardian bungalows like Alec's or in pleasant Georgian houses with windows open to gardens and birdsong, where sunlight lay perpetually on shelves of dusty first editions. These drawing-rooms were the property of older people, amateur poets and philosophers of private means like Arland Ussher, who had known Yeats or had moved in circles tangential to his; and, though we were happiest in O'Neill's with Alec booming away, we were conscious too of a continuity with the unpubbable Yeatsian past. Alec's holiday home was a disused lighthouse in Greece, though whether he had Yeatsian towers in mind when he chose it, he never said.

Those of us who were at Trinity in the early sixties and starting to write contributed to *Icarus*, which we edited in rotation, so I think of us as 'the *Icarus* crowd'. We included Michael Longley (a slightly older Instonian), Edna Broderick, Brendan Kennelly, Eavan Boland, Ronnie Wathen, Jeremy Lewis and Deborah de Vere White. Not all were Yeatsians necessarily: Longley and Wathen were Gravesians, and Kennelly was a Kavanagh man. Up at UCD too they were Kavanagh people, as well as Joyceans, and our contemporaries there – Michael Hartnett, Paul Durcan, Macdara Woods, Eamon Grennan – could sometimes even be seen sitting nervously at Kavanagh's table in McDaid's. One of the fun things about the *Icarus* crowd was its gregariousness. We were a mixed bunch, from everywhere including India and Nigeria, and knocked about together with the natural camaraderie of youth – while cultivating, of course, all sorts of privacies and solitudes of the soul. Something of that inclusiveness is evident in Brendan's later remarks about Yeats, where he praises his capacity 'to discover unity where so many before and since have perceived and perpetuated discord and division'. This is an obvious but valuable point, and one to be emphasized; for Yeats incorporated aspects of most known traditions into the imaginative structure and wove into the patchwork, together with oriental silks and 'grey Connemara cloth', a few threads from the sash some fathers wore.

Longley and I, like other Northerners in Dublin, returned regularly to Belfast and environs, where our families lived, and often hung out with students from Queen's, some of whom we'd known at school; so a typical Saturday night in Belfast, especially around Christmas time, would find us in Kelly's Cellars or Lavery's back bar (the 'Cobbles') off Shaftesbury Square, with our QUB opposite numbers. There we met student activists like Eamonn McCann and other literary types like James Simmons and Seamus Heaney. Belfast-fashion, there was much sectarian banter, idiotic in a place where so many have exogamous relations: my own non-Protestant auntie, Lily Lavery, I presumed to be related, however remotely, to the 'wine trade' and even to the great Sir John, husband of Hazel. There too we met an Englishman, a recently appointed lecturer at Queen's, called Philip Hobsbaum, a Cambridge man who had known the London 'Group' and now established a Belfast branch. Philip in person was an exhilarating presence and fitted in very well to the rather rackety local milieu; for he was a challenging, rambunctious figure, fond of drink and controversy, and given to self-dramatizing pronouncements like 'Things happen wherever I go; fights break out' and 'I bet I could take Mahon's girlfriend away from him'. About the fights it was certainly true, and we cherished him for it; but in his critical attitudes he espoused a moral earnestness, an insistence on 'felt experience' and a literal-mindedness that were dogmatic and doctrinaire in the extreme. You didn't disagree with Philip, or not for long; you learned to listen to his opinion, think your own thoughts, and keep your own counsel. Much guff has been written about Philip's 'Group', whose combative meetings aroused limited interest. Though we hit it off in informal situations, I myself attended only once and never went back. 'Group' guff was an invention of English journalists, critics, commentators, who had no idea of the circumstances, and I think there's a reason for this, a political one. Conscious of a loosening grip, English culture (always retentive) seizes upon whatever it can claim, however residually, as its own; and so it has been with the recent Ulster poetry. The Limerick-born actor Richard Harris used to say that if he won an award the London papers would run the headline 'British Actor Wins Award'; but if he misbehaved they would say, 'Irish Actor

Thrown Out of Night Club'.

While Belfast discourse was cheerfully abrasive, a more polished variety was characteristic of Dublin, where the rhetorical arts still flourished. Famous windbags abounded, and self-appointed 'wits'; extravagant gesture was much admired, parliamentary vehemence cultivated. The university debating societies, where aspiring barristers and politicians practised their oratory, flashed with profile and attitude; everyone thought he was Edmund Burke. These performances were exclusively masculine and stylistically conservative. Women were not encouraged, not that any sane woman would have wanted to take part, though she might have found the spectacle revealing; for here, on noisy nights, one could hear the voice of authority being formed (or so they hoped) in the inflections of an earlier time. They were all longing for an opportunity to exclaim, 'Let no man write my epitaph!' or 'You have disgraced yourselves again!' The tradition died, however. The debating-society stuff was already archaic; for even in Ireland the sixties brought new developments. We're all provincials of our own time, and the decade probably brought little that hadn't occurred before, in the forties or in the twenties; but it seemed evident to us that a new age had dawned, and one or two of the brighter hippies noticed a relevance to their own concerns in some of Yeats's prophetic utterances. Gyres and the like were bound to appeal to a generation devoted to Tao and *The Tibetan Book of the Dead*.

Yeats himself, in *A Vision*, describes his strange ideas as 'stylistic arrangements of experience' comparable to the cubes of Wyndham Lewis and the ovoids of Brancusi. If he has taken such ideas literally, he reports, 'my reason has soon recovered'. This is reassuring to us sceptics, and gives us the perfect excuse to pay minimal attention to his magical system. But perhaps we miss out on something by being too quick to ignore the implications; for *A Vision* is really a sort of political book. Yeats described it as mythology rather than philosophy, much as Graves later described *The White Goddess* as 'an historical grammar of poetic myth'. But both are political books, or perhaps I should say ecological books. I think it probable that Yeats considered *A Vision* to be in effect a Nietzschean prophecy like Spengler's now largely forgotten *Decline of the West,* so fashionable at that time; and he may have thought it better to publish a fanciful work than a pompous one. The gyres have come in for a lot of stick over the years; but aren't they really a way of asking questions like 'Is there a shape to history?' and 'Where do we go from here?', questions not in themselves ridiculous. Besides, in his curiously practical fashion, Yeats was epistemologically sound; he always 'saved the phenomena', as scientists say.

Another problem area is the archaism: linguistic certainly; social too, of course, but also what we might call environmental:

> Beloved books that famous hands have bound,
> Old marble heads, old pictures everywhere.

The tower itself is an ivory one, figuratively of course; he wishes to 'set eyes on nothing' not sanctified by time, like Sato's sword. A tall order in the modern world, and there's something painful about the great national poet staring with 'hatred' (his own word) at the lights of Dublin. He studiously ignored many modern developments; much had to be excluded from consciousness, especially if it had an electrical or mechanical origin. We know his philosophical aversion to mechanism. Perhaps in the long run he will be proved right, and some future post-industrial society will turn for endorsement to his ecological purism; but even so he misses out on an exciting feature of the period. Readers of the future, exploring the texture of twentieth-century life, will find little of it in Yeats. True, the Middleton freighters sailed to Constantinople ('All my dreams were ships'); but there are no cinemas or aircraft in his work, the obvious exception being Robert Gregory's biplane in 'An Irish Airman Foresees His Death' – though even here the plane is more like the *picture* of a plane. There's none of the 'oil-rinsed bearings' of Hart Crane's 'Cape Hatteras'. Crane, another Platonist, also writing in the twenties, likens the cinema to Plato's cave with 'multitudes bent toward some flashing screen', and proposes, in futuristic mode, 'the articulation of the contemporary human consciousness *sub specie aeternitatis*'. Yeats preferred his eternity unadulterated; yet he recommends 'the baptism of the gutter' – an example of his ability to make words mean different things in different contexts. 'Arrogance' and 'bitterness', for example, can be good or bad depending on the persons involved. He is hostile to the notion (his own) that the 'abounding gutter' might be Helicon; while for many, including himself, this has been an article of faith. He talks frequently about 'the book of the people' and 'the common tongue'; and one can easily imagine him, in another context, using a phrase like 'the abounding gutter' with a positive and even festive intention. The list of modern poets whose Helicon has been, precisely, the abounding gutter, *vox populi vox Dei*, is a long one, and I need only mention MacDiarmid, Brecht and Pasolini to show with what eloquence the idea has been celebrated. Yeats knew this too, of course, as later poems like 'Lapis Lazuli' go to show: everything is dialectic, truth and counter-truth.

Other objections might be that there is too much 'fury'; that his heroism is too relentless; that his standards of beauty and performance are too elevated to be humanly interesting. There is a singular character defect too: the will to 'win'. He was too interested in winning; so it comes as no surprise that his brother Jack was the more winning personality and his father, in many ways, the wiser man. Yeats learned much, perhaps most, from his father, as a reading of the old man's letters to his son make clear. Writing from New York in April 1913, JBY says, 'Rhetoric expresses other people's feelings, poetry one's own' – a remark which, duly pondered by the poet, emerges five years later, in *Per Amica Silentia Lunae*: 'We make, out of the quarrel with others, rhetoric; out of the quarrel with ourselves, poetry'; and there are many such examples. 'The world will not be right', says JBY, 'till poetry is pronounced to be life itself, our being but its shadow and poor imitation'; and in June 1921, eight months before his death, he again writes to Willie: 'It is easier to write poetry that is far from life, but it is *infinitely more exciting* to write *the poetry of life*, and that is what the whole world is crying out for. I bet it is what your wife wants – ask her. She will know what I mean and drive it home.'

The mask compels reductive curiosity: what was Yeats 'really' like? Who was the bundle of incoherence that sat down to breakfast? Did he ever play football, go for a swim? Had he a phone, a radio? He would have played football at school, though it seems like a 'mobbish' kind of game for a solitary; so it comes as no surprise to learn, from the *Autobiographies*, that as a boy he followed athletics, where individual excellence is the thing, not team spirit, where the individual competes against himself, as in any form of art. He himself drew, or implied, the parallel: 'I followed the career of a certain professional runner for months, buying papers that would tell me if he had won or lost. I had seen him described as "the bright particular star of American athletics", and the wonderful phrase had thrown enchantment over him. Had he been called the particular bright star, I should have cared nothing for him. I didn't understand the symptom for years after ...' He swam constantly in youth at Rosses Point (indeed, he swam into middle age when occasion offered); interestingly too, also in youth, he was a keen sailor, sometimes setting off at dawn in a cousin's boat and spending whole days on the water. We know that later he had a phone and a 'wireless', answering back to broadcast voices he disagreed with. Did he ever push a pram? I don't know that he ever pushed one, but I think he's at least minding one in 'A Prayer for my Daughter', one of the great pram poems together with Coleridge's 'Frost at Midnight'. Watching his baby daughter, he entertains thoughts of 'natural kindness'; and it's worth remembering that, for all his abstract urgency and hauteur, these ordinary things were central to him – indeed, they have much to do with the 'unity of being'.

We came to think of him as a monument, even as a statue. Yeats himself, like Pound, perfected 'the sculpture of rhyme', and had a taste for lapidary inscriptions: 'Swift's Epitaph', 'To Be Carved on a Stone at Thoor Ballylee', 'Cast a cold eye ...'. To be cold, somehow beyond human reach, especially 'the daily spite of this unmannerly town' (Dublin), became a personal necessity, though one which didn't rule out the 'passionate'; on the contrary, the ideas fused in his mind. To be somehow beyond critical detraction was also a stylistic (and creative) imperative, and we came to think of him as unassailable where the poetry itself was concerned, if open to serious question in matters of politics and philosophy; but the scholarly snow precipitated by his own coldly passionate dreams disfigured his dream-statue in our minds; he 'became his admirers'. The myths took shape, the critical books piled up, and somehow the man himself ceased to exist. Such was the force and ingenuity of his self-creation (a trick learnt from Wilde), he seemed to have spirited himself away until only the work remained, a monument of its own magnificence. He really did seem to be 'out of nature', one who had never taken his bodily form from 'any natural thing' – a ludicrous thought when one considers his own emphasis on the physical. It was a triumph of masquerade, heroic in its intensity; but the deconstructionists came to Sligo, and now he is human again.

Montague, Simmons, all of us indeed, have echoed Yeats; Heaney, too, echoes Yeats echoing Shakespeare: 'Every wind that blows'; 'The end of art is peace'. All this intertextuality is nothing new: 'Works of art are always begotten by previous works of art.' We inherit his example, to use Seamus's word. What we haven't inherited, or only residually, is his deep structure; for we were born at a later time, into changed conditions, and have often felt it necessary to resist the Yeatsian charm and authority. He was, of course, proud with a pride many called arrogance; but, though no 'wit' in the traditional sense, thank God, he obviously had a rich vein of fun, besides giving an important place to 'gaiety' in his hierarchy of values. Humour he recognized as an enemy of his kind of poetry, so he avoided it in verse almost entirely; but gaiety is a different thing, capable as it is of condoning madness, lust and rage. The Chinese sages in 'Lapis Lazuli' and the lords and ladies of Byzantium and Ben Bulben are gay in that sense; and so too was Yeats, as the later photographs testify. No doubt he could be affected and insufferable, yet how come such a man had so many friends? As for the admirers he has become, they increase daily. He has left us phrases like talismans, consolatory and inspiring ('a lonely impulse of delight'; 'our proper dark'), an ideal of audacity and empowerment, and a paradigm of transfiguration, personal and historical. His example shames and ennobles us all.

(Autumn 2002)

Crossing the Delaware

CHRISTINA HUNT MAHONY

When I was eleven I started to take piano lessons from a man named Eddie Hatrack. He lived in a gaunt house around the corner, alone except for his withdrawn teenage son whom most of us never saw. A Juilliard graduate of great promise, Eddie had played piano for Ernie Kovacs, first on the radio and then on live television. But that was years earlier. He had hands that spanned twelfths, which meant he could play Dave Brubeck as written. Now Eddie Hatrack taught people like me.

I had started lessons quite late, but when a scholarship exam came up a couple of years later it was decided I would try for it. Success meant a private convent-school education a cut above the archdiocesan alternative. There was an academic scholarship exam too; that part was easy. The musical audition took place at the school's dark Victorian mansion under surreal conditions, and was terrifying. I played a Chopin nocturne. Recently I heard the piece, played by Rubenstein in a classic recording. I was stuck in traffic, listening to the car radio. Every note reverberated through my skull, with love, panic and total recall. Every pause, every adagio. I could smell the furniture wax from the day of the audition.

I told the nuns at my elementary school that I had won. No one from the school had ever won a scholarship. The principal was beaming, and sent me immediately to the pastor, Thomas E. Kearney. When I rang the bell at the rectory I was ushered in by the elderly housekeeper, who never spoke in anything but a whisper. Fr Kearney always wore the belt of his soutane under his belly. I think he was from Clare. 'I've won a scholarship to the Villa. For music and academics – half tuition – Sr St Joseph said I should come and tell you.' He was red-faced and white-haired, and didn't miss a beat: 'Hope you like spaghetti.' He was talking about the Italians.

The school was run by an order of nuns who had been brought over to teach the children of Italian immigrants. It was situated on the banks of the Delaware. I remember being fascinated by the term 'riparian rights', something the school retained. Private access to waterfront property was no longer allowed, but the school's deeds predated the legislation. The house had been part of the old Fisk estate, and a lot of people still called it that. It had been built with money from the gains of the Credit Mobilier scandal under President Grant. Its purchase by the Church had been arranged by Diamond Jim Brady, a Gilded Age tycoon and gourmand who favoured diamonds for himself, not for the ladies, and whose name was once a byword for nouveau riche ostentation. In appreciation for Diamond Jim's efforts the school had been named the Villa Victoria, after his wife. The story was told that she had died young, and I had always thought it was a sad, romantic story, and felt sorry for him. Somehow I had the idea that he had built the house for his bride. I knew the true story, but I preferred my own version. I was thirteen by then.

The Victorian Gothic mansion was where the nuns and the boarders lived, and where we had our music lessons. Scattered about were a number of outbuildings, some old, and some new and ugly, including a Quonset hut for the sciences, which weren't a priority. The elementary school was housed in a charming bungalow with a screened porch, set in a small apple orchard; it had been the groundskeeper's house. There was no playground. The little ones played in the orchard at recess, and I always thought their building was much nicer than ours. All the classes were very small. There were only fifteen freshmen who entered in my year, and the school's traditions were elaborate. For First Communion the little girls wore ankle-length gowns with long veils, and carried sprays of fresh flowers like baby brides. When we performed in recitals, and even for graduation, we wore white ball gowns. For graduation, girls also had to wear long white gloves.

The chaplain, a German monk, came straight out of central casting, rotund with a tonsure. He occupied a tiny cottage, no more than a hut, in the pine woods at the rear of the campus. He was a Franciscan, always surrounded by dogs, and rather comically fond of critters – the school cats, and even Sister Lillian's inexplicable flock of white ducks. They had imprinted on her at birth, and scurried after her whenever she left the Quonset hut, her domain. I guessed the chaplain took the Franciscan thing seriously enough. That his name was Godfrey Wolf simply added to the mystique. He was the only man there, but there were other Franciscans in town so I suppose he had company when he wanted it.

I went from being an ordinary girl in my neighbourhood of clapboard houses and kids who played on the sidewalk, to being someone who was whisked off by bus early each morning to an exotic venue about which the neighbours were curious and knew nothing. I wore a school uniform that no one could readily identify. All my friends went to other schools. Gradually I lost track of them and they of me. Lou, the bus driver, was my friend. I was picked up first, as I lived the farthest away. I had been urged to accept the free boarding that went with the scholarship, but I wasn't ready to live away from home. Boarding school was a rarity in my world, it was for rich kids with divorced parents. We didn't know anyone who was divorced.

Lou called me 'Red'. Every morning he would open the door of the bus with the huge cranking metal arm, and he and I would have freewheeling conversations at 7 a.m. He also called me his 'paysan'. I didn't know what that meant, but I knew it was a compliment, and when I asked my father he laughed and said Lou must like me. Lou didn't like the rich girls on the bus who treated him like a servant, never talking with him or even looking at him as they passed by and took their seats, opening pocket mirrors to make sure their hair hadn't blown.

I was skinny and red-haired and from an Irish family; it seemed all the other girls at the school were Italian-American, and had figures and boyfriends. Later I learned there were more exotic boarders – wildly privileged older girls from Caracas and Buenos Aires. They actually had apartments in New York, or rather their parents did. During the week their duennas lived there, and came to collect them on Friday afternoons to take the train back to Manhattan. The duennas disapproved of the convent food, and monitored the girls' intake religiously. They were being groomed for rich husbands after a year or two of acquiring English. They would return after shopping expeditions to Henri Bendel with silk underwear and suede pumps. They held hands and giggled in Spanish. There was one boarder with an Irish name, motherless, with a father an army officer. She had lived as a pet in the convent for years. Her name was Margaret, but everyone called her Happy. She became a nun and died of cancer at twenty.

First thing every morning we had singing. Mother Superior was from an exalted family in Rome. It was rumoured she was titled. Tall, thin, pale and elegant, she exhorted us to breathe, suggesting, not entirely discreetly, that it would be good for developing our breasts. I loved the music and sang with gusto and high hopes. I have a decent voice, but my real value in these sessions was that I have relative pitch and could be counted upon to come in on key in either the second soprano or alto range. We sang Italian operas as though our lives depended upon it. In ways they did. Mother Superior filled in edited versions of the passionate story lines, and we were suckers. This was as close as I got in those days to passion.

'Miserere d'un'alma già vicina alla partenza che non ha ritorno!' – I can still do it. My problem was that I never knew Italian, and since nearly everyone else came from an Italian background the language was not taught in the school. My mother begged them. They were polite, but they didn't get it. So I learned the syllables off by heart. There always seemed to be months and months of preparing for recitals, tensions building, tempers getting shorter. Certain star performers took to developing strange illnesses. But ours weren't always the usual school concerts. Sometimes we got to play in places like the old Carnegie Hall. I played *Finlandia* – six pianos, twelve girls, twenty-four hands. That one still gives me a start when I hear it too: especially the part where I was supposed to come in. A vast Cuban girl called Carmen, whose parents had come to the States at the end of the Batista regime, led us all. She went on to the Southern concert circuit – Montevideo, Nairobi, Sydney. She was powerful at the keyboard, unlike most young women, and could handle the Grieg piano concerto admirably, even then.

The pianists, myself among them to a lesser degree, were brainiacs. We all did well, naturally, in math. The dancers were something else. Scraping through the academic subjects, they lived another life within those limited grounds with their formal garden and fountain, and the big iron gates on the road to Princeton. One of them was also an Irish girl, and our fathers had gone to school together. She asked me in our final year to be her accompanist for an audition. We practised together for weeks, every day after school. Eventually we went to Manhattan on the big day, and I played while Jeannie danced. She made the cut and went into Harkness House, a good company that no longer exists. The process was incredibly cruel. There were names on a huge chalkboard high up. If you didn't make the cut, someone came along with an eraser on a long rod and swished your name away. Girls were crying everywhere. That's all I remember: girls crying in the halls and throwing up in the bathrooms. I don't even remember Jeannie being glad, but she must have been.

I remember that there was another Jeannie. She was the one who entered our French class one morning late and blurted out that the president had been shot. Sister Dolores was Canadian, half French, half Italian, and she said calmly, but sternly, 'Jean, take your seat please, that's a dreadful rumour to spread.' Nicknames were not permitted.

There was a gilt harp in the main drawing room, and only one girl who played. When she left the school I was asked to learn. I never learned well, but the harp was only used incidentally in concerts. Meanwhile my career as a pianist wasn't taking off. In my third year I was changed from lessons with Mother Superior to her sub-altern, who was not the least bit inspiring. Sister Stella was small, dark and dour. I knew it was a demotion and was demoralized. Years later I read a Carson McCullers story, 'Wunderkind', in which the lone girl with a vaguely WASP background studies music in a world of Mitteleuropean males. She is given MacDowell to play in an act of desperation on the part of her well-meaning teacher after she seems to lose her touch for the music. He hopes she will regain her confidence and have a rapport with a composer who had an inspiration closer to what she knows. She doesn't. I was given MacDowell to play too, all those years earlier, by nuns who were Mediterranean and saw my heritage as being something that was alien. Does anyone ever play or listen to MacDowell anymore? I never hear him on the classical music stations.

One day before the demotion I was having my usual lesson with Mother Superior in her lavish study with its concert grand. There was a velvet drape over the piano to muffle the sound. The other practice rooms, many in converted porches which extended for three sides around the mansion, had uprights. We were working on a Scarlatti piece, and I thought I understood it, could feel it instinctively. It was a day of flutter, as one of the patrons of the school had arrived earlier in a limousine, and had disappeared into the convent for lunch. She was handed out of the car, dressed in white fur. These festive meals in the convent were a revelation to me when I first arrived at the Villa, because I saw the wine merchant's station wagon arrive at regular intervals. The nuns in primary school certainly never drank wine, but most of the nuns at the Villa were Italian born and the idea of meals without wine would never have occurred to them.

We had only got a glimpse of the patron. She was to speak to us at an assembly before we went home. Mother Superior was in good humour, but distracted. She smiled more than usual, and I was encouraged. And then the door opened quietly. The scent of perfume was immediately apparent (we were forbidden to wear scent, and of course the nuns didn't). But the scent heralded much more. A woman, not tall, arrived on high heels which clicked on the parquet floors until she reached the oriental carpet secured under the piano. She seemed wrapped rather than dressed. There were shawls and jewels, maybe feathers. But the whole effect was of wrapping, packaging, as though she were an elaborate gift. Even her head was swathed in a turban, also white against her fiercely black hair visible in the front. She had arched, heavy, pencilled eyebrows, a white face and fiery eyes. Her lips were also pencilled around the edges and filled in with a deep red lipstick. Her long nails were varnished in an equally bloody carmine. This was the era of pale make-up and Carnaby Street fashions, and rather than being arrested by her glamour, I thought her ugly and ghoulish. I had never seen anyone dressed as she was. Her hands weren't nice, stubby, and everything on her seemed to glitter, but not welcomingly. She had a strange European accent, which at the time I could only have recognized as 'foreign'. As an adult I would learn that she had grown up in New York and acquired this speaking voice later in life. In early recordings she had the usual formal American radio voice of the era.

'Continue, continue, don't let me interrupt. I must see, Elisabetta, how you spend your days. And this is one of your fine pupils.' She settled into a leather chair and crossed her legs showing a lot of shiny black silk stocking.

Mother Superior wasn't pleased. I wasn't one of her best to show off. I had risen and curtsied, and nearly fallen off the piano bench while trying to sit down again. I kept thinking that I should have been one of the Italian girls with a figure, who would have at least looked promising as a woman, if not as a musician. Or that Carmen should have been there, in all her girth, to bat out Rachmaninoff and silence all questions of worth. But there I was, all the wrong color and shape, and aware that one knee sock was drooping. I really tried with the Scarlatti, and did a creditable job. Mother Superior relaxed and threw me a slightly appreciative look. At least I hadn't fallen apart or disgraced either one of us. When 'Madame' asked my name, I replied 'Christina'. It somehow seemed better than if it had been Deirdre, my sister's name. What would she have made of that?

'Ah Christina, you play with emotion, and that is what we musicians must always have.' She then rose, and spoke briefly with Mother Superior, calling her again by her first name, and touching her. They left together, arms linked and laughing quietly. I just hoped they weren't laughing at my Scarlatti.

Madame could be seen walking across the gardens to the auditorium later that afternoon. She didn't really walk, she seemed to glide or sweep. People, mostly nuns, were swarming around her, and they all seemed smaller, although she wasn't a large woman. She could have been sailing; her white turban made her look like a figurehead. I looked at the river close by, and thought of George Washington and his soldiers crossing the Delaware right there on Christmas Day, and how they had changed the course of the Revolutionary War. If you grew up in that part of the world you had the story off by heart. (The Hessian soldiers who fought on the British side were barracked about a mile away. The building is still there.) The painting of the scene of Washington and his troops isn't distinguished, but it is iconic. I couldn't have identified many paintings when I was thirteen, but I knew that one. I imagined Madame at the prow of a boat on the river with huddled figures behind her, changing the course of lives simply by her presence. My parents were later thrilled to hear the story of the unexpected guest at my lesson. My mother told the neighbours, my father tried to tell the men at work. Mostly people didn't understand, except some of their Italian friends. I knew who she was, of course, just like I knew the real story of Diamond Jim Brady and his wife. I had heard her sing on the Ed Sullivan show. My mother had repeated the name of the aria for me – 'Casta Diva'. But on that day I preferred to think of Maria Callas crossing the Delaware.

(Spring 2004)

Shalom à la crème

IAN SANSOM

My father is standing at the front of the church, welcoming the congregation to the Christmas service. He is wearing his blue nylon blazer with the plastic gold-coloured buttons, a blue-and-white striped shirt, a shiny striped blue tie, and grey slacks. He has a silky powder-blue handkerchief tucked into his blazer pocket and his shoes – brown shoes of that peculiar plastic-soled, exceedingly soft and squidgy kind available only from discount shoe shops and much favoured by pensioners and people on low incomes, the shoes, I know, of my own future – are highly polished. There are liver spots – brown liver spots – on his hands and all over the top of his bald head, *my* head in years to come. He looks like a kindly old second-hand car salesman, the paterfamilias perhaps of a tidy little business operating on a corner-site just off the A13 down towards Pitsea, or a speaker at a Rotary Club dinner.

'Welcome,' he is saying, putting on what I recognize as his telephone voice, 'Welcome to our Christmas Service.' He has a slight, soft lisp – 'Crispmass' – that's partly a result of fifty years of pipe smoking and partly the remains of his old-fashioned Ron-Moody-as-Fagin London accent. 'Welcome to our Christmas Service at St Margaret's Church, Worthing, in Norfolk.'

I'm not at all clear how we got here. Or rather, I know how we got here, this morning, to this place in particular: we walked up the lane from my parents' house to the church, past the ploughed fields and the sheep, the children running on ahead, my mum walking slowly behind, talking to Nancy the next-door neighbour, and me pushing the buggy with my little year-old nephew, my wife following on with my sister and her partner. What I don't know is how we got here in general, together, to a church, on Christmas day. How any of us have ended up here is a complete mystery.

We always go to my parents' for Christmas; it's tradition. But until a few years ago none of us went to church at Christmas. Until a few years ago most of us would never have darkened the door of a church under any circumstances – my sister and her partner on principle, my parents out of mere disinterest, my wife, an Ulster Protestant, through sheer surfeit, and me personally because I'd had more than enough of church throughout my late teens and early twenties when I somehow ended up leaving school and working as a full-time proselytizing charismatic evangelical, travelling up and down the country bringing Good News to the poor and glad tidings of great joy about the little baby born in the manger, who was born that we might have life, and life eternal. Back then I wore thirteen-hole Doctor Marten boots, had long hair, and read only the Bible, and when I visited home at Christmas to see my parents I'd have heated arguments about religion with my father at the dinner table: he was more Richard Dawkins then than Richard Dawkins is now.

'It's just a phase you're going through,' he would say, pausing between mouthfuls of turkey and Brussels sprouts. 'You'll see.'

'I would like to extend a particular welcome this morning,' my dad is saying, up front, 'to people who have travelled a long way to worship with us. There are some people here from Sydney, Australia, I believe.' A slight murmuring acknowledgement from the Australians in the congregation. 'My own family are here from Ireland.' Excited glances among my children. 'And some of you, I believe' – this is a ministerial-type joke now – 'have come from as far away as Foxley.' Foxley's about two miles away; the locals have a little laugh.

My father started going to church when my sister and I left home and he and my mother moved out of suburban Essex and up to rural Norfolk. They moved initially for my dad's work but he was soon made redundant, and so my parents found themselves in a new place under new circumstances, and maybe it was the shock that sent my dad to church, just as it sent my mother into a long depression – far from her family, in a new house, and stuck with my dad all day every day for the first time ever – or maybe it was the fresh country air, though neither of my parents ever walk anywhere, and the house is double-glazed throughout and so intensely centrally-heated that even in the middle of winter my wife and I have to throw open all the windows at night and toss off everything except a nylon sheet to cover us, and even then it's still too hot and we have to remove the plastic mattress protector that my mum put on when my nan was dying of cancer and double incontinent and staying here in the little spare room, with its miniature wardrobe containing the hoover, and the MDF bedside table.

They live in a tiny village, my parents – a dozen houses at most, down a byway, with no pub and no shop, no pavements, no streetlights, no nothing at all except for the big East Anglian skies outside the double-glazed windows, and this tiny little Saxon church with its round tower and its flint walls and its graveyard at the end of the lane.

'He's gone all obsessed with it,' says my mum, who doesn't really approve of church-going and who accompanies my father only out of a sense of loyalty and for something to do. 'There's nothing good on TV on Sundays,' she says, trying to justify her own unexpected church-going to us and to herself. There's nothing good on TV any day of the week anymore though, according to my mum, except perhaps *The Catherine Tate Show*, which she likes a lot. 'Am I bovvered?' she says to my dad on Boxing Day when he's grumbling about no one having emptied the bins. 'Do I look bovvered? Is my face bovvered?' He goes to communion every week now, apparently, my dad – my mum skips communion, regarding it as a step too far – and he attends services sometimes twice on a Sunday. He is the secretary of the parochial church council, and he cuts the grass in the churchyard. He is also a member of the local Health Centre's patient care group, and seems to be a member of two Masonic lodges, though owing to the secretive nature of Masonic lodges this is impossible to verify. His retirement has worked out OK; he has become, in old age, and to his own surprise, and ours, a pillar of the community. He gives out hymn books; he cleans and polishes the old oak pews and the brasses; he is a stalwart of the fêtes and the fund-raising events. But this Christmas service is something special; this is his first Christmas service up at the front.

The first hymn is 'It Came Upon a Midnight Clear'.

'That's ironic,' I whisper to my wife.

It has been the foggiest Christmas that anyone can remember. We only just made it through to Stansted airport from Belfast City; we were lucky; a lot of flights were cancelled. Our hire car for the journey from Stansted up to Norfolk is a Renault.

'I hope it has fog lights!' I say to the lady working at the hire-car desk.

'Sorry?' she says.

'Just ...' I say, giving up. I'm too tired to be pleasant. We left home at 6 a.m.

'Nice little car,' I say to my wife, once we're all loaded.

'Do you know where the fog lights are?' she says.

'Don't worry. I'll find them. They'll be here somewhere,' I say.

'Do you know where you're going?' she says. 'Do you need a map?'

'I know this journey with my eyes shut,' I say.

The road layout has changed around Stansted since the last time I was here. And I can't find the fog lights.

'Where are the fog lights?' I say. 'Can you find the fog lights for me? Is it that little switch over there?'

The fog on the M11 and the A11 and the A14 and through Thetford Forest is enough to make your eyes water; visibility's down to about five metres; we're averaging 30–40 m.p.h.; at this rate we won't make it to my parents' until teatime. Years ago, travelling the same journey just before Christmas, thick snow began to fall and we got caught in a traffic jam heading up towards Watton. Our eldest son, who'd just started attending playgroup back then and had been exposed to Christian teaching for the first time, kept calling out, 'God save us! Please Jesus, let us get to granny and granddad's. Please, Jesus! Please!'

'Do you remember that time we got stuck here in the snow,' my wife asks the children, 'and you were praying that we got to granny's for Christmas?'

'Was I born then?' says our daughter.

'Was she born?' asks my wife.

None of us can remember.

Driving in fog is worse than driving in snow – it's a lot less exciting but you have to concentrate just as hard, and by the time we reach my parents' it's late afternoon and I have a terrible headache. My wife has been on her mobile the whole time; she'd been waiting for news about a promotion at work and she didn't get the promotion and her manager is giving her 'feedback' over the phone. The children are wanting to listen to the radio, but instead we've all been listening to my wife saying 'Uh-huh', and 'Yes', and 'Of course, I take your point …'

'It Came Upon a Midnight Clear' is not going well; we're all out of sync. There's no organ in the church any more. There never really was an organ – just a kind of harmonium thing. And now there's not even the harmonium – it's disappeared.

'Maybe someone's sold it on eBay,' I say to my wife.

'Don't be silly,' says my wife.

The organist has disappeared too, moved away to be nearer her children, and so the church wardens, Nikki and Steve – who aren't married but who are living in a committed monogamous relationship, and who are both really young, younger than me anyway, maybe in their early thirties, which seems young these days, certainly young to be a church warden – have put some kind of karaoke carol thing on an iPod and rigged it up to the speaker system. It's not bad but by the time we get to the second verse of 'It Came Upon a Midnight Clear' ('Still through the cloven skies they come, / With peaceful wings unfurled') we're all over the shop. The carol karaoke lacks the sensitivity of even the most insensitive church organist and it's cracking along at a hell of a pace, heedless of the congregation; we're about half a line behind, partly because we're all following the service using a pamphlet in which the words of the carols have been done in some kind of olde worlde font, making it look as though you're reading a menu in a mock-Tudor Inne.

After the carol there are prayers. People bow their heads into what I as a proselytizing charismatic evangelical used to call the 'shampoo position', bending slightly forward as though washing their hair in a sink. Nobody kneels. Do people kneel in church anymore? I used to like it when people kneeled. I always used to kneel. I was a great kneeler; one of the best. These days I don't even do the shampoo position. I just sit there looking around. My eldest son is sitting there looking around too; he looks at me, and I look at him, and I wink, but he stares at me blankly. He's not a happy chappy. (My wife does not like me using the phrase 'happy chappy'. 'It sounds ridiculous,' she says. 'You sound like you're putting it on.' She also does not like me calling women 'dear', or 'darling', or 'sweetheart', or referring to men as 'geezer' or 'matey'. 'You're not down Romford Market,' she says. 'You've got a degree, for goodness sake.' 'Maybe,' I say. 'But you'll always be my sweetheart, sweetheart.' This does not make her laugh. She really doesn't like it.) The night before, Christmas Eve, our son asked if 'Santa – or anyone?' would be getting him an Xbox for Christmas; we most certainly have not bought him an Xbox for Christmas.

'I didn't know you wanted an Xbox,' I say.

'Of course I want an Xbox,' he says. 'All my friends have mobile phones and PlayStations. Do you not want me to have what they have?' he says.

'No,' I say.

My wife is worried that he's not going to have a good Christmas. We've bought him some books, and a puzzle, and a T-shirt.

'It's fine,' I say. 'Christmas is not about presents. We're the gift at Christmas.'

Our son does not appreciate this. He is only ten. He is appalled by the books, and the puzzle, and the T-shirt.

'We could get him an Xbox next year,' I say to my wife.

'He won't want an Xbox next year!' she says.

'Precisely!' I say.

The first reading is Genesis 22, verses 15–18, which is all about Abraham's seed. 'And in thy seed shall all the nations of the earth be blessed; because thou has obeyed my voice.'

'Didn't you think that was weird?' I say to my wife after the service. 'The bit about Abraham's sperm, reading that out in a family Christmas service? Isn't that weird?'

'It's not about Abraham's sperm,' says my wife.

'It is.'

'It's metaphorical,' she says.

'Metaphorical seed?'

'Exactly,' she says.

I don't know about metaphorical seed. My father was born to a Jewish mother and a Gentile father in the East End of London almost exactly seventy-one years ago; his birthday is on Christmas Eve. As a child I always thought this made him special, almost like Jesus, a kind of precursor or forerunner, a bit like John the Baptist. We're a Christmas birthday kind of a family: my grandmother was born on Boxing Day, I'm a couple of weeks before Christmas, and so is my sister, and my wife and her sister are the week after. My mother, a January baby, is also, like my father, half or possibly all Jewish, depending on your definition of a Jew. It turns that out my wife has a Jewish grandmother – a fact she discovered only last year when her father went to visit his elderly long-lost sister in Canada and she said to him, 'Well, now you're here, and since we're not likely to see each other again, it's time you knew some of the family history ...'; he always thought his mother was a good Ulster Prod. It can be confusing. My own grandparents spoke bits of Yiddish around the house – bobs and tags just, *shlummocks* and *schlemiels* and what have you – but none of them were religious in any way, or ever went either to church or to synagogue. One of my dad's brothers used to work on Friday nights as what was called a 'Shabbes goy', tending fires and doing cooking for the Sabbath meals for East End Orthodox Jews. When I tell my father that my wife and I have started lighting candles on the Sabbath – we find it cheering – he says, completely reversing the meaning of the phrase, that we're turning into a couple of 'Shabbes goys'. Before the service I had suggested to him that he might want to greet the congregation by saying 'Shalom aleichem'. He repeats this out loud several times, deliberately mispronouncing it.

'Oh yes,' he says. 'That'd be good. Shalom à la crème! Shalom à la crème!'

On Boxing Day, when we're having the traditional cold meats with piccalilli, my father offers round a jar of gherkins.

'My mother used to love those,' he says. 'Big wallies. The old pickle-munching Jewess!' He says this with a great deal of affection.

The second carol is 'As with Gladness Men of Old'. It's about death, like most hymns. 'Holy Jesus, every day, / Keep us in the narrow way; / And, when earthly things are past, / Bring our ransomed souls at last, / Where they need no star to guide, / Where no clouds Thy glory hide.'

My sister and I have agreed this year not to talk to my parents about moving. My sister recently bought some land in Australia so that she and her Australian partner and their little baby son can move over and build a house and make their home there. She shows us a video of the land on her mobile phone. It looks like paradise: a one-acre plot by the beach, surrounded by woods, in a small town full of coffee shops and surf shops and shops selling organic vegetables and jewellery made out of shells. My sister has been trying to persuade my mum and dad for years to move with them to Australia, but my mum and dad have no intention of moving to Australia.

'Too hot,' says my mum, 'and too far away.'

'Far away from where?' says my sister.

'From here!' says my mum.

I occasionally suggest to my mother that since they're getting older and they've no family around to look after them and they're not going to move to Australia they might like to consider moving over to be near us in Northern Ireland.

'I wouldn't want to die in that dreadful place,' she says. 'Never mind live there.'

So that's the end of that conversation.

The second reading is Isaiah 9, verses 2–7, which I believe is understood in Christian exegesis to be Isaiah foretelling Christ's birth and kingdom – 'For unto us a child is born, unto us a son is given.'

'Christmas is all about the children,' says my mum on Christmas Eve as we're wrapping up a few stocking presents, and she's absolutely right, of course: the baby Jesus, the Slaughter of the Innocents, elves, et cetera. Me and my sister spend a lot of our Christmas remembering other Christmases, Christmases when we were children; talking about the Christmas when my mother cut her finger while carving the turkey and fainted, and how everyone decided to just keep on eating and leave her be, recovering on the sofa; and the Christmases when my granddad would dress up as Santa for the works' Christmas do. To be honest I don't know if we're actually remembering these things at all or just retelling stories that we've been told many times over; the stories, like children, and childhoods, and religions, could be complete inventions, comforting fictions. But I don't care; I like comforting fictions. On Boxing Day we're out for a walk to give my parents a little bit of peace in the house – eight extra people to feed is beginning to prove a strain – and I'm talking to my sister and her partner about a dilemma they're facing, not something I feel able or qualified to offer an intelligent opinion about, but I say something waffly about how life always finds a way, and my sister greets this with the guffaw it obviously deserves and goes off to play with my children on the swings.

'Don't,' she says, 'give me all that Pollyanna shit.'

*

The third carol is 'Once in Royal David's City'. I'm really having trouble with the carols. In this one you have to swoop right down from 'Mary was that mother mild' to 'Jesus Christ, her little child', and in order to reach the notes I have to go from a wobbly falsetto down to a kind of basso profundo; it sounds terrible. After the service my sister says to me, 'Do you think they had higher voices in the eighteenth century?'

'Yeah. I think so. And they used to drink sherry for breakfast.'

'Sounds like a good idea,' says my sister. We've all been drinking advocaat since 10 a.m.

'I would have loved to have lived in the eighteenth century,' I say.

'It probably would have suited you,' says my sister.

'Everything was different back then,' I say.

'Everything's always different,' says my sister.

'And His shelter was a stable,' I'm singing, 'And His cradle was a stall,' and while my voice is cracking on that 'cradle' I'm thinking about the beggars on the street back home, the big wide-hipped women in their colourful skirts and their headscarves with the little children in their laps. We've never had beggars in town before, but this year for the first time there's been a little crowd who turn up once or twice a week on Main Street, outside Eason's, or by the Heatherlea Bakery. I don't know if they're Romanian or where they're from; they look Romanian. Actually, no, they don't look Romanian, they look like Roma; they look like gypsies. I've been to Romania a couple of times, and I try talking to the ladies in the big skirts, but they don't understand my Romanian – which admittedly is limited to 'Hello!' (*'Salut!'*) and 'Do you speak English?' (*'Vorbiti engleza?'*). Unfortunately I don't speak any Romany, so we don't get very far. I'm usually clutching a pan loaf and some traybakes or a *Belfast Telegraph* when I see them, so of course I feel guilty and usually give them a couple of pounds, and I like to do this; I like living in a town with beggars. When we arrived at Stansted the arrivals area was deserted except for people from our flight, about half of whom looked like Poles – but what do Poles look like? And Poles, on a flight over to England from Belfast? Is it possible? In fact it's more than likely; even in our scabby wee seaside town in the north of the north of Ireland there are suddenly Poles.

'But this is the best thing that's ever happened to Northern Ireland!' I am enthusing to my in-laws one Sunday afternoon. 'Think of the influx of culture, and languages, and the great food!' My in-laws are sceptical.

Just before Christmas a shop advertising itself as a 'European Food Hall' opened up on Central Avenue. I'm very excited. I tell all my friends about it. I go there the first week it opens. The shop is selling only cigarettes, paprika-flavoured crisps, packets of Knorr soup, and tins of Heinz baked beans.

'Are you Polish?' I ask the man behind the counter.

'Yes,' he says.

I can't think of a good follow-up question.

The third reading is Luke 2, verses 1–7. My father had asked me to do the reading. I am not that comfortable with reading in public. He says, 'It's not reading in public. It's reading in church.' I suggest instead that my wife might like to do a reading; she has a nice voice; the accent and everything. So my father asks my wife to do the reading. My wife says wouldn't it be better if my sister did a reading? It's turning into a game of what my children call 'Hot Tomato', where they throw a tomato to one another and whoever ends up with the tomato at the end of a minute is the loser. None of us is willing to participate, so there's nothing else for it: on Christmas Eve we have an *X-Factor*-style audition to choose who's going to have the honour of reading Luke 2, verses 1–7, in church on Christmas morning.

My wife does the first audition: we're in my parents' front room, gathered round the telly; we've turned off the main light; it's just lamps; it's better than church. My wife reads very well: 'And it came to pass in those days, that there went out a decree from Caesar Augustus, that all the world should be taxed.' My sister reads well also, and her partner. When it's my turn I read the passage in a funny voice.

'Is that supposed to be Nelson Mandela?' says my dad.

'I think it's supposed to be Mao Tse-Tung,' says my sister's partner.

I'm trying to do Kenneth Williams in *Round the Horne*.

'If you try to disqualify yourself you automatically have to do it,' says my sister. I try reading it in another funny voice – a *Goon Show* sort of voice – but to be honest I just can't do funny voices, so I read it in my normal voice. I lack conviction.

My dad pretends to be Simon Cowell. My mum is Sharon Osbourne. My son is Louis Walsh. They all really get into their roles.

'I thought you were a one-trick pony,' says my son to my sister. 'But tonight you've proved me wrong.'

'I thought you could have put a bit of emotion into it,' says my mum to my wife.

'That was … rubbish!' says my dad to my sister's partner.

We have a vote. It's a tie between my sister and her partner. In order to choose a winner we switch from one reality TV show format to another and decide to have a danceathon. We've all had a few drinks by this time. My sister and her partner have to perform a dance to Take That's current number-one single, 'Patience'. I have bought the single for my wife as a good luck present for the promotion she was applying for at work, the promotion she didn't get; the song's sentiment suddenly seems depressingly appropriate. My sister does a brilliant interpretative dance which involves the picking of a lot of imaginary flowers from the air. She ends up on the floor in an ecstatic swoon. She wins. She's doing the reading.

The fourth carol is 'While Shepherds Watched Their Flocks by Night'; the olde worlde font makes it look like 'Slocks by night'. This is my favourite carol, the story of an angel coming down and visiting a bunch of shepherds sitting around; you can just imagine them playing cards and having a few drinks, none of them quite able to believe what's happened. It makes the supernatural seem natural, the extraordinary ordinary, and vice versa. My sister's little boy has been wandering up and down the aisle and during this carol he suddenly makes a break to get under the altar cloth. My sister's partner goes up front and fishes him out. My dad isn't fussed; I like the way he's doing the service; it's kind of casual; smart casual; blazer casual. The person who used to take the Christmas service was a man named George, a lay reader with a booming voice who used to wear a big black cassock. You couldn't really imagine children wandering up and down the aisle while George took the service. But George is long away now; he moved from the village, which is how my dad ended up taking the service; they're short of lay readers in Norfolk and although my dad is not a lay reader he is the next best thing; he's nice, and he's enthusiastic. He used to live in the big house, George, with his wife and their little dog, and they had a swimming pool in the garden, and when we came to visit my parents each summer he'd let us all use the pool, like the lord of the manor.

'Marvellous,' he would say, dispensing his considerable largesse, when he heard us splashing around. 'Lovely to hear children enjoying themselves.'

This summer was our last summer in the pool; the new owners of the big house are having it filled in.

There are a few more carols ('O Come All Ye Faithful' and 'Hark the Herald Angels Sing') and readings (John 1: 1–14) and prayers ('Let us approach the throne of heaven,' suggests my dad), but eventually the service comes to an end and on the way out I'm talking to my mother. She did the flowers in church, with Val and Nancy, and all during the service I've been trying to work out which are hers. I ask her, and it turns out I was right; I picked them out from all the other arrangements; hers are the yellow chrysanthemums and the gladioli, with lots of greenery. It's definitely the best arrangement.

'He did very well, didn't he,' I say.

'Well,' says my mum. 'It keeps him out of mischief.'

My dad stays behind at the church, shaking hands with people and wishing them a hearty Merry Christmas, and as we're walking away, out of the graveyard, along the path – though there is no path, just a worn patch through the grass – I say to my mum, 'What do you think? Maybe you should come to us next year for Christmas?'

'Maybe,' she says. 'We'll see what happens.'

(Spring 2007)

This is what libraries are for

CIARAN CARSON

I see myself, some time about 1955, carrying two pillow-slips stuffed with rags to the ragman's yard at the corner of Cairns Street, off the Lower Falls Road in Belfast. I 'see' myself, that is, with the eye of memory, which seems to occupy, in a hovery, havering kind of way, both the inside of my present head (aged $52^1/_2$) and that of the boy back then (7 plus a couple of weeks, maybe, for I sense a late-Octoberish, coming-up-to-Hallowe'en feeling in the air of 1955, an atmosphere of squibs and bonfires, and my birthday is October 9th). That being so, I cannot view the complete boy. This is not an out-of-body experience. I get glimpses of hands, shod feet, a short-flannel-trouser-clad leg (is there a scab on the knee?), yet when I try to concentrate on these features in order to determine their specific gravities and contours, their textures and their colours, they tend to blur, drifting out of focus, getting lost in the corner of the eye. This is only a manner of speaking. The eye has no corner, and the view has no straight edges like those of a photograph. The eye is not a camera, the eye of memory still less so. There is no fixed viewpoint. The eye flits and flickers around all over the place, taking in bits of this and that, weaving in and out, picking, choosing, shuffling, negotiating, building up a picture that is never static, for everything moves through time and space. In fact ordinary seeing is all memory, too.

At a certain point I felt I was beginning to exhaust the ideas which got me interested in photography in the first place. But before I abandoned the work, I wanted to try to deal with memory in a photograph, so you could see memory, as well as everything else that's there. I made pictures of a walk in a Zen garden, and later on in a street in Kyoto, where I attempted to show the experience of walking, so that one might see the entire experience, in time. It means that you must look with your memory. Then it led me to believe that we're always looking with our memory, as memory is always present. Memory is a part of vision – it's inescapable. I came to the conclusion that there is no such thing as objective vision. There never can be, because even the memory of the first instant of looking is then a part of the perception, and it adds up and it adds up. (David Hockney)

Now I find myself remembering the ragman's premises, I visualize the brick floor of the covered yard, slightly tacky or greasy underfoot, scattered with wisps of lint and wool. Grey light seeps through the sooty glass roof. Bundles of rags are heaped against the sweating brick walls. The ragman himself has a looming, musty presence I can't fully put a face or body to, but I think of him as robed in a long black overcoat belted with a piece of rope. The transaction must only occupy a minute or two, as he weighs the rags on a big cast-iron scales – one lot of woollens, the other linens and cottons – and pays me in heavy pre-decimal coin; yet I have remembered this occasion on many occasions in the past, for very many minutes, possibly for many hours altogether, not to mention the time I'm spending now writing about it, and re-reading it to make sure it corresponds to the truth of the matter, realizing as I do so that the matter is inevitably compromised by writing about it, and remembering it. And I don't really know what made me remember this brief, dim encounter in the first place, beyond the context of this essay; but now that I imagine that the linen and cotton rags, for instance, were most likely collected for their value as papermaking materials, I am led to contemplate another memory, which is indissolubly linked to the smell of paper – or, more accurately, the smell of certain books.

I have only to stretch my hand up to the bookshelves above my desk and pick out a book, and open it, and plunge my nose between its pages, to retrieve that smell. The book is *The Captain's Death Bed and Other Essays*, by Virginia Woolf, published in 1950, which I bought a couple of years ago at the Belfast Public Libraries' annual sale. When I inhale, I am transported back to the 1950s and the Falls Road Library, where I get the allied aroma of polished linoleum and varnished shelving. I detect a gleam of brass here, too, coming from the handles of the big doors, but also from the little pulls of the filing-cabinet drawers, and I wonder if they are implicated in the overall smell. They would be polished, yes, but the brass itself ... I remember a reference somewhere to a 'Roman connoisseur' who could distinguish among five kinds of patina on bronze by the smell, and, searching for it in a likely book, Roy Bedichek's *The Sense of Smell* – it's on the same shelf as the Woolf, which gives you some idea of the apparently random, but personally associative, organization of some areas of my library – I come across this quotation from Helen Keller:

The sense of smell has told me of a coming storm hours before there was any sign of it visible. I notice first a throb of expectancy, a slight quiver, a concentration in my nostrils. As the storm draws near my nostrils dilate, the better to receive the flood of earth odours which seem to multiply and extend, until I feel a splash of rain against my cheek. As the tempest departs, receding farther and farther, the odours fade, become fainter and fainter, and die away beyond the bar of space.

'In the same connection,' writes Bedichek, 'she tells of smelling from a distance the destruction of a grove of trees of which she was fond. "I know," she continues, "the kind of house we enter. I have recognised an old-fashioned country house because it has several layers of odours, left by a succession of families, of plants, perfumes and draperies."'

As for the Roman connoisseur, there is no more information about him beyond Bedichek's noting that 'it is the nose, not the substance, that is remarkable'; but in the next breath he mentions a H.T. Finck, whose 'identification of books and newspapers by odour is an unusual achievement, although he declares that many people do'. Turning to the bibliography, I find that Henry T. Finck is the author of *Food and Flavor* (New York: The Century Company, 1913), *Romantic Love and Personal Beauty* (London: Macmillan, 1912), and 'The Gastronomic Value of Odours' (*The Contemporary Review*, Nov. 1886): could a blindfolded Finck, we wonder, identify those books, that article, by their specific aromas? How far did this olfactory classification extend? Could a library be organized along these lines? Opening and sniffing a number of books on my shelves at random, I find that it is possible to say that each has a more or less unique odour; but it is a different matter entirely to remember which odour belongs to which book, and I wonder if a specially gifted mnemonist could construct a system based on aromatic association. For example, a copy of Cary's translation of Dante's *Divina Commedia*, published in New York by Hurst & Co. (n.d., but it looks 1880s), has a slightly acrid sooty brownstone smell, which seems appropriate to the subject-matter of the *Inferno*, at least; but then the Jefferson Butler Fletcher translation of 1931, in a 1967 reprint by the Columbia University Press, reveals a pleasurable aroma of cedar wood, or the interior of certain American homes, whose construction is much more wood-based than ours; it also reminds me of American central heating, the sort where the hot air comes up through an iron grille in the wooden floor. A London edition (W.W. Gibbings, 18, Bury Street, W.C., 1891) of the Cary translation seems to have a faint tobacco incense emanating from its pages. The new translation (Doubleday, December 2000) by Robert and Jean Hollander, which I bought in a Borders bookstore in Brookline, Massachusetts, does have a definite smell – of what, I can't think, but it leads me to the scent of the nearby underground trolley station: iron, rubber, electricity, a claustrophobic heat. Having said all that, I comprehensively failed to identify these books in a blind test (I shut my eyes while my wife, Deirdre, presented the open book to my nose).

I was, however, successful with the Woolf. Examining it again, I find that its aroma derives as much from its leatherette library binding as the paper of its pages. (I have other items from the same book sale on my shelves, and they smell more or less the same, so that I would have great difficulty in singling out the Woolf from this com-

pany.) And, as I sniff and sniff again, I am returned again to the Falls
Road Library, or to the larger realm of the Belfast Central Library in
Royal Avenue, some time in the late '50s, when I first began to read
Rider Haggard; and yesterday, in order to research this article you
are reading, I had occasion to go the Central Library to find a copy
of Haggard's *She*. Regrettably, the copy I was loaned – the only one
in the library's possession – is nowhere near an appropriately
Victorian edition, but a Penguin, re-bound by the library in laminated boards. But it contains the same story, and the passage I'd
been looking for:

'Thou wilt presently understand,' said Ayesha, with a little laugh, when
Leo asked her; and certainly we did. Scarcely were the words out of her
mouth when from every point we saw dark forms rushing up, each
bearing with him what we at first took to be an enormous flaming
torch. Whatever they were, they were burning furiously, for the flames
stood out a yard or more behind each bearer. On they came, fifty or
more of them, carrying their blazing burdens and looking like so many
devils from hell. Leo was the first to discover what these burdens were.
    'Great heaven!' he said, 'they are corpses on fire!'
    I stared and stared again – he was perfectly right – the torches that
were to light our entertainment were human mummies from the caves!
    On rushed the bearers of the flaming corpses, and, meeting at a spot
twenty paces in front of us, built their ghastly burdens crossways into a
huge bonfire. Heavens! how they roared and flared! No tar barrel could
have burnt as those mummies did. Nor was this all. Suddenly I saw one
great fellow seize a flaming human arm that had fallen from its parent
frame, and rush into the darkness. Presently he stopped, and a tall
streak of fire shot up into the air, illumining the gloom, and also the
lamp from which it sprang. The lamp was the mummy of a woman tied
to a stout stake let into the rock, and he had fired her hair. On he went
a few paces and touched a second, then a third, and a fourth, till at last
we were surrounded on all three sides by a great ring of bodies flaring
furiously, the material with which they were preserved having rendered them so inflammable that the flames would literally spout out of
the ears and mouth in tongues of fire a foot or more in length.

    I say I was looking for this passage; more accurately, I was fol-
lowing up a brief reference in Nicholson Baker's *Double Fold: Libraries*

and the *Assault on Paper* (the ostensible subject of this review, essay, or ramification). That mummies were indeed used as fuel is corroborated by the 11th edition of the *Encyclopaedia Brittanica*:

In Lower Egypt practically all the mummies have perished; but in Upper Egypt, as they were put out of reach of the inundation, the cemeteries, in spite of rifling and burning, yield immense numbers of preserved bodies and skeletons.

More specifically, as Baker notes,

Combustion this intense could generate steam. The railroad from Cairo to Alexandria, imposed on the Abbas Pasha by the English in the early 1850s, runs through several bustling necropolises; Egypt had no indigenous coal and very little wood. A small item in the September 27, 1859, edition of the Syracuse *Daily Standard* reads: 'Egypt has 300 miles of railroad. On the first locomotive run, mummies were used for fuel, making a hot fire. The supply of mummies is said to be almost inexhaustible, and [they] are used by the cord.'

Mark Twain, visiting Egypt in 1867, recorded some of his impressions:

I shall not speak of the railway, for it is like any other railway – I shall only say that the fuel they use is composed of mummies three thousand years old, purchased by the ton or by the graveyard for that purpose, and that sometimes one hears the profane engineer call out pettishly, 'D—n these plebeians, they don't burn worth a cent – pass out a King'.

The English *mummy* is from *mum*, or *mumia*, the Persian/Arabic word for wax, bitumen, or pitch – highly inflammable materials. In late antiquity, bitumen was thought to be a powerful medicament, the Persian kind being specially prized as a panacea, and it was then further accepted that the pitch-like substances (not true bitumen, in fact, but resinous compounds) discovered in embalmed bodies were of similar virtue. By the eleventh century, certain Arab authorities had begun to ascribe the therapeutic values of *mumia* to the actual flesh of the embalmed. By the beginning of the sixteenth century 'mummy' was so highly regarded that François I of France was accustomed, says Belon, to carry a little packet containing 'mummy' mixed with powdered rhubarb, in case of accident. 'Mummy is become merchandise, Mizraim cures wounds, and Pharaoh is sold for balsams', wrote Thomas Browne. There were different grades and flavours; the best was generally acknowledged to be that which was hard but easily pulverized, dark brown to black in colour, with a bitter taste and a strong smell. Roquefort alleges that the French found '*fille vierge*' to be particularly desirable. In 1564 Guy de la Fontaine, physician to the King of Navarre, discovered that the Alexandrian mummy-traffickers were wont to eke out their supply with the bodies of executed criminals and the dead from hospitals, hastily prepared by stuffing with asphalt and then distressed by drying in the sun. In this context, it is worth noting that bitumen, dissolved in oil or turpentine, was used as a brown oil paint up until the nineteenth century; that it shows undesirable characteristics on ageing, as it never completely dries, and when applied in a thick film forms a network of broad cracks resembling an alligator's skin; and that finely powdered 'mummy' itself was used as a pigment, a single corpse sufficing to supply one colourman's customers for twenty years.

Such were some of the uses of the remains of the Ancient Egyptians. In 1855 a New York scientist, Dr Isaiah Deck, advanced the idea that the wrappings of Egyptian mummies could be used in making paper, which at that time was entirely manufactured from rags – linen and cotton castoffs. A sheet of rag paper might contain fibres from any number of garments: shirts, blouses, semmits, dresses, petticoats, unmentionables; used bandages were not exempt.

Arriving at a typical early-nineteenth-century paper mill, bales of rags were opened and thrashed to remove loose dust and dirt; rag-room attendants opened seams, and snipped off fasteners and decayed sections. They cut the rags into pieces about four inches square on scythe blades attached to posts. Then they sorted them according to type of material, colour, amount of wear, degree of cleanliness, and so on. Sometimes the sorted rags were stored for weeks to allow them to rot and soften before being broken down into individual fibres in a 'Hollander' beater, so called because it was invented, like so many other useful things, by the ingenious Dutch. The beater consisted of an oval wooden tub, in which revolved a solid wooden roll made from the trunk of a tree and fitted with about thirty metal knives. The rags circulated around the tub and were lacerated by the action of the knives revolving over a metal or stone bed-plate; the material was kept in constant motion given by a backfall and by the rotation of the roll. The resulting pulp was fed into a vat. Here the paper was made. Before mechanization, the process, as described by Judith A. McGaw, went as follows (I like to think that the protagonist is a remote ancestor of mine):

As vatman, Carson placed a narrow wooden frame, called a deckle, on the upper rim of the paper mold. Holding mold and deckle firmly together at each end, he dipped the mold perpendicularly into the vat, flattened it, and raised it covered with a smooth, even layer of macerated fiber. The slight suction created by the wedge-shaped ribs drew water out of the bottom of the mold, while the deckle kept the fiber from running over the edges. By tipping and flattening the mold at various intervals, Carson created paper of various thicknesses. By shaking the mold from side to side and back and forth, he caused the fibers to intertwine, making sheets with equal tearing strength in both directions. He then removed the deckle, set the mold on a rack, and quickly withdrew his hands so as to avoid spotting the newly formed sheet with water. Years of observation and practice gave his movements their necessary precision and rapidity.

Rags, increasingly, were in short supply. Bamboo waste, old rope, corncobs, grass and straw were important American pulp additives; European research had roamed farther afield. In the 1770s Jacob Christian Schäffer, an authority on the fungi of Bavaria, printed a series of pamphlets on papermaking which included sheets of paper made from such diverse materials as wasps' nests, moss, vines, hemp, bark, cabbage stalks, asbestos, thistles, mallow, St John's Wort, pinecones, tulip leaves, turf, and potatoes (both the skin and the flesh). In 1854 an Englishman named Hill produced a paper made from horseradish; also one from manure, 'bleached and reduced to pulp by the usual modes'. Everything, it appeared, was grist to the mill. During the American Civil War the papermaker I. Augustus Stanford, possibly acting on Dr Deck's suggestions, imported mummies from Egypt to his mill in Gardiner, Maine, where he pulped their bandages as well as their papyrus fillings, and made them into wrapping paper, thus destroying an unknowable number of ancient texts. As C.H. Robert notes,

... the great mass of our papyri (for example those from Oxyrhynchus and Arsinoë) were thrown away as so much waste paper. The oddest transformation has been suffered by those papyri which were converted into a kind of papier mâché, and used to form the covering or stuffing of mummies, whether of men or crocodiles; from one such emerged the earliest fragments of any manuscript of the Bible – the Manchester papyrus of Deuteronomy – which were found covered with glue and wrapped in some pieces of the first book of the *Iliad* ...

Another enthusiastic manufacturer, M. Szelelmey, about the same time as Stanford was turning mummies into paper, was making coffins from paper: his so-called 'Zopissa' casket of the late 1860s, made of compressed and laminated paper, closely resembled an Ancient Egyptian mummy case.

The coffin remembers the person it contains, and books are a monument to human thought: yet all will decay and putrefy. In the long run, everything will be carbonized, and turn into star-dust. Under the microscope, the interwoven tendrils, tangles, and filaments of paper look like galaxies, or a synaptic map of the brain, replete with the threadlike extensions of the nerve cells known as dendrons, from the Greek for 'tree'. Trees, mashed and macerated into wood-pulp, provide the material for most papers nowadays; and wood-pulp paper is apt to decay sooner than that made from rags. 'Sooner' is a flexible word: for generations, librarians have been arguing that material printed on wood-pulp paper is liable to crumble into dust any minute – any day – soon – in a couple of years; and since the 1950s, as argued by Nicholson Baker in *Double Fold*,[1] the librarians of the USA, following a policy of 'destroying to preserve', have methodically dismantled their collections of original bound newspapers, cut up thousands of so-called brittle books, and replaced them with microfilmed copies – bad photographs that are difficult to read, lack all the colour and quality of the original paper and illustrations, and deteriorate with age. Yet, as Baker demonstrates,

the originals didn't crumble into dust. Keyes Metcalf, a microfilm pioneer and the director of the libraries at Harvard, in 1941 predicted that the 'total space requirements' of research libraries 'will be reduced by paper disintegration'. Then five, ten, twenty years went by, and the paper – even the supposedly ephemeral newsprint – was still there. So librarians began getting rid of it anyway. If you destroy the physical evidence, nobody will know how skewed your predictions are.

Space, or lack of it, is the enemy of the librarian, since, in the jargon, 'every time you buy a book, you buy a space cost'. In the USA, tons of books were used as landfill, or as fuel for incinerators. The policy of the Belfast Public Libraries, in selling off what it perceives as surplus stock, has been somewhat more benign; but it has resulted in unique copies of books being lost to the public domain. At the book sale where I got *The Captain's Death Bed* I also bought the following: Woolf's *The Death of the Moth and Other Essays*; *Stars and Atoms*, by A.S. Eddington (Oxford, 1928); *Modern Prose Style*, by Bonamy Dobrée (Oxford, 1934); *Textile Fibers and their Use*, by Katherine Paddock Hess, M.S., Associate Professor of Clothing and Textiles, Kansas State College of Agriculture and Applied Science (J.B. Lippincott, Chicago & Philadelphia, 1931); and *Crooks are Human Too*, by Daniel J. Campion with Myron M. Stearns, the memoirs of a New York cop (Prentice-Hall, Inc., New Jersey, 1957). When I was borrowing *She*, I thought I'd look up these books in the Central Library's computerized catalogue. With the exception of the two Woolf titles, there are now no longer any copies of these books in the entire Belfast Public Library system. There is *nothing* by Sir Arthur Eddington, the foremost British theoretical astronomer of his generation (and a pioneer of popular-science writing, quoted as an example of an expository prose style by Dobrée). Perhaps

Eddington's science is out of date; perhaps the extract from James Joyce's *Work in Progress* that concludes Dobrée's survey is no longer the last word in 'experiment', or maybe it still is; perhaps fibre technology has moved on since Katherine Hess's day; perhaps criminal activity has become more sophisticated since Danny Campion walked the streets of the Gas House District. Certainly, these books are old-fashioned; and that is precisely why they should be in a library, for you'll get them nowhere else. This is what libraries are for: to provide us with a window to the past.

As for the two Woolf titles – saved, I suppose, from total oblivion by their status as 'literature' – there is one of each, reprinted by Hogarth of London in 1981. These are nice copies, but they are not the true originals, the first editions now owned by me – *The Captain's Death Bed* published in 1950, *The Death of the Moth* in 1942, the latter printed on wartime recycled paper, but perfectly serviceable, beautiful even in its austerity, with its little oatmeal flecks. What must it have been like to read the following, in London, in wartime?

How beautiful a London street is then, with its islands of light, and its long groves of darkness, and on one side of it perhaps some tree-sprinkled, grass-grown space where night is folding herself to sleep naturally and, as one passes the iron railing, one hears those little cracklings and stirrings of leaf and twig which seem to suppose the silence of fields all around them, an owl hooting, and far away the rattle of a train in the valley. But this is London, we are reminded; high among the bare trees are hung oblong frames of reddish yellow light – windows; there are points of brilliance burning steadily like low stars – lamps; this empty ground, which holds the country in it and its peace, is only a London square, set about by offices and houses where at this hour fierce lights burn over maps, over documents, over desks where clerks sit turning with wetted forefinger the files of endless correspondences; or more suffusedly the firelight wavers and the lamplight falls upon the privacy of some drawing-room, its easy chairs, its papers, its china, its inlaid table, and the figure of a woman, accurately measuring out the precise number of spoons of tea which— She looks at the door as if she heard a ring downstairs and somebody asking, is she in?

But here we must stop peremptorily …

More to the point, what is it like to read this now? I can tell you what it's like: it's like Helen Keller's breathing in the layered odours of a country house; it's like sensing, as one reads, the breathing of others who bent over these pages before you. The paper is grainy, textured, its microscopic bumps and hollows saturated with the weight of others' DNA, with the odour of Belfast libraries, the smell of the Blitz and broken brick, coal-dust, smog, the perfume of finger-tips; it holds a residue of ropeworks dust and lint, horse-dung, peat. As I concentrate on Virginia Woolf's essay, these impressions fade into the background, and I enter another realm. 'Street Haunting: a London Adventure' is a description of her going out to buy a pencil – a beautiful ramble through various spaces and times. This is the beauty of a text. It is a textile thing, a weave. And I, as reader, weave myself through space and time; I am both here and there:

Passing, glimpsing ... Standing out on the street, one may build up all the chambers of an imaginary house and furnish them at one's will with sofa, table, carpet. That rug will do for the hall. That alabaster bowl shall stand in a carved table in the window. Our merrymaking shall be reflected in that thick round mirror. But, having built and furnished the house, one is happily under no obligation to possess it; one can dismantle it in the twinkling of an eye, and build and furnish another house with other chairs and other glasses.

The week before I sat down to write this piece I had to travel to Aberdeen on some literature business. I was met at the airport by a man who identified himself as a librarian. He had just been on a course, he told me, in which he and his fellow librarians were told that in the future everyone would have only one book. But this book was a magic book, for it would contain every book. The book would have a little screen, and some buttons. The reader would punch in a code, a title, and thereby summon up, Aladdin-like, any book, from any one of all the libraries in the world.

But what, I asked him, will happen to the smells?

He looked at me as if I was quite mad.

NOTE

1. For an explanation of Baker's title, see pp. 152–7, e.g., 'Anyone can do it. Open a book at random and fold its lower right corner in toward you, forming a triangle against the paper, until you feel it crease under your thumb. Then fold it back in the opposite direction until it folds against the far side of the page. That is one double fold. Do that until the paper breaks, or until you reach some stopping point, as specified by your library's preservation department – one double fold, two, four, five. Double folding may seem oddly familiar to some, for it is how kindergarteners are taught to divide a piece of paper without scissors. Now, however, it is used to survey research collections in order to determine their "usability" and hence their fate.'

REFERENCES

David Hockney, On Photography: a lecture at the Victoria & Albert Museum, November 1983; National Museum of Photography, Film and Television.

Roy Bedichek, The Sense of Smell, Michael Joseph, London, 1960.

Nicholson Baker, Double Fold: Libraries and the Assault on Paper, Random House, New York, 2001.

Mark Twain, The Innocents Abroad, 1869.

J.R. Harris, 'Medicine', in The Legacy of Egypt, ed. Harris, Oxford, 1987. (The paragraph beginning 'The English mummy …' is taken almost verbatim from this source.)

Judith A. McGaw, Most Wonderful Machine: Mechanization and Social Change in Berkshire Paper Making, 1801–1855, Princeton University Press, Princeton, N.J., 1987.

Dard Hunter, Papermaking, The Cresset Press, London, 1957. (See this source for Jacob Christian Schäffer.)

C.H. Robert, 'The Greek Papyri', in The Legacy of Egypt, op. cit.

(Autumn 2001)

Good works for the locals

MAURICE WALSH

1

There was a dust storm on our first morning in Ndjamena and the city – so warm and dark the night before – took on an air of sickliness, as if something worse was expected to happen. The light was grey and a shroud of dust hung where the sky used to be. In the streets, people seemed discomfited, squinting against the little eddies of sand thrown up now and again by light gusts of wind. Even though it was only midday there was an impression that everybody was on their way home early, the men who sped by on their motorbikes and the women who walked on the pavements carrying baskets on their heads. Many of the streets were unpaved and the buildings were low and colourless and it was difficult to get any vivid sense that this was a city at all.

Ndjamena has an area called the 'European Quarter'; usually it is easy to tell the difference between those well-to-do streets where the expats live and the other neighbourhoods, but this city is so flattened out that it was not immediately possible to distinguish the strip of French restaurants and supermarkets, the small bookstore and the airline offices at Avenue Charles de Gaulle as a place for the wealthy. The city presents itself to the visitor in a series of little pictures: a man with a beard reading the Koran to a group kneeling under a tent; Pernod and vegetable oil bottles full of petrol on sale at tables placed at the side of the road; small wooden shacks surrounded by old cars with their bonnets raised, oily engines and machine parts; kiosks selling cigarettes and phone cards and, on every wooden or corrugated fence, signs for the mobile phone company, Celtel.

At the offices where we went to get our papers, a soldier in a green uniform walked across the broad front yard where a car with no wheels appeared to have sunk into the sand. The dark and poky rooms were bare save for dust-covered filing cabinets and an unsteady metal-framed chair with yellow foam sprouting from the seat. Bored men laboured over enormous typewriters under the cooling breeze of a whirring fan. In one room stacks of old papers were piled high all along one wall, bound together in dusty grey bundles like forgotten bank-notes, tattered at the edges as if rats had nibbled them. The sound of motorbikes and the smell of petrol fumes came and went. On the cracked cement pavement a barefoot boy passed holding out a box of eggs for sale in the palm of his hand. He was followed by another boy holding a set of silver tools in the crook of one arm, like a game-show compère displaying a prize to an audience. In his other hand he gripped a canvas bag containing a bicycle pump and a machete.

On our way back to the hotel we drove past a crowd of people across the road from the French consulate. Soldiers or policemen stood by the entrance tapping long wooden sticks against the heels of their shoes. The crowd, men in ragged shirts and trousers, were relations of veterans of French campaigns from Vietnam to Algeria, waiting to collect pensions. Most were still there the next day and the day after that. Chad was invented by France at the end of the last century as its more adventurous colonialists pushed in from their conquests on the west coast of Africa. Until 1973 Ndjamena was called Fort Lamy, after the French commander who was killed while trying to subdue the Africans. For the white soldier or administrator Fort Lamy was an unforgiving outpost of French Equatorial Africa, seven hundred miles from the Atlantic in a vast space of desert and scrub. In the mid 1920s a traveller setting out from Paris would take four or five months to reach Chad, where he would find only a handful of French merchants. But from here the French created a country, drawing borders that pulled together different clans, religions and traditions. Muslims from the north became fellow-countrymen with southerners whom they used to enslave. In some places the French imposed themselves brutally; in others they were hardly seen. One of the French commanders who had once celebrated the conquest of Chad as a great achievement later confessed to second thoughts: 'I said to myself, when I was alone, that it truly was not worth having killed so many and having suffered so much to conquer such a forsaken country.' Since independence in 1960, the French have pulled the strings of Chad's history when it suits them, a state of affairs described by one historian as 'sovereignty under surveillance'.

2

Chad is still one of the poorest countries in the world, most of its territory arid mountain and desert. It has no access to the sea and no railway. But it has found oil. Last year, from an oilfield in the south, a consortium led by Esso began pumping around two hundred thousand barrels a day through more than a thousand kilometres of pipeline to tankers off the coast of Cameroon. It's the biggest single investment of any kind in sub-Saharan Africa. The government of Chad stands to earn a hundred million dollars a year over the next decade or two. In a new version of 'sovereignty under surveillance', the country has made a deal with the World Bank under which it will spend the money on reducing poverty. The Bank is supposed to help local groups to make sure that the money is spent wisely. But although the civil wars that convulsed Chad after independence ended fourteen years ago, the idea of checks and balances is still very fragile. Three years ago President Idriss Déby put all the main opposition leaders in jail after a dispute over an election. He released them after a phone call from the president of the World Bank. The Bank is so powerful because Chad is dependent on foreign aid. Some Chadians urged it not to give its sanction to the oil exploration until political institutions were much stronger; they fear the oil money will be used to strengthen a repressive government or even reignite the wars of the past.

Ndjamena has been fought over many times, but it is getting more difficult to find the marks of war. Grass and weeds have grown up around bomb sites; occasionally, passing the same corner for the third or fourth time, it is possible to notice bullet marks on a crumbling gable end. Every morning around half past eight, two French Mirage jets would scorch their way across the sky above our hotel. At lunchtime the pilots would come sauntering into the lobby. And in the afternoon they would be found drinking beer in the bar beside the swimming pool.

Much of the violence that broke out after the French left formally in 1960 had its origins in how they had ruled – in the way they had set the south against the north, for instance. At first, the French sent Legionnaires for brief campaigns to protect their favoured factions. But in the late seventies Libya invaded the Muslim north and within a couple of years Colonel Qaddafi's troops controlled two thirds of Chad. This got the Americans interested: General Alexander Haig, President Reagan's Secretary of State, talked of giving Qaddafi 'a bloody nose'. The French and the Americans supported Hissen Habre, the victor in the civil war of 1982, and slowly the Libyans were pushed back. For as long as they could they turned a blind eye to Habre's repression; he is said to have killed forty thousand people. After Habre was challenged by his best commander, Idriss Déby, who had beaten the Libyans across the desert, the French switched sides again. Déby took power in 1990.

The oil minister of Chad, Jusuf Abasallah, wasn't in the country then; his family had sent him to Germany to escape the war and he studied law there. At his office in an ugly, modern building towards the edge of Ndjamena, he wears a dark blue suit and is young, confident and friendly. It's odd, then, to notice on his desk a little ceramic red and yellow pick-up truck crowded with little miniture soldiers with guns. Whenever we have a break in our interview he lights a cigarette. I asked him what he would say if, when he stopped to buy cigarettes on his way home, a stallholder asked him to explain how the oil would make life better. He took a puff of the cigarette and said he would explain to the man in the kiosk that he needed to see the impact of the oil with an economist's eye: if you wait ten years you will have better roads, electricity in your house and maybe a telephone. This is the kind of thing the World Bank likes to hear. But we also met an older, less charming man called Quoroom Kabaddi, who is referred to as the 'Oil Co-Ordinator' and has a more powerful position than Mr Abasallah, being responsible for negotiating with Esso and the World Bank on President Déby's behalf. So long as there were no security problems, Mr Kabaddi said, then the oil money would be spent on improving life for stallholders and other ordinary people. But nobody could predict the future and in exceptional circumstances the money could be used for the security of the state. 'When the government has to defend itself there is no minimum price', Mr Kabaddi said.

3

Esso has its own little terminal at the edge of the airport where you're checked in, searched and given yellow laminated boarding cards for the one-hour flight on a small plane to the oilfield at Kome in the south. Many of the people here at seven o'clock on a Saturday morning were foreign oil workers. When we flew into Chad from Paris the Air France plane was full of Americans with southern accents who were talking to each other about the price of cows in Louisiana and what kind of mileage they got from their pick-up trucks. When they get to Ndjamena they check in for the night in the Novotel and then pick up the company flight to the oilfield, where they stay for eight weeks before flying back home for eight weeks' rest.

Most of the flight was through a cloud of dust. When we began to descend, the Longone river opened out below us, patches of green stretching away from its banks. We could see little villages and herds of cattle. Here and there neat rectangles of red dirt stood out like tidy garden plots, some of them marked with white picket fencing. These were the sites prepared for new drilling. We landed on an airstrip of laterite and were taken on a minibus to the Esso offices, elaborate prefabs constructed from materials shipped from the United States and carried on hundreds of trucks and train carriages from the Cameroon coast.

We had come on the plane with Ron Royal, the boss of Esso in Chad, a Canadian who has spent most of his life working in the oil business. In contrast to the others on board, who were casually dressed, Ron was wearing a navy business suit, a white shirt and tie and polished black city shoes which, though he was a tall man in his late fifties, made him look dainty as he walked across the red clay. On the plane he had sat by himself in the front seat. Ron's pitch was that Chad was very lucky Esso had even considered coming here. He liked to say that the economics of the oilfield were not 'robust'; in his thirty-five years with Esso he had never seen a project with such low returns. But he hinted that Esso was looking beyond immediate gain: the exploration teams had found that new satellite wells looked even more promising than the base from where the oil started pumping in late 2003.

Ron talked of meeting President Déby as if these encounters between the Canadian oil executive who wore his navy suit in the bush on a Saturday and an all-powerful president who had spent most of his life making war in the desert were between two worldly-wise old stagers. Ron had reminded the president that even income of $100 million a year, when divided up among Chad's population of nine million, left only $12 a head per year. 'That rang a few bells.' Nonetheless he could see how Chad was growing prosperous. When he came to Ndjamena from the Esso office in Bordeaux a couple of years ago, Ron left his sixteen-year-old Mercedes behind for fear of being too ostentatious. Now, he said with the air of a man impressed by a shiny car, he had recently seen a 7-series BMW and a brand-new Mercedes on the same street.

We spent most of an afternoon with Ron touring the villages

around the oilfield where, in recognition of disturbance caused by the heavy machinery and the wide trench dug for the pipeline, Esso was engaged in good works for the locals. Some of the discarded wood from packing cases had made desks in a school classroom in one village; in another they were building a solar-powered water pump to replace the hand pump. Ron was genial in the presence of half-naked children and their mothers. Later, though, on the bus, he confessed to finding rural Chad a shock. When his friends back in Canada had asked him about it the best way he could describe it to them was by saying it was like a National Geographic TV special.

To judge from his account on the bus, he spent most of his time telling the Chadians what Esso couldn't do for them. Local officials had asked Ron if he could give them four-wheel-drives to come to meetings, and he had said no. The Chadians had asked for a hundred thousand dollars to pave the roads but he had said no. The government wanted eighty kilometres of paved road; Esso was building nine. We drove along a wide dirt road carved through the flat, recently green plain. Occasionally lorries and trucks roared by. Mostly it was empty. Then we caught up with a small boy pushing another boy in a kind of wheelchair with pedals. A man was ploughing a little plot to plant ground nuts. In front of us a tanker lorry trundled along, spreading a mixture of water and molasses to keep down the dust. We passed a tree where a bicycle had been left; smoke was rising from the grass nearby.

As we arrived back at the oilfield Ron was urgently called aside by one of the American managers as he got off the bus; we had been waiting on the plane for a while before he reappeared. When we landed once again in Ndjamena, flying in over hundreds of corrugated iron roofs, he rushed away again, barely saying goodbye.

4

The next day we discovered the cause of this little panic. A rumour was going around that the President of Cameroon, the country where Esso's pipeline ended up, had died suddenly while playing golf in Switzerland. The rumour turned out to be untrue, but it was the kind of unexpected news that Ron and the other Esso executives dreaded. A few weeks previously there had been a mutiny at an army barracks in Ndjamena. International telephone lines had been cut for forty-eight hours. The official story was that the mutiny had been staged by a group of disaffected soldiers seeking more pay. Other people had their own stories that they would share: that the rebellious soldiers wanted President Déby to go to war on behalf of the Africans in Darfur in Sudan; that some of the soldiers had taken their weapons and disappeared into the interior of the country.

Certainly there was an air of insecurity in Ndjamena. At the World Bank offices a sign had been recently affixed to one of the doors: 'For security reasons due to recent events in Ndjamena staff and visiting missions are advised not to stay in the office later than 7pm.' One evening we had gone to dinner at a local (that is to say, African) restaurant much further out of town than the three or four places run by French expatriates that were usually favoured by foreign visitors. On the way back, our taxi, driven by an old man, was pulled over by several men in military uniforms near a roundabout. Out of my window on the passenger side I could see two men being pushed around. A soldier or policeman – it was difficult to tell which – put his head through the driver's side and asked for our passports. Then another soldier pulled open the driver's door and dragged the old man outside. One of us had no passport, and the very agitated soldier, clearly drunk, screamed at him in the back seat: 'C'est très grave! C'est très grave!' He turned towards me again and said, more wheedling than screaming, that he needed to eat, bringing his thumb and fingers towards his mouth. I gave him five thousand Central African Francs and that was enough. The driver returned and we set off again. Approaching the centre of town the driver saw another military truck approaching and took off down side streets.

The biggest paradox of Chad as an oil producer is that most of the streets of Ndjamena are dark after six o'clock, the kind of darkness that, relieved by occasional flickers of lamps and candles, gives the sensation of a permanent power cut. The headlights of the car make a small tunnel of light through the murk: cyclists and pedestrians appear from nowhere. People gather at candlelit tables by the roadside or do their grocery shopping at markets where dozens of little kerosene lights barely illuminate slabs of fish and bags of rice laid out on rows of tables. The city's power plant has about half the capacity of the plant that runs Ron Royal's oilfield. They say that at night the oilfield can be seen from space.

(Winter 2004–5)

Five, four, three, two, one

ANNE ENRIGHT

Amniotic fluid smells like tea. When I say this to Martin, he says, 'I thought that was just tea.' Of course a hospital should smell of tea; a hospital should smell of bleach. Unit 3 in Holles Street smells of tea and a little bit of ammonia, whether human or industrial is hard to tell. There is a lot of amniotic fluid in Unit 3. At least three of the women have had their waters broken that afternoon, and as the evening approaches we sit draining into strips of unbleached cotton and watching each other, jealously, for signs of pain.

There is a little something extra in there, sharp and herbal – green tea maybe, or gunpowder tea. Pregnancy smelt like grass. Sort of. It certainly smelt of something growing; a distinctive and lovely smell, that belongs to that family of grass, and ironed cotton, and asparagus pee. But the smell of tea is beginning to get to me. There are pints of it. I'm like some Burco boiler with the tap left open. It flows slowly, but it will not stop. For hours I have been waiting for it to stop, and the mess of the bed is upsetting me. It upsets the housekeeper in me and it upsets the schoolgirl in me. The sanitary pads they hand you are school-issue and all the nurses are turning into nuns.

The breaking of the waters was fine. The nurse did whatever magic makes sheets appear under you, while other things are folded back, and the obstetrician did something deft with a crochet hook. There was the sense of pressure against a membrane, and then *pop* – a bit tougher, but not much different than bursting a bubble on plastic bubble-wrap. It felt quite satisfying, and the rush of hot liquid that followed made me laugh. I don't think a lot of women laugh at this stage in Unit 3, but why not? We were on our way.

After which, there was nothing to do but wait. As the afternoon wears on, the pink curtains are pulled around the beds. The ward is full of breathing; the sharp intake of breath and the groaning exhalation, as though we were all asleep, or having sex in our sleep. One woman sobs behind her curtain. From the bed beside me the submarine sound of the Doppler looking for a foetal heartbeat and endlessly failing – a sonic rip as it is pulled away, then bleeping, breathing; the sigh and rush of an unseen woman's electronic blood.

Then there is tea. Actual tea. The men are sent out, for some reason, and the women sit around the long table in the middle of the ward. It's a school tea. There is a woman with high blood pressure, a couple of diabetics, one barely pregnant woman who has such bad nausea she has to be put on a drip. There are at least three other women on the brink, but they stay in bed and will not eat. I am all excited and want to talk. I am very keen to compare dressing-gowns – it took me so long to find this one, and I'm quite pleased with it, but when I get up after the meal, the back of it is stained a watery red. I am beginning to hate Unit 3.

After tea is the football. Portugal are playing France and when a goal is scored, the men all come out from behind the curtains to watch the replay. Then they go back in again to their groaning, sighing women. I keep the curtain open and watch Martin while he watches the game. I am keeping track of my contractions, if they are contractions. At 9.35, Martin looks at me over the back of his chair. He gives me a thumbs up as if to say 'Isn't this a blast? And there's football on the telly!' At 9.35 and twenty seconds I am, for the first time, in serious pain. I am in a rage with him for missing it, and call to him quietly over the sound of the game.

A woman in a dressing-gown comes to talk to me. She is very big. I ask her if she is due tonight but she says she is not due until September, which is three months away. She is the woman from the next bed, the one with the Doppler machine. They couldn't find the foetal heartbeat because of the fat. She stands at the end of the bed and lists her symptoms, which are many. She has come up from Tipperary. She is going to have a Caesarean at thirty-one weeks. I am trying to be sympathetic, but I think I hate her. She is a weakness in the room.

When I have a contraction I lurch out of bed, endlessly convinced that I have to go to the toilet – endlessly, stupidly convinced, every five minutes, that there is a crap I have to take, new and surprising as the first crap Adam took on his second day in the world. This journey to the toilet is full of obstacles, the first one being Martin, whose patience is endless and whose feet are huge. When I get into the cubicle at the end of the ward, I sit uselessly on the toilet, try to mop up the mess, and listen to the woman on the other side of the partition, who is louder than me, and who doesn't seem to bother going back to her bed anymore.

This has been happening, on and off, for a week. There is nothing inside me by way of food; there hasn't been for days. I am in what Americans call pre-labour, what the Irish are too macho to call anything at all. 'If you can talk through it, then it's not a contraction,' my obstetrician said when I came in a week ago, convinced that I was on my way. This week, she says she will induce me because my blood pressure is up; but it may be simple charity. Ten days ago I wanted a natural birth, now I want a general anaesthetic. Fuck aromatherapy, I would do anything to make this stop – up to, and including, putting my head in the road, with my belly up on the kerb.

A woman answers her mobile. 'No Ma, nothing yet. Stop calling! Nothing yet.' Pain overtakes the woman two beds down and the curtains are drawn. When they are pulled back, you can tell she is delighted. Oh this is it. This *must* be it. Oh Oh I'm going to have a baby. Then more pain – agony, it looks like. 'Oh good girl! Good girl!' shouts the midwife, as the man collects her things and she is helped out of the Ante-Room To Hell that is Unit 3. I am jealous, but I wish her well. The room is full of miracles waiting to happen, whether months or hours away. Another bed is empty – the woman on the other side of the toilet partition, is she in labour too? 'She went out, anyway,' says Martin. 'Hanging on to the wall.'

It is a theatre of pain. It is a pain competition (and I am losing). Martin says that Beckett would have loved Unit 3. We wonder whether this is the worst place we have ever been, but decide that the prize still goes to the bus station in Nasca, the time we went to Peru and didn't bring any jumpers. All the paper pants I brought have torn and I sit knickerless on the unbleached sheet, which I have rolled up into a huge wad under me. My bump has shrunk and gone slack. When I put my hand on it, there is the baby; very close now under the skin. I just know it is a girl. I feel her shoulder and an arm. For some reason I think of a skinned rabbit. I wonder are her eyes open, and if she is waiting, like me. I have loved this child in a drowsy sort of way, but now I feel a big want in me for her, for this particular baby – the one that I am touching through my skin. 'Oh, when will I see you?' I say.

This could be the phrase of the night, but instead it is a song that repeats in my head. 'What sends her home hanging on to the wall? Boozin! Bloody well boo–oozin.' I stop getting out of bed every five minutes and start breathing, the way they told us to in the antenatal class. I count backwards from five when the pain hits, and then from five again. Was I in labour yet? Was this enough pain? 'If you can talk, then it's not labour.' So I try to keep talking, but by eleven o'clock the lights are switched off, I am lurching into sleep between my (non)contractions for three or five minutes at a time, and Martin is nodding off in the chair.

My cervix has to do five things: it has to come forward, it has to shorten, it has to soften, it has to thin out, it has to open. A week earlier the obstetrician recited this list and told me that it had already done three of them. In the reaches of the night I try to remember which ones I have left to do, but I can't recall the order they come in, and there is always, as I press my counting fingers into the sheet, one that I have forgotten. My cervix, my cervix. Is it soft but not short? Is it soft and thin, but not yet forward? Is it short and hard, but open anyway? I have no sense that this is not a list but a sequence. I have lost my grasp of cause and effect. My cervix, my cervix: it will open like the clouds open, to let the sun come shining through. It will open like the iris of an eye, like the iris when you open the back of a camera. I could see it thinning, the tiny veins stretching and breaking. I could see it opening like something out of *Alien*. I could see it open as simple as a door that you don't know you've opened, until you are halfway across the room. I could see all this, but my cervix stayed shut.

At 2.30 a.m. I give in and Martin goes off to ask for some Pethidine. I know I will only be allowed two doses of this stuff, so it better last a long time. I want to save the second for the birth, but in my heart of hearts I know I'm on my way to an epidural now. I don't know why I wanted to do without one, I suppose it was that Irishwoman macho again. Mná na hÉireann. MNÁ na hÉireann. FIVE four three two … one. Fiiiive four three two one. Five. Four. Three. Two. One.

Once I give in and start to whimper, the (non)contractions are unbearable. The Pethidine does not come. At 3 a.m. there is a shrieking from down the corridor, and I realize how close we are to the labour ward. The noise is ghastly, Victorian: it tears through the hospital dark. Someone is really giving it soprano. I think nothing of it. I do not wonder if the woman is mad, or if the baby has died, but that is what I wonder as I write this now.

Footsteps approach but they are not for me, they are for the woman from Tipperary, who has started crying, with a great expenditure of snot, in the bed next door. The nurse comforts her. 'I'm just frikened,' she says. 'She just frikened me.' I want to shout that it's all right for her, she's going to have a fucking Caesarean, but it is forty-five minutes since I realized that I could not do this any more, that the pain I had been riding was about to ride over me, and I needed something to get me back on top, or I would be destroyed by it, I would go under – in some spiritual and very real sense, I would die.

The footsteps go away again. They do not return. I look at Martin who is listening, as I am listening, and he disappears silently through the curtain. At 3.30 a.m., I get the Pethidine.

After this, I do not count through the (non)contractions, or try to manage my breathing. I moan, with my mouth a little open. I *low*. I almost enjoy it. I sleep all the time now, between times. I have given in. I have untied my little boat and gone floating downstream.

At 5 a.m. a new woman comes along and tells Martin he must go home. There follows a complicated and slow conversation as I stand up to her (we are, after all, back in school). I say that I need him here, and she smiles. 'What for? What do you need him for?' (For saving me from women like you, *Missis*.) In the end, she tells us that there are mattresses he can sleep on in a room down the hall. Oh. Why didn't she say so? Maybe she's mad. It's 5 a.m., I'm tripping on Pethidine, at the raw end of a sleepless week, and this woman is a little old-fashioned, in a mad sort of way. Wow. We kiss. He goes. From now on, I stay under, not even opening my eyes when the pain comes.

I think I low through breakfast. They promise me a bed in the labour ward at half past ten, so I can stop lowing and start screaming, but that doesn't seem to be happening really. I am sitting up and smiling for the ward round, which is nice, but I am afraid that they will notice that the contractions are fading, and I'll have to start all over again, somehow. Then the contractions come back again, and by now my body is all out of Pethidine. I spend the minutes after half past ten amused by my rage, astonished by how bad I feel. Are these the worst hundred seconds I have ever been through? How about the next hundred seconds – let's give them a go.

At twelve o'clock, I nip into the cubicle for one last contraction, and we are out of Unit 3. The whole ward lifts as we leave, wishing us well – another one on her way. I realize I have been lowing all night, keeping these women from sleep.

The room on the labour ward is extremely posh, with its own bathroom and a high-tech bed. I like the look of the midwife; she is the kind of woman you'd want to go for a few pints with. She is tired. She asks if I have a birth plan and I say I want to do everything as natural as possible. She says, 'Well you've made a good start, anyway,' which I think is possibly sarcastic, given the crochet hook, and the Pethidine, and now an oxytocin drip. Martin goes back to pack up our stuff, and I start to talk. She keeps a half-ironic silence. For months, I had the idea that if I could do a bit of research, get a bit of chat out of the midwife, then that would take my mind off things – what is the worst thing that anyone ever said? or the wierdest? – but she won't play ball. I run out of natter and have a little cry. She says, 'Are you all right?' I say, 'I just didn't think I would ever get this far, that's all.' And I feel her soften, behind me.

I don't remember everything that followed, but I do remember the white, fresh light. I also remember the feelings in the room. I could sense a shift in mood, or intention, in the women who tended me, with great clarity. It was like being in a painting. Every smile mattered: the way people were arranged in the space, the gestures they made.

I have stopped talking. The midwife is behind me, arranging things on a stand. Martin is gone, there is silence in the room. She is thinking about something. She isn't happy. It is very peaceful.

Or: She tries to put in the needle for the drip. Martin is on my right-hand side. I seem to co-operate but I won't turn my hand around. The stain from the missed vein starts to spread and she tries again. I am completely uninterested in the pain from the needle.

Or: A woman walks in, looks at me, glances between my legs. 'Well done!' she says, and walks back out again. Perhaps she just walked into the wrong room.

Even at a low dose, the oxytocin works fast. It is bucking through my system, the contractions gathering speed: the donkey who is kicking me is getting really, really annoyed. The midwife goes to turn up the drip and I say, 'You're not touching that until I get my epidural.' A joke.

A woman puts her head round the door, then edges into the room. She says something to the midwife, but they are really talking about something else. She half turns to me with a smile. There is something wrong with one of the blood tests. She tells me this, then she tells the midwife that we can go ahead anyway. The midwife relaxes. I realize that, sometimes, they don't give you an epidural. Even if you want one. They just can't. Then everyone has a bad morning.

The midwife goes to the phone. Martin helps to turn me on my side. The contractions now are almost continuous. Within minutes, a woman in surgical greens walks in. 'Hi!' she says. 'I'm your pain-relief consultant.' She reaches over my bare backside to shake my hand. This is a woman who loves her job. Martin cups my heels and pushes my knees up towards my chest, while she sticks the needle in my spine, speaking clearly and loudly, and working at speed. I am bellowing by now, pretty much. FIVE, I roar (which seems to surprise them – five what?). FOUR. THREE. (Oh good woman! That's it!) TWO. One. FIVE. They hold me like an animal that is trying to kick free, but I am not, I am doing this, I am getting this done. When it is over, the anaesthetist breaks it to me that it might be another ten minutes before I feel the full effect. I do not have ten minutes to spare, I want to tell her this, but fortunately, the pain has already begun to dull.

The room turns to me. The anaesthetist brushes down her gown and smiles: a job well done. She is used to the most abject gratitude, but I thank the midwife instead, for getting the timing spot on. The woman who talked about my blood tests has come back and the midwife tells me that she is finishing up now, Sarah will see me through. This is a minor sort of betrayal, but I feel it quite keenly. Everyone leaves. Martin goes for a sandwich and Sarah runs ice cubes up my belly to check the line of the epidural. There is no more pain.

Sarah is lovely: sweetness itself. She is the kind of woman who is good all the way through. It is perhaps half past one and in the white light, with no pain, I am having the time of my life. Orla, the obstetrician, tells me my cervix has gone from practically zero to eight centimetres open, in no time flat. The heavens have opened, the sun has come through. Martin is called back from the canteen. He watches the machines as they register the pain that I can not feel anymore. He says the contractions are off the scale now. We chat a bit and have a laugh, and quite soon Sarah says it is time to push. Already.

For twenty hours women have been telling me I am wonderful, but I did not believe them until now. I know how to do this, I have done it in my dreams. I ask to sit up a bit and the bed rises with a whirr. Martin is invited to 'take a leg' and he politely accepts: 'Oh, thank you.' Sarah takes the other one, and braces it – my shin against her ribs. Push! They both lean into me. I wait for the top of the contraction, catch it, and ride the wave. I can feel the head, deliciously large under my pubic bone. I can feel it as it eases further down. I look at Martin all the while – here is a present for you, Mister, this one is for you – but he is busy watching the business end. Orla is back, and everyone willing me on like football hooligans, Go on! Go on! One more now! Push! Good woman! Good girl! I can hear the knocking of the baby's heartbeat on the foetal monitor, and the dreadful silence as I push. Then, long before I expect it, Sarah says, 'I want you to pant through this one. Pant.' The child has come down, the child is there, Orla says, yes, you can see the head. I send Martin down to check the colour of the hair. (A joke?) Another push. I ask may I touch, and there is the top of the head, slimy and hot and – what is most terrifying – soft. Bizarrely, I pick up Martin's finger to check that it is clean, then tell him he must feel how soft it is. So he does. After which – enough nonsense now – it is back to pushing. Sarah reaches in with her flat-bladed scissors and Martin, watching, lets my leg go suddenly slack. We are mid-push. I kick out, and he braces against me again. Orla, delighted, commands me to 'Look down now, and see your baby being born'. I tilt my head to the maximum; and there is the back of the baby's head, easing out beyond my belly's horizon line. It is black and red, and wet. On the next push, machine perfect, it slowly turns. And here it comes – my child; my child's profile. A look of intense concentration, the nose tilted up, mouth and eyes tentatively shut. A blind man's face, vivid with sensation. On the next push Sarah catches the shoulders and lifts the baby out and up – in the middle of which movement the mouth opens, quite simply, for a first breath. It simply starts to breathe.

'It's a girl!' Sarah says afterwards that we were very quiet when she came out. But I didn't want to say the first thing that came to mind – which was 'Is it? Are you sure?' Newborns' genitals are swollen and red and a bit peculiar looking, and the cord was surprisingly grey, and twisted like a baroque pillar. Besides, I was shy. How to make the introduction? I think I eventually said, 'Oh I knew you would be.' I think I also said, 'Oh come here to me, darling.' She was handed to me, smeared as she was with something a bit stickier than cream cheese. I laid her on the top of my stomach and pulled at my T-shirt to clear a place for her on my breast. She opened her eyes for the first time, looking into my face, her irises cloudy. She blinked and found my eyes. It was a very suspicious, grumpy look, and I was devastated.

Martin, doing the honours at a festive dinner, cut the cord. After I pushed out the placenta, Orla held it up for inspection, twirling it on her hand like a conoisseur: a bloody hair net, though heavier, and more slippy.

The baby was long. Her face looked like mine. I had not prepared myself for this: this really astonished me. I said, 'She looks like me,' and Martin said (an old joke), 'Yeah, but she's got my legs.' At some stage, she was wrapped rigid in a blue blanket, which was a mercy, because I could hardly bear the smallness of her. At some stage, they slipped out, leaving us to say, 'Oh my God,' a lot. I put her to a nipple and she suckled. 'Oh my *God*', said Martin. I looked at him as if to say, 'Well, what did you expect?' I rang my mother, who said, 'Welcome to the happiest day of your life,' and started to cry. I thought this was a little over the top. In a photograph taken at this time, I look pragmatic and unsurprised, like I had just cleaned the oven and was about to tackle the fridge.

I am not stricken until they wheel us down to the ward. The child looks at the passing scene with alert pleasure. She is so clear and sharp. She is saturated with life, she is intensely alive. Her face is a little triangle and her eyes are shaped like leaves, and she looks out of them, liking the world.

Two hours later I am in the shower. When I clean between my legs I am surprised to find everything numb and mushy. I wonder why that is. Then I remember that a baby's head came out of there, actually came out. When I come to, I am sitting on a nurse. She is sitting on the toilet beside the shower. The shower is still going. I am very wet. She is saying, 'You're alright, you're alright, I've got you.' I think I am saying, 'I just had a baby. I just had a baby,' but I might be trying to say it, and not saying anything at all.

(Winter 2000–1)

Lost time accidents

BRIAN DILLON

The story of the pebbles

Travelling, initially, west-south-west along the coast from the Kentish
port of Folkestone, then arcing slowly south towards the shingle
spur of Dungeness, I am gradually, as I try to match the OS map on
my knee to the bus window's jolting vistas, becoming conscious of a
singular fact: I have never seen so many stones. To my left, the morning's mist has cleared, and the English Channel glints like a full car
park. To my right, the intricately channeled and sporadically settled
expanse of Romney Marsh is so flat that the sea looks askew by comparison. Having lived in this part of south-eastern England for
several years, I have grown used to the flint: to every sinking of a
gardener's spade striking stone an inch below the surface, to the
way every footpath is a mass of chalky rubbish, to the sparks raised
after sunset by a flint tossed onto the seashore. But none of it has
prepared me for the gravelly oddness of this section of the coastline.
Everything appears to be made of flint, including the sea wall that
towers to several decks' height above my bus. A refurbished
Martello tower, made blind by the wall, is bordered by a path of the
same substance; a caravan park is similarly surrounded. Just outside
of Hythe, the road curves inland for a couple of miles, enclosing a
long stretch of shingle, fenced off and sparsely dotted with the low
brick buildings, wooden huts and watchtowers of a military firing
range. At the furthest, narrowest end, a row of roughly pebble-
dashed council houses faces, across the stones and through the
fence, a two-dimensional simulacrum of a garish seaside town. The

road turns to meet the coast again, and larger detached houses spring up to my right; almost every one stands guard over its own bright patch of pebbles.

The ageing iconography of the English seaside is all more or less intact and legible along this stretch of the coast, although it is rather muted compared with the Regency paradise of Brighton, up ahead, or the Victorian dreamland of Margate, far behind. So familiar is the scurf of chip shops, amusement arcades, gift emporia and pub gardens (these last often inhabited by huge plastic dinosaurs) that it has all come to seem, on this Saturday morning in April, the first properly bright day of the year, a natural spring flourishing of the landscape. Far stranger is the stuff of which the territory itself is composed: as I near my destination, I start to catch sight, between the Italianate double garages of flaking villas, of a land made entirely of rounded stones you could hold in your hand. Can it really be natural, this vast acreage of gravel? I have half begun to suspect, as I glance at the mottled triangle on my map, that the whole thing has been designed and dredged up here by some monumentally ambitious land artist, a conceptualist's joke at the expense of a visitor foolish enough to set out to make sense of it. I think of the artist Robert Smithson, who wrote of the prodigious earthworks he produced in the late sixties: 'Words and rocks contain a language that follows a syntax of splits and ruptures. Look at any word long enough and you will see it open up into a series of faults, into a terrain of particles each containing its own void.' At Dungeness, every stone is a discarded word, or an orphaned phoneme, in the story of the making of the place. To attempt to describe it is to experience what Smithson calls 'a sedimentation of the mind'.

Dungeness, according to a leaflet put out jointly by British Nuclear Fuels Ltd and English Nature (as we shall see, the encounter between landscape and technology is especially stark here), has the largest discrete surface area of shingle in Europe, and probably in the world. Its pointed mass, measuring six by twelve kilometres, is made of six hundred separate ridges, layered up over the past five thousand years. Its substance is, of course, almost infinitely older:

chalk formed over ninety million years ago was eroded during the ice ages of the last two to three million years, allowing the harder flint to be washed to the floor of the English Channel. From there, as the ice melted and the sea level rose, it was dashed diagonally against the land by waves from the west. The resulting ridges were thrust into being in a textbook example of the process of longshore drift: the stepped movement of a particle along the coastline, a process whose key terms – 'swash' and 'backwash' – reproduce, in their acoustic precision, the exact action in question. The surface of Dungeness, in other words, is in constant motion. Its western side is continually being scooped out and smuggled round the corner to the north, skirting the sentinel beam of a lighthouse just inland of the southernmost edge. In the gardens of the houses I pass as I near the end of my bus ride, I spot numerous model lighthouses, some of them three or four feet tall, surrounded by neatly raked shingle. Perhaps it is only by the seashore that householders feel the need to fashion placatory copies of the landscape in which they live, as if it might otherwise, with a sinister swash and backwash, be sucked from under their feet. A similar invigilation is required with regard to the landscape at large, especially since the construction, in the mid-sixties, of a nuclear power station on the southern coast (it was followed, a decade later, by a second). Each year, one hundred thousand cubic metres of shingle must be transported from the eastern side and dumped in a massive new ridge to the west of the power station, in a patch my map simply calls 'Danger Area'. By this surgical expedient, the ness – the suffix denotes a headland or promontory, and is only a couple of etymological twitches away from a nose – maintains its Roman profile and resists a natural urge to wrinkle upwards to the north-east.

I get off the bus before it turns west and heads into the marsh. As I round the Pilot Inn, a long, low, nondescript and flat-roofed building that appears to lack a doorway, I get my first glimpse of the twin power stations in the distance. From this vantage, Dungeness A and B are the only objects in the landscape still washed out by the mist, as if a slightly overexposed photograph of them has been stuck on the horizon. It will be some hours before I can examine it closely.

A series of signs, decorated with local flora, announces that I am now entering the privately owned Estate of Dungeness, and that from this point on the territory is especially to be respected by the likes of me, the casual visitor. A sign also tells me that here I will find six hundred separate species of plant, which is to say one third of those extant in Britain. I realize as I head into the estate that even with the aid of the fading but helpful signage I will probably not be able to tell sea kale from sea campion, curled dock from common sorrel, Viper's Bugloss from Red Valerian. I will fare a little better with the fauna: there are more species of bumble-bee here than anywhere in the British Isles, and something apparently the size and colouring of a tabby kitten is already aloft and purring towards my head. My desultory advance research into the plant and animal life of Dungeness has yielded one or two useful facts. I can at least distinguish the largest plants: broom and gorse. The latter, I am told, has colonized mostly disturbed ground, and disturbed ground is precisely what I am looking for. Then, of the numerous species of bird to be found here, I have decided that the black redstart (though I would scarcely be able to recognize it) will be my mascot today. This bird, rarely seen in Britain before the 1940s, took a liking first to the bomb sites of the Second World War, later to industrial and derelict buildings, and finally to the new nuclear power stations dotted around the coast. The black redstart is my unlikely ally: a lover of the last century's abandoned, obsolete or blasted places, a connoisseur of ruins.

A tour of the monuments

I aim to stick closely, for now, to the path that, according to my map, will take me through the populous part of the ness, between the two lighthouses at its base and onto a narrow ridge that sepa-rates the power stations from the sea. To my left, beyond low

mounds of shingle, I can see the buildings, cranes and vessels of the
Dungeness fishing fleet. Its history, like those of most such commu-
nities, is long, arduous and punctuated by tragedy. But its material
traces are indistinguishable from any other deceptively picturesque
tangle of old and new fishing equipment. The particular mystery of
the fishing families of Dungeness is not to be found in their peren-
nial struggle with the sea, but slightly inland, on either side of this
path, where they have chosen to live. Many of the cottages I pass are
still inhabited by fishermen and their families; others, especially in
the last decade, have been bought by outsiders lured here by the
area's strange glamour, its reputation for a special sort of solitude,
its lunar aspect. The houses have in common a sense of imperma-
nence that one often finds in such places, but which is further
heightened by the territory itself. Dwellings here seem as unstable
as the earth. Many of them are actually old railway carriages appro-
priated in the twenties and thirties; even now, settled into the
stones and having sprouted all manner of ramshackle extensions,
they look as though you could tow them away, noisily, towards the
gates of the estate.

But it is in their relationship to the shingle that the buildings of
Dungeness seem somehow implausible. The cottages are traditionally painted black. (In a slightly too knowing twist on this
convention, a recently renovated house has been clad entirely –
except, sensibly, for its chimney – in black rubber.) Houses look as
if they have sprouted naturally from beneath the stones and at the
same time as though they have been dumped here or washed up by
the tide: the natural and the artificial abut oddly. The borders
between plots are impossible to discern. At one point I come across
a tiny sign driven between the stones: 'Keep Out, Private Property';
but there is nothing to show where this 'property' might begin or
end. I pass a cottage whose peeling white boards make it look like
it has been cobbled together out of driftwood. In front of it, six enormous blocks of reinforced concrete – each at least a metre across –
compose a bizarre sort of garden ornament. They are in various
stages of decay; from the centre of the most decrepit, which has

eroded unevenly from its upper surface so that it now resembles in miniature the aftermath of a landslide, a rusted spike protrudes: the church spire of a buried village. The whole austere and melancholy ensemble is literally grotesque: it emerges straight from that aesthetic, cultivated by the poets, painters and garden designers of the eighteenth century, which thrills to the chilly echo of ruins and caves, and seeks to reproduce their dank atmospheres in domestic landscaping. But this garden – there is no other word for it – outdoes all of that in its abject affinity with the stones on which it stands. The blocks have clearly been made from the shingle itself: it is impossible to tell, at their edges, what is concrete and what is natural. In fact, you might as easily think the entire arrangement (from a distance, a clump of dissolving sugar cubes) a weird new agglomeration of the surrounding stones as the remnant of some ancient industrial or military structure. All over Dungeness, one finds similar scraps of decaying concrete: fat slabs slowly vanishing; rounded lumps melting like snowballs; enigmatic channels sunk into the gravel and now filled with it, indistinguishable; perfectly smooth concrete poles felled and flensed to reveal their pebbly interiors.

This garden – I have just noticed that the house is called 'Shingleton' – is only the most alarming (at once broodingly Modernist and brutally Romantic) example of an aesthetic for which Dungeness has garnered a certain celebrity. Its most famous – though not, it seems clear, its first – adherent was the filmmaker, painter and writer Derek Jarman, who bought Prospect Cottage, formerly a fisherman's quarters, in 1986. Until his death in 1994, Jarman tended an eccentric planting of local flora and found objects. His garden was the setting, and in part the subject, of his 1990 film *The Garden*. A constant presence in the diaries he published towards the end of his life, it was luminously photographed by his friend Howard Sooley for another book, since repackaged as a popular coffee-table volume. It is probable that the British public knows Jarman now primarily as a diarist and gardener, not as the director of the notorious punk film *Jubilee*, of a camp and manic rendering of *The Tempest*, or of a violent and homoerotic study of

Caravaggio. I came to Dungeness first nearly a decade ago, solely to see this garden. (Strangely, I have forgotten almost everything about how the landscape looked that day.) Jarman was then not long dead, and it seemed disloyal, given how his films had once warped and emboldened my teenage soul, not to make the journey down from the other end of Kent to walk among the spirals of flint, swaying blooms of rust and jauntily phallic spikes of steel and wood with which the artist had decorated the earth about his cottage. Today, I am somewhat less sure of my right to pay my respects by disturbing this ground, though it must surely attract hundreds like me each year. The front door is open; spotting somebody seated by the window to the left, I decide to risk asking if I may wander in the garden. I regret it almost immediately: the figure inside doesn't stir in response to my knock, and I realize, with shame, that what I was really hoping for was to be invited inside. I stand there feeling foolish for at least a minute before stepping, as quietly as I can, back across the shingle to the path.

The history of the official architecture of Dungeness, like that of its domestic, is a stony palimpsest. It seems that without the pressure of restricted space, obsolete and decommissioned structures have simply been left where they stand. In the late fifties, as plans for Dungeness A took shape, it was discovered that, once complete, the power station would obscure from a crucial angle the view of a lighthouse erected in 1904. A replacement lighthouse, finished in 1960, stands a few hundred metres to the east of its precursor. Fully automatic, it seems impossibly slim against the sky. Its working end disappears as I move towards the surrounding fence; it looks from here, its upper reaches flaring out to hide the lamp at the top, like an old-fashioned electric torch placed on end with its beam to the sky. A leisurely concrete spiral steadies it at its base: a walkway that resembles, curiously, the elegant curving paths of the celebrated Penguin Pool built in 1935 for London Zoo by the modernist architect Berthold Lubektin. I put my face to the wire for a couple of minutes, half expecting something black and white to come waddling round the ramp.

One hundred and sixty-nine steps take me from the ground floor of the nearby Old Lighthouse to an enclosed gallery that surrounds the lenses of its one-million-candle-power lamp. Many of those steps encircle the terrifyingly open interior; I find that if I keep my gaze fixed on the next step, I can reduce the tremor that has overtaken my whole body just sufficiently to focus, on reaching each of the building's three floors, on the sights for which I have paid: a set of huge lenses, cased in brass, that circle the nearby power station in red and green; three framed and fading pages that depict the profiles of Soviet battleships, cruisers and submarines; a yellowed photograph of a mobile foghorn from the early years of the last century. This last, a squat, bulbous object, sits awkwardly on the shingle, looking remarkably like the monstrous meeting of animal and boiler in Max Ernst's painting of 1921, *The Elephant Celebes*. Outside, the remains of the last foghorn station attached to this lighthouse can still be seen, fenced off like so much of the area's official heritage, a little way down the beach. A few single-storey brick and concrete buildings are dwarfed by a white-painted (now badly rusted) lookout platform. A pair of thin, rusted tramlines runs the length of the compound; nearby lies a sort of squared trumpet, of a finer concrete than I have so far seen. The foghorn itself stands just inside the perimeter. Six more concrete trumpets face the sea and comprise the foghorn itself: two columns of three each, the squares alternately painted black and white, so that from a distance it seems a fraction of a vast chess board has been upended on the beach. At the centre of each square, a pale metal protrusion is ringed with rust. The whole has a slightly sinister air, as though from the rusted depths of each speaker a ghostly voice might warn me away from the fence.

Outfall Avenue

Trudging back up the shingle towards the Old Lighthouse and the path that will take me around the perimeter of the power station, I decide to stop for lunch at a green and cream-coloured wooden building announcing itself as The Railway Café. The café is also the terminal station of the Romney, Hythe and Dymchurch Railway, a service that has run out almost to the edge of the ness since 1927. I have already crossed its tracks on my way into the estate. As I sit down, a train pulls in and I am amazed to observe that it is carrying a group of malformed giants, their hydrocephalic heads looming in the carriage windows. I have quite forgotten that it is a miniature railway. As these monsters detrain and suddenly shrink to normal proportions, I notice the posters above my head: 'the world's only miniature mainline railway ... so much to see, so much to enjoy!' Over the counter, another sign announces: 'Sucka Slush, so cool you can't rush it'. Underneath, in a pair of clear plastic vats, toxically green and red liquids rise and fall, alternately urging their foamy tides upwards. Beside them, on the glass counter-top, four or five lurid plastic aliens hover proprietorially. The café fills up rapidly, the three sorts of visitor immediately fanning out as far from each other as possible: birdwatchers in expensive rain gear, a few hefting shiny tripods between the tables; young families, probably local to Kent, some with attached grandparents whose task is apparently to nod approvingly as sepia photographs of old Dungeness are pointed out, though they are all clearly decades too young to recall the era depicted; finally, a couple in their late twenties, the woman carrying a glossy guide to *Weekend Breaks*: they move three times before settling at a relatively clean table. The room is suddenly hot with noise, and my bacon sandwich falls apart before I've taken a bite.

'Nuclear Installations Act 1965, Licensed Site Boundary': the sign is a fading plate stuck to the fence in front of Dungeness A. Below it, a bright addendum has recently been attached: 'Please Take Your Rubbish Home'. After several letters, emails and telephoned enquiries to the management and PR offices of both stations, I have failed to solicit any sort of access to either. The same phrase emanates from each office or individual I try: 'the current security situation' has necessitated the closure of the site's Visitor Centre. The centre's last remnants, I suppose, are the brochures I have received in recent days, explaining the workings of a Magnox reactor and detailing the conservation projects supported by the owners of Dungeness A and B (British Nuclear Fuels and British Energy, respectively). A publicist at the B station briefly canvassed the intriguing notion that I might be allowed to view a simulation of the main control room, but the plan evaporated at the next stage in my enquiries.

Turning the corner at the south-eastern extremity of the site so that I am now walking directly due west, I pass on my right an enclosure that from a distance I had taken for a car park. It turns out to contain several long, low, rusted frames, laid parallel to the shore, against which have been propped sheets of corrugated metal, painted in bright colours and arranged so that they face both sun and sea. The woman who took my money at the lighthouse had said something about 'all kinds of tests' being carried out here by 'all sorts of companies', including paint manufacturers. I suppose that these are samples of different paints, exposed to the caustic air of Dungeness to test their longevity. But how long have these experiments been going on? Even allowing for the speed with which metal must corrode here and paint crack, these planes of colour look ancient, like an abstract rendering of elderly sunbathers mottling painfully in the harsh light. I leave them behind and climb the ridge of stones, perhaps twenty feet high, that separates the station from the sea. At the top, with the sun in my eyes, I almost trip over a dark oblong on the shingle: an actual elderly couple, stretched awkwardly across the stones. It seems an unattractive spot to loaf in the sunshine, but then I notice the others: below me on the beach, a couple of dozen dark figures are standing or sitting, all staring out to sea, some of them attached to telescopes, binoculars or the camera tripods I had seen back at the café. And what they are watching is this: a hundred metres out from the shore, two vast patches of the sea are churning violently. Thousands of seabirds have congregated over the area. The noise is astonishing, competing even with the constant roar of the A station behind me. Below my feet, hundreds of thousands of litres of water per second are being drawn into the station's cooling system and gushing out again. (The disturbed area to the left must be the outlet: here, the warm water has attracted twice as many birds as the adjacent maelstrom, which must lie above the intake.) Just inside the boundary fence, a sign on the nearest building reads 'Outfall Avenue'.

Between the open shingle and the power station site proper, a sort of no-man's-land encloses the whole facility: a ribbon of stones a few feet across, bordered by wire on both sides and punctuated by the supports for an electric fence, slim poles that hold security cameras and (these seem a recent addition) some svelte and gleaming black monoliths that I take to be part of an infra-red alarm or warning system. In the awkward lexicon of contemporary prison design, this space is an 'inertia': its gravelled surface is intended to slow a potential escapee (or, in this case, intruder). Here, it seems itself a sort of invasion, as if the surrounding territory has started to creep under the wire. The authorities appear to have responded to this inhuman encroachment with a preposterous display of sympathetic magic. Within a flint's lob of the wire, they have constructed a brutalist garden, laid with suspiciously plant-free shingle, dotted with chunks of incongruous granite and bordered by some anonymous bushes which are neither broom nor gorse. There are no flowers; the only colour comes from some metal seats painted the jarring mauve of the British Energy livery. One might almost suspect a subversive wit at work here: in a final gesture of recursive allegorizing, the garden has itself been fenced off from the rest of the compound.

I have left the A station behind now, and have to turn back to remind myself of its precise shape. In truth, despite its pallid bulk, it is formally unremarkable: a collection of variously sized box-like buildings that give no hint of the unthinkable processes at work inside. Dungeness B, by contrast, has more of the cathedral grace and modernist confidence that one expects from a power station. In fact, with slim vertical windows running almost the whole height of its two thickly joined cylinders, it is not unrelated to the flourishing of a particular kind of Catholic modernism in the second half of the last century. It would not look out of place in the futuristic cityscape of Brasilia, for example, and it bears a passing resemblance to the fluted elegance of Liverpool's Catholic cathedral of the 1960s. As for its interior, we have now to rely on the extraordinary published work of a local photographer, Nigel Green, to assure ourselves that the impression of a sacred space is carried on inside and is not just a kitsch projection. In Green's photographs of the B station, it looks as if something that was once alive here – the spirit of mid-century technological optimism, the ghost of a nuclear dream – has leached away into the shingle. The power station looks deconsecrated. The A station is to be decommissioned in 2006, but in Green's images of its twin's untended machinery and vacant control rooms, the impish atom might already have absconded, leaving the whole edifice shuddering and bereft. Atop a lofty gantry, a spray-painted smiley-face grins knowingly like the labyrinthine station's own Piranesi, about to duck out of sight and leave us alone with his atrocious invention. The most immediately impressive of Green's photographs are those which conjure the scale of the interiors. But his images are alive too to the installation's leakage of energy and meaning across the landscape outside. In a series of small black and white studies, he sends his camera scuttling across the shingle in search of a mutant, stunted, alien's-eye view.

'the rags of time'

By the time I think I have spotted some of Nigel Green's scrubland subjects – a series of desiccated bramble bushes that look somehow sentient, as though patiently awaiting a vivifying charge that will start them scrabbling over the stony ground – I have already inadvertently passed the western limit of the power station site. I have failed to notice that the high fence to my right, which has for a few hundred yards enclosed only empty shingle, is now completely rusted and will soon come to a stop. I pre-empt the end of the fence and duck through a gap, assuming that, although the occasional sign here still appeals to the Act of 1965, this area must no longer belong to the power station. The newer fencing starts again, several hundred metres on, around what I have decided will be my final destination in this direction. I have guessed, from my map, that it is a transformer station: two rows of pylons extend from the northern side of the power station complex to the eastern edge of the almost featureless grey building in front of me. When I reach it, the low static hum that I could already hear by the seashore has become an almost unbearable amalgam of roaring and crackling. I am no longer hearing this sound so much as feeling it with every nerve, every startled cell in my body. A strong wind is blowing from behind me as I place my hands flat against the fencing – not far from a sign that says 'Danger of Death' – and I cannot tell whether the vibration running through my fingers comes from the wind or from the huge ceramic, glass and metal housings of the cables running over my head. I imagine that at any moment these supports might fail and the wires start whipping angrily in the salt air.

I draw back from the fence and approach, gingerly, an enigmatic metal frame that has been sunk into the ground a few metres from the perimeter of the transformer station. It appears to have been used to test the sort of cable that is currently swaying above me. Five thick ropes of metal are laid loosely across it a metre or so above the ground, each about four metres long and securely bolted at both ends. The whole thing looks a lot like certain minimalist sculptures by Antony Caro, in particular his 1967 work *Prairie*, in which four slim and extremely long rods of steel are suspended above a notional landscape. The lines, as here, remind us of the implacable human energies expended to traverse and tame the natural world. A couple of the wires in front of me extend beyond their attachment to the frame and seem to have burrowed between the stones. I let my hand brush against the nearest cable. Then, with the air as if suddenly charged around me, and a feeling that the electric buzzing is now coming from my own heart, I grab hold of it and pull it taut. A rush of adrenalin earths me to the shingle.

Dungeness has been traversed, throughout its history, by several sorts of current. The landscape is everywhere pitted and striated by the evidence of these crossings. The instability of the place, the constant slow swirl of the shingle around the point, seems to draw energy into its circuit. There is a sense, crossing the stony ground, that all of these historically disparate forces, some of them supposedly long discharged, are still alive here. This is no fanciful stab at a seaside psychogeography, no conjecture regarding occult intensities at work beneath the stones. It is simply to say that the territory, by virtue of its emptiness, has retained to a remarkable extent the remnants of past movements across its surface. It is impossible to walk this land without feeling oneself at the nexus of these energies: the slow edging of the settlement itself out towards the point; the fishing fleet's ancient slipways; the routes of at least three railway lines; the beams of several lighthouses, now destroyed, that predated that of 1904; the sounds of their foghorns; the memory of a huge pipeline that ran into the sea here and, in the last year of the Second World War, supplied petrol to the Allied forces on the other side of the Channel; the surge of electricity overhead and the hidden forces by which it is generated. The only thing not in constant movement here, strangely, is water. Dungeness is unique among areas of coastal shingle: the stones are so tightly compacted that they form a barrier between the sea and the several small freshwater lakes at its eastern edge. This place, so friable and in flux on its surface, is apparently, a few feet below, wholly impermeable.

After my adventure at the edge of the energy field of the ness, it is at first a relief to return along the path by the power station. Something out there seems to have unsettled me: my walk back to the gates of the estate is fraught with misreadings and botched calculations. On the other side of the fence, a large electronic sign has been affixed to a wall not far from the neurotic garden. It details some statistics regarding the daily running of the site, and has presumably been placed here to catch the attention of workers and public alike. Its categories compose a poetics of possible disaster, and I find myself mouthing these resonant phrases: 'reportable event', 'unplanned auto-trip', 'days since last lost time accident'. But the information is missing: the power to the sign has been switched off. I feel as though something in me has been tripped too: I have stopped making sense of the landscape. On the way back, I stumble into a wide foveal dent in the shingle; heading towards the opposite bank, I get lost in some sort of wire and wood-framed passageway and wander around for several minutes before it dawns on me where I am: at the centre of a large abandoned aviary. The buildings around me seem suddenly illegible. I stop for ages in front of an apparently formless wooden object which might be a shed or a woodpile, I cannot tell. Then I peer a little closer at the tattered flag hoisted above it, with its sun-bleached logo: 'British Ener ...'. I look up at the pale monument humming on the horizon, and back at this chaotic mound: is it possible that it is meant to be a model of the power station? The community's (or the landscape's) wry rejoinder to that ludicrous garden, that sorry stretch of captive earth at the centre of the station's carceral maze?

Passing by Prospect Cottage again, I remember that Jarman inscribed the text of John Donne's poem 'The Sunne Rising' on a south-facing gable. Approaching the house from the other side, I had quite missed it this morning. Now, standing at the edge of the garden, I can just make out the black letters raised from the black wall. Although I know this poem well, and can half read, half recall most of its thirty lines, I can neither properly discern nor remember the last line of the first stanza. At least, not until I have almost reached the entrance of the estate again, where I turn for a last look back at the ness, with its complex web of competing histories: 'Nor houres, dayes, moneths, which are the rags of time'.

Testing ground

It is mid-afternoon when I leave the estate, and although I have been walking the shingle for hours now, I have just enough time and energy left to visit the last of the famous monuments of Dungeness. (There are lesser wonders, visible on my map, further inland on the edges of the marsh: old water towers, disused gravel works, the remains of another railway station.) I head north along the coast road by which my bus approached the ness, through the tiny village of Lydd-on-Sea and towards Greatstone, where, on the map, the minute dots and lozenges that denote the shingle finally disappear. The stretch of road between these two villages is flanked on my left by the occasional meticulously presented bed-and-breakfast, but mostly the houses, though more sturdily built in the thirties, have all the tumbledown eccentricity of the cottages behind me at Dungeness. Neat pre-war bungalows have had rambling, baroque extensions added: glassed-in verandas that, for all their Mediterranean aspirations, are really no more than makeshift lean-tos. As I pass an especially decrepit example (not far from a nursing home called 'Memories'), I notice an old woman slumped in an armchair inside; her head is flung back and her mouth hangs open. Behind her, against the wall, crates of Coke have been piled almost to the ceiling; a large, dirty, blond dog is pacing around its mistress's chair. I keep walking, but glancing back a moment later I notice that the woman's face is grey as concrete. I slow my pace, turn, dawdle, look out to sea and check that there is nobody else on this stretch of the road, before walking back to look at her again. She has definitely not moved; I squint, trying to see if she is breathing, but the veranda is too far away, across a garden full of rubbish and a couple of dingy towels dried stiff across the fence. I remember passing this house on my way down the coast, telling myself I should have a closer look on the way back. Now I'm reaching into my rucksack for my mobile phone, wondering how long I can stand here glancing furtively at what I have by now convinced myself is a corpse. There is, of course, only one way to find out, but I'm not yet ready to approach the window. If the woman is alive, and maybe even awake and regarding me with mounting alarm through slitted eyelids, she might summon help before me. Or the next passerby will be justifiably suspicious of this agitated figure on the pavement, alternately peering at a sleeping old woman and pretending to address some nonexistent object on the empty shore. I have still not resolved what to do when the gaping mouth begins, very slowly, to close.

What you think is dead here will turn out, always, to be merely dormant. The particular relics whose energies I am now hoping to resurrect are to be found at the end of one of the short residential roads that run inland at right angles to the shore. The place is invisible from the coastal route, obscured by a fat ridge running across the road: it is presumably a speed bump, though it looks more as if the tarmac has buckled in response to some seismic shift far below. As I reach its summit, I can see the shingle – less often mixed, here, with steadying soil, not so easily negotiated – stretching a few hundred metres to the edge of a lake. The lake is the result of several decades of gravel extraction. Its nearest shore, running north–south, is almost completely straight, and separated from a nearby caravan park by high fencing that is topped with barbed wire. I have stepped over a couple of collapsed and rusted fences already, one of them barely a reddish-brown stain among the stones. In front of me, a sturdy recent addition to the site's spiky enclosures will soon cut off my approach to the lake. To my right, a mobile-phone mast is the most securely enclosed object I have seen all day, more impregnable even than Dungeness A and B. The signals it relays across this desolate but teeming landscape add to its history a further crackling stratum of invisible energy. The water in the lake, cut off from the sea, looks black, depthless, worried. The wind has raised tiny waves, like gooseflesh, across its surface. I thought that out here, for the first time today, the territory itself might fall silent around my noisy progress. But the water keeps up a constant chatter against the shore, like clapping in an auditorium with bad acoustics.

I feel like applauding the view across the lake. Directly opposite me, thrust out into the water on a pebbled promontory, is a spectacular arc of grey concrete, curving sleek and low around a forecourt that slopes and narrows to a point by the water. To the right of this amazing construction – which looks as though it has been cut out, like a slice of pie, from a Greek amphitheatre – a huge concrete bowl, turned diagonally towards the sky, is supported by a thickly buttressed base. Further right (that is, north) again, a much smaller slab of the same material, like an upright, flattened satellite dish, is leaning perilously from its lakeside position. These are the 'sound mirrors' of Dungeness: a few of the last remaining artifacts from a programme of acoustic research carried out by the British military in the years leading up to the Second World War. Together, these and others like them, built along the south-eastern coast of England, made up an early-warning system designed to detect enemy aircraft as they approached across the English Channel. A central controlling station, installed in a Post Office building near St Paul's Cathedral in London, would await telephoned messages from the coastal outposts. The project, which had its origins in listening trenches sunk by military engineers in the battlefields of the First World War, met with some limited success before the competing technology of radar overtook it in the late 1930s. The man behind the system, William Sansome Tucker, had already, in the mid-thirties, run into trouble here at Dungeness. The acoustic field that the three sound reflectors erected here were supposed to survey and condense towards special microphones of Tucker's invention, had by this time become distinctly unruly. Houses had begun to appear along the coast in front of the listening stations; the sound of the neighbouring holiday camp was encroaching into the fragile cone of sound focused on the largest of the three structures. It was, Tucker wrote, 'sensitive to any impulsive sounds which some ill disposed person might be capable of creating, and would be considerably affected by car traffic'. Fortunately, the holidaymakers a few hundred yards away went to bed early, but, as Tucker noted, 'should a band start up, matters would be different'. Imposing and sinister (this largest one is two hundred feet long), the sound mirrors seem at the same time to have been excessively sensitive, almost neurasthenic, in their workings. The young soldiers who operated them, sitting cramped and cold in the listening stations to the rear of the larger mirrors, could listen for no more than forty minutes at a time: any longer and they would, wrote Tucker, become so 'irritated' that they could not be relied upon.

I will not be able to get any closer to the sound mirrors today.

The site has recently been acquired by English Heritage. Already, the narrow isthmus by which one reaches the two-hundred-foot mirror has been fenced off; before long, it will be excavated so that a narrow body of water separates the structure from the land, and a bridge will allow for controlled access. The mirrors have attracted the wrong sort of visitor in recent years: the two larger, in particular, have been daubed with graffiti. Two years ago, after some hours negotiating the chaos of fencing, impassable ditches and wrong turns that left me time and again stranded and staring at the mirrors from across a few metres of water, I finally discovered the shingle path that led to the rear of the largest. Its advanced state of decay was sadly evident: a small concrete hut, the listening station attached to the back of the structure, had obviously collapsed decades ago. Only the remains of its chimney were intact on the ground; the rest had begun to dissolve, like so much of the area's built environment, into the pebbles. A few of the vast buttresses at the rear had also started to disintegrate, revealing, obscenely, their rusted reinforcing innards. But coming out onto the mirror's forecourt, this impression of decay was quickly overtaken by a sense of the geometric grace of the thing. Suddenly sheltered from the wind, I felt the form curving around and above me. Here, I sensed that I had discovered the heart of this whole landscape, a heat sink for all the stray historical forces still circulating among the stones, a monument to the spectral energies of the ness. The sound mirrors, the ruins of a possible future, are the perfect image of the enigma of Dungeness. Their mystery is that of the obsolete precursor. Like so much of this place, they were rapidly constructed, quickly abandoned and left here to live too long. Later, looking through the photographs I had taken of the two-hundred-foot mirror, I noticed for the first time, almost lost in the profusion of grafitti, this message scrawled faintly on its surface in letters a foot tall: 'I hate myself and I want to die'.

In 1938, in *The Air Defence of Britain*, a book hastily and cheaply published by Penguin as part of a series devoted to the nature of the inevitable conflict to come, Air-Commodore L.E.O. Charlton set out the full implications of 'the new factor in warfare'. He wrote with regretful realism: 'An efficient warning organization is an impracticability at present out of sight of land, and will remain so until our physicists can produce a detecting ray which will probe the distance. We will, therefore, only be able to rely on a period of notification which will commence when the invaders are sighted from off the coast and end with their arrival inland, a matter or ten or twelve minutes.' This is the perilously brief interlude that the sound mirrors were designed to extend. A sense of imminent emergency has long afflicted this stretch of the English coast. Consequently, even in peace time, it seems still to function as a kind of testing ground, not only for the technologies that might stall invasion, but for the very fear of invasion itself. That fear is a weapon in its own right, a force that the landscape of my journey north from Dungeness expressed with startling frankness. In Hythe, twenty miles along the coast, I spotted the earliest sign of a crude rhetorical barrier that in the weeks to come would stretch across this and other towns around the country. It was the first billboard I had seen in advance of the general election, and it read simply: 'How would you feel if a bloke on early release attacked your daughter?' Almost a month later the Conservative party would announce its policy of putting an end to the early release of prisoners. In the meantime, the party's leader, Michael Howard, the Member of Parliament for this part of Kent (he is photographed, crouched in the shingle, in the brochure for Dungeness power station and its nature reserve), would declare his party's rigorous attitude to the matter of immigration, a message designed in part to appeal to his own constituents. He would be pictured on television, on the streets of the county's market towns, being urged by supporters to 'do something about it'. The billboard I spotted in Hythe would be joined, across the country, by another: 'It's not racist to impose limits on immigration'. I realize now what I was looking at as I sat, exhausted, on the upper deck of the bus back from Dungeness. It was another burst of short-lived energy dispatched across this landscape, an experiment carried out at the edge of England, to determine its vulnerability, to gauge the porousness of its psyche, to measure how far the message could be made to sink into the stones.

(Summer 2005)

The shadow line

AMIT CHAUDHURI

1

Once, in 1973, a Switzerland-bound train I was in with my parents stopped for a few minutes at Bonn. A soldier came into our compartment and sat opposite us, and got off at the next stop: it seems fantastic, but it is true. For many years, this was my only claim to having been in Germany.

It's now more than a month since I entered Berlin for the first time. We flew into the Tegel airport; oddly, for a capital city, there is no pre-eminent international airport in Berlin. This is in keeping with its history; its complexity; its shyness of landmarks and its proliferation of them; its dubious but continuing fascination with its emblems of the past; its being situated in a constant narrative of relocation – mental, ideological, physical, geographic. So, there is the 'old' city centre and the 'new' city centre, the 'old' town hall and the 'new' town hall; but these inscriptions of 'old' and 'new' are themselves fairly recent. The expected movements of history have been compressed unnaturally; it's a little like being in Calcutta during the Pujas, but on a long-term basis, so that one might almost hope to become inured (who knows?) to an intertwining of the banal, the historic, the allegorical and the domestic.

It was a brilliant summer. It took me by surprise: this natural affluence of daylight in the midst of such palpable material affluence was difficult to digest. I thought, blinking in the sun, of those pre-war summers when Stephen Spender and company descended on Berlin, to sunbathe with god-like blonde boys, and also of the vanishing, in an instant, of sensual innocence, political blindness, devastating pain, into the vacancy of this present-day, new-millennial happiness. Bathed in light, I was there with Spender, in the Thirties, as I could never have been if I had lived then, and I was here, in post-unification, post-Schroeder, post-Iraq Berlin.

We stayed in a lovely flat in Schoeneberg ('beautiful hill', apparently, though there was no hill in sight) with large windows and wooden floors, and that most unEnglish of promontories, a balcony; the flat was spacious enough for a dog, let alone humans, to be content in. There was no dog; but my new friend's 'children' – a blonde sixteen-year-old boy and a dark-haired nineteen-year-old girl – kept coming in, going out. My friend and his wife no longer lived with each other; they spoke to each other on the phone and shared the children; they had become blood relations. His name was Reinhold ('Call me Reini'), and he taught English at the University of Magdeburg in the former East Germany, where, in four days, I was to read out my stories.

I went out and stood on the balcony and surveyed the buildings opposite. More reticent but no less compelling than cathedrals and temples, they wouldn't give up their secrets in a glance. Schoeneberg, Reini said, had been a mixture of economic classes and religions before the war; people of varying income groups had lived here, and not a small number of Jews. (I discovered later that the area used to be called the 'Jewish Switzerland', and had a sizeable upper-middle-class Jewish population at the turn of the century.) 'Tagore might have come here,' he beamed. Why? 'Einstein lived here. If they met in Berlin, it might have been here!'

The houses I saw from the balcony, like the building I was in, had been erected in the Twenties; they had miraculously survived the bombing. Thus, some of the residential areas of Berlin, which escaped both the bombs and the social levelling of East Berlin, have an extraordinarily ambiguous 'inner weather'. There are certain cities whose residential districts are even more revelatory to the outsider than their monuments and landmarks. Calcutta, I'd say, is one, for a walk in Mandeville Gardens or a drive through Bhowanipore or

Alipore is much more instructive and charged with excitement for the visitor than a pilgrimage to the Victoria Memorial. Berlin, I think, is another.

Next morning (again, glorious), Reini said he'd take us – me, my wife, our daughter – for a walk around Schoeneberg. On a plaque at the bottom of the façade of a nearby block of flats, partly hidden by the undergrowth, was the message that Einstein had resided here. We crossed the main road, further rows of buildings, and a bridge. We came to the 'old' town hall and the 'old' city centre. Before the wall fell, the Schoeneberg town hall had been the town hall of West Berlin. Happy to be at the secure centre of an American colony, it displayed lapidary words from John F. Kennedy addressed to West Germans. At midday, the stentorian chimes of the 'freedom bell' rang out, as they had for fifty years, once a signal to benighted East Berliners that liberty and democracy would one day be theirs. Unlike the Iraqis, the West Germans, till recently anyway, were happy with their liberators (and had chosen to forget their Russian ones).

On our way back our companion pointed out signs that hung from posts on the pavement, black German words on a white background. I recognized only 'Juden' as common to them all. These signs were meant to remind you of the exact day when, say, Jews became barred from taking PhDs. Another proclaimed the date when they were deemed ineligible to become professional classical musicians. Another recorded the day when Jews were denied access to well-known areas of recreation. The dates ranged from the late Twenties to the late Thirties.

Thinking of those signs, I'm reminded of Walter Benjamin and his essay 'Theses on the Philosophy of History', for two related reasons. The first is obvious: Benjamin's own history, his destiny and aborted career, his suicide after the fall of Paris in 1940, are inextricable from the history the signs narrate. It is only after walking around Schoeneberg that I understand something of the panic that fuelled his eloquence: 'The tradition of the oppressed teaches us that the "state of emergency" in which we live is not an exception but the rule'; and, 'The current amazement that the things we are experiencing [that is, fascism] are "still" possible in the twentieth century is not philosophical'.

Part of Benjamin's critique of what he calls the 'empty, homogeneous time' of Western history – of the idea that Western history, with its narrative of rationality and progress, stands as a universal paradigm of history itself – surely involves his violently endangered Jewish identity. It was the inability of German liberals and opponents of fascism to imagine outside that paradigm, to imagine in what way fascism might be happening beyond and outside it, that helps bring fascism, in Benjamin's eyes, into existence. The same might be said of many secular individuals and political parties in India – the problem is not just the calculated connivance with fascism, but the inability to imagine it is really present, to acknowledge that it is not an element in our secular history with which we can quarrel on our own terms.

The other thing that struck me gradually, as I looked at these signs – astonishing, estranging, and puzzling – is the profound, as-yet-unfathomed importance of the Holocaust to European identity and self-consciousness. This is something I hadn't quite grasped till I travelled to Berlin. Obscene though it might be to say so, it seems that the obsessive righteousness, memorialization and remorse surrounding the Holocaust – in Berlin, in Germany, but also everywhere in Europe – suggest that it, too, has become an all-important component of that 'empty, homogeneous time' without which history would be unimaginable (although it is imaginable without many other traumas of the twentieth century). The Holocaust cannot be replicated or repeated; it has been universalized, almost aestheticized, with the authority only Europe has, or has had, to universalize and aestheticize. Both Jew and European non-Jew are hurt and outraged if any comparison is made, say, between what is happening in Israel and Palestine and what happened in Europe. 'The "state of emergency" in which we live is not the exception but the rule', but, ironically, this statement is doomed to be proven true only in retrospect.

2

In the afternoon, we slept. We were heavy with jet-lag. When we woke, we found Reini was waiting for us. We set out in his car from Schoeneberg at about half-past four. Summer days in Europe are interminable; as the afternoon expanded, it seemed we'd woken up at an untimely hour in the latter half of the day not only to a new time zone, but to the extension of possibility.

Reini drove us to Nollendorfstrasse, where, in a rented room, Isherwood met and became familiar with some of the characters in *Goodbye to Berlin*, and with the 'deep, solemn, massive street' itself. His pressing reason for being in Berlin – his search for working-class boys – is, of course, mentioned in neither of the Berlin novels. Is it this story of unspoken desire that gives the language of these novels, especially *Goodbye to Berlin*, its character, its deceptive transparency, its constant, low-key melody; for what's literary style but a negotiation between the sayable and the unsayable? The unsayable, in the Thirties, was a way of life.

The next day, I'd return here with my wife and daughter, walk down Nollendorfplatz with its shops and restaurants, eat there, and walk back to Nollendorfstrasse. Not far from Isherwood's abode, a man was arranging things for a jumble sale. Mainly furniture and household objects, which had an exquisiteness that, my wife observed, only European objects once had. We asked how much a small white porcelain swan, its neck and head bent over the edge of a table as if it were about to drink, would cost us. Its delicacy – the pleated wings, the pale yellow of the beak, its whiteness, which, if it were an illustration in a book, would have made it merge into the page – made it look like something from the Twenties. It would need to be placed always at the edge of something, like a basin in a bathroom, because its head and neck were stooped at such an angle that they must necessarily inhabit empty space. We waited for a vast figure. Four euros, came the reply. We decided to buy it. It was wrapped in a polythene bag for travel.

That brief encounter with bric-à-brac dislocated me. Recounting the experience of walking in the Parisian arcades, Walter Benjamin said, famously, that some time in the late nineteenth century Paris had become a great interior; the introduction of gas-lit lamps had, in a sense, removed the sky over the city, turning it into a ceiling, and to stroll as flâneur or dandy through the arcades was in a way to roam about in your own room. In Nollendorfstrasse, buying the swan, hovering over the furniture, I felt something of that confusion, and felt, too, that my being there was charged with significance. It was as if I were in someone's house, but the house had been made invisible. On Nollendorfstrasse itself, buildings had been razed in the bombing, then swiftly replaced in post-war reconstruction by what Reini called 'prefabricated' houses. These were juxtaposed with the buildings that had survived, with their balconies, their drawing rooms with chandeliers.

The swan might have belonged to one of those houses. In my mind, the history of the bombing had set it free. Certainly, the bombing must have once added to the flâneur's experience of urban rambling, with its interchangeability of inside and outside, a dimension Benjamin couldn't have imagined. This ambiguous extra dimension informs this sentence, about London after the war, from Muriel Spark's *The Girls of Slender Means*: 'Some bomb-ripped buildings looked like the ruins of ancient castles until, at a closer view, the wallpapers of various quite normal rooms would be visible, room above room, exposed, as on a stage, with one wall missing; sometimes a lavatory chain would dangle over nothing from a fourth- or fifth-floor ceiling; most of all the staircases survived, like a new art-form, leading up and up to an unspecified destination ...' This self-aware aestheticization, with its comedy of absences and its juxtapositions of castles and wallpaper, takes me back to Benjamin's view of bourgeois Paris. The meandering sentence might not know it, but it is a child of that vision.

3

That sentence, which I'd read several years ago, prepared me for the Kaiser Wilhelm Memorial Church in the Kurfurstendamm. The latter is a long avenue of shops, cafes, and restaurants, Berlin's Champs Elysées, albeit on a smaller scale; the church, built at the end of the nineteenth century in memory of Wilhelm II, was bombed in the war. The main structure has been largely left as it was; the sudden impact of devastation, the bruises wrought by a single moment, are permanently on display. It was added to later, and its interior is open to tourists; before it, like a futuristic offspring, is a new bell-tower, modernist in conception, a tall hexagon. The contiguity between the two buildings is astonishing and provocative. The old church, perhaps affectionately, is called the 'rotten tooth'; it looked to me uncannily like Brueghel's picture of the Tower of Babel, with its burst centre, except that it, unlike the Tower, overwhelmingly represents silence.

From here, Reini drove us to the Reichstag, which, during the era of the two Berlins, had been disowned by both sides, partly because it stood on the border that separated them; it was now revived as a conference centre and a tourist attraction. We stared at it and walked across the now-impalpable dividing line; there was no wall here; it was at this point that the border most approximated the phrase with which Isherwood so movingly evoked it in his account of a post-war visit: the 'shadow line'.

I have never encountered the past as I did when I was in Berlin. It was not only I who saw the ghost; my wife did too. 'It's amazing,' she said. If only one of us had seen it, we could say that the person in question had imagined it; but both of us couldn't have had the same dream. Every city gives you a past which is, of course, a construct. But, here, the construct is curious. You are meant to confront the past everywhere, but are kept from what is surely the universal human instinct toward it – to mourn it; to commemorate it. Instead, you are dislocated by it in a series of encounters.

We crossed the 'shadow line' in Reini's blue car as the sun began to go down; he took us into the former East Berlin and showed us rows of prefabricated houses, and old official buildings the government still didn't know what to with; it is as though they are still awaiting repatriation. 'Don't quote me,' said Reini, 'but some of the profit-making companies of the East were bought over and discontinued by companies from the West to weed out competition.' From there to checkpoint Charlie, the Wall inscribed with artists' graffiti, the avenue of resplendent and still-threatening 'Stalinist' architecture, the Muscovite buildings looking like a great army without a general.

Can one see a city in a day? Can one absorb it? Certainly, in great Modernist texts – *Ulysses, Mrs Dalloway, Under the Volcano* – a day is all that is given; and, in that day, a break is made in Benjamin's 'empty, homogeneous time of history'. Benjamin conceived of that break as a 'now': '*Jetztzeit*'; a revolutionary, but also a mystical, moment in the present. The following is from his eighteenth thesis on the 'philosophy of history':

'In relation to the history of organic life on earth,' writes a modern biologist, 'the paltry fifty millennia of *homo sapiens* constitute something like two seconds at the close of a twenty-four-hour day. On this scale, the history of civilized mankind would fill one-fifth of the last second of the last hour.' The present, which … comprises the entire history of mankind in an enormous abridgement, coincides exactly with the stature which the history of mankind has in the universe.

This is a bit like the Hindu notion of human history as a blink in the eye of a *yuga*; it is also a fair definition of the day in a Modernist classic. A day is at once infinitesimal and endless.

4

Magdeburg is in what was called vaguely, until fourteen years ago, 'East Germany'. It is well known for being an important pre-war industrial town; for being thoroughly bombed during the war; for a very old cathedral; and for Otto von Guericke, after whom the university is named. This man was a scientist who is renowned for an experiment: he joined two empty hemispheres together and filled them with a vacuum. Then, in an odd tug-of-war, he had teams of horses try to pull them apart. They failed.

As we stepped out of the railway station into the strong light of six o'clock in the evening, Reini made us turn around and look at the building. It was the most magnificent structure in the area, something that might have been erected at the end of the nineteenth century; one could imagine it as a great terminus for horse-drawn carriages. From it to our hotel was a mere two minutes' walk. The hotel resembled an American motel, and was just the place for the conference visitor: well-equipped, efficient, unlovely, and turn of the century (the twentieth, not the nineteenth). We washed our faces and combed our hair in a brightly-lit bathroom before emerging for our walk with Reini.

Our walks give me the illusion of knowing Reini better than I do. His beard, his granny glasses, his long hair, coming down to well below his collar, suggest – and I confirmed this from a black and white picture in his kitchen – that, although he's probably modulated his politics, he's largely left the incarnation he found himself in during the student radicalism of the late Sixties, when he was at Berlin's Free University, untouched.

Naturally, he's put on weight. No sign of his residual left-wing propensities is to be found in his beautiful Berlin flat. In the course of conversation, a professed enthusiasm for Stuart Hall and Raymond Williams betrays not so much an allegiance to a programme as a private romanticism. He lived for years in China; he has been to India; among the pictures in his kitchen is a postcard that shows a place I believed I'd seen before – was it Rome? Only after repeated glances at the brown stone buildings, the lovely urban arc of traffic around an ancient European statue, did I recognize the Flora Fountain in Bombay, which I used to pass every day on my way to school.

In the black and white photo, Reini is smoking a cigarette. Like radicalism, cigarette smoking made an exit from bourgeois European society in the Eighties. The new religion is life; not just the pursuit of happiness, but of health. In this regard, Reini's unfashionable paunch – I could see, from old photographs, that he's had it for a while – proclaims, more than any political opinion, his anomalousness. I don't know what his relationship to the contemporary world is, but I suspect it isn't an entirely normal one; I suspect that, in spite of his joviality, his apparent satisfaction with his routine of work and leisure, he is secretly bemused by the fallout of the Cold War.

I think that he belonged to a particular sub-group in that generation of Europeans that was defined by the Cold War in profound and contradictory ways; that, while he'd never have given up the pleasures and freedoms of capitalist society, or doubted the veracity of democracy, or the futility of the division of Europe into East or West, the flame of some pure, Marxist nostalgia would have been fed, without his being even fully conscious of it, by the existence of the Soviet Union that otherwise, in the daylight of reason, so appalled him. The fall of the Wall and the collapse of the Soviet Union must have left him off-kilter; ever so slightly, in comparison with his counterparts in the East, but off-kilter nevertheless.

That's why, maybe, he likes taking visitors for these walks; why he's such a good guide. I wouldn't mind him as a companion in purgatory. I asked him if he ever found it a nuisance showing people around. No, he enjoyed seeing familiar things through others' eyes. I think the walks, punctuated by jokes and gestures of the hand, are a sort of circling round history, a pattern of confirmation and distancing. Because they are an improvised, rather than an actual, form of mapping, they must accrue, rather than lose, significance with repetition.

The walk that sunlit evening too traced a sort of circle. We started from the hotel, went past the station, turned right at Pizza Hut, passed a group of academics who'd come here for the conference on post-colonial literatures, walked down an immense road with tramlines in the middle, then right, into a long featureless avenue that led us to the cathedral – dark, huge, one of Europe's oldest. From there we turned back, past another old and peculiar building, the General Post Office, and, finally, made our way through a path that, by some sleight of hand, returned us to our post-modern hotel.

By our second evening, our last, my wife and I had become well-acquainted with this arc. Nowadays, I find it takes me only a day or two to form an emotional link with a place I'm passing through. It's as if I've entered yet another suburb of an indefinite but persistent metropolis I'll never escape. This suburb is different from the one I was last in, but not wholly strange. I begin to find my way in it; at first, like a blind man; then, with a mixture of circumspection and trepidation, like someone who's never strayed from the route to a particular destination over many years, but who has never found that route boring. All this happens in approximately a day. When I was a child, I recall, I went to Athens, but never felt like seeing the Parthenon. Now, I find that a city like Magdeburg compels me to discover it.

My reading, on the second day, was at 7 p.m.; we had the rest of the day to ourselves. We visited a pharmacy; chanced upon an open market in a town square; photographed the statue of a man on horseback; and ran into an Indian selling knick-knacks. He told me he'd been a taxi driver in Punjab; he had married a German tourist and come here eleven years ago. They were now divorced; he'd stayed on. My discovery of this man, my compatriot, was, to me, astonishing, for I'd begun to imagine I was the only Indian man in Magdeburg. These days, no one stares at you in the West; eye-contact is a potential precursor to assault; when it occurs, it's nearly always domesticated by a nod and a smile. In Magdeburg, though, my family and I were stared at intently.

Five minutes before the encounter with the Indian vendor, we were resting on a bench before a fountain; a tramp with a can of lager in one hand sat on the neighbouring bench. 'Indien?' he said suddenly. Disarmed, I nodded. He then asked me a series of questions in German. 'No Deutsch, no Deutsch,' I replied. He embarked upon a hoarse, rapid monologue. Finally, he raised his arm in the old Nazi salute. What had this man done and thought, I wondered, during those forty-odd years of communism?

Reini tells me that most East Germans, in a fit of collective amnesia, forgot the legacy of socialism overnight. Although an Indian friend tells me that she found an older generation in Dresden still insisting on speaking Russian as a second language, the second language in question now is not Russian, but English; and, as the Head of the English Department shrugged and sighed, 'These Easterners know no English.'

It seems a knowledge of English, or the lack of it, has become a metaphor, in certain circles in Germany, for a figurative barrier, a silence that keeps, like Isherwood's 'shadow line', one side from the other. Most of the teachers at Magdeburg's English department are, indeed, 'Westerners', and, thus, commuters. Just as Reini's life was an intersection in my journey, my journey must have been an intersection in the constant travelling of which his life is composed, the weekly to-ing and fro-ing on the autobahn between West Berlin and what he once laughingly called, in a moment of levity, 'darkest Europe'.

(Autumn 2004)

Boarders

LIA MILLS

The first time I was expelled from boarding school I was eight years old. It happened because I ran away, with a friend, at night. We walked across the city to my house in the dark, and by the time we got there the police had been called out to look for us.

We did it because we were in trouble. We'd been exposed as the brains behind a planned midnight feast and we didn't want to say who else was involved. The nuns were determined to find out and things turned ugly very fast. They had all the advantages in the situation. They even had the threat of purgatory, if not actual hell, on their side, and we knew that sooner or later they'd get those names out of us if we didn't do something drastic.

Midnight feasts and refusing to sneak on your friends are in the very best tradition of Enid Blyton and her ilk, our preferred reading at the time. Enid Blyton believed in girls and their potential, told us to believe in ourselves. Well, it was a long time ago and we were very young; we had to take our inspiration where we found it. We never even noticed that her schools were set in England, or in the past. The fact that they were boarding schools was good enough for us.

My friend, who was from another country and whose parents were on the other side of the world, was taken back to school almost immediately. It took a little longer with me. Imagine my surprise, when I did go back, to discover that the entire oeuvre of Enid Blyton had been banned from the junior school as a result of our escapade. Even then, I knew that she was on the side of authority: her interesting characters always ended up as prefects. The nuns had missed the point completely. Those books would wait for us on bookshelves at home and in libraries and in the shops of the outside world.

I was sent away to school when I was six. I would be a boarder, at different schools around the country, until I got my Leaving Cert at sixteen.

That first school was an enormous grey building with narrow-paned windows, behind high stone walls. There were about a hundred of us. I was the youngest girl there when I started.

It was overwhelming. The sheer size of the building, the crowds of other girls, of all shapes and sizes. Rules. Time parcelled out in bells. Knowing that you had to be in certain places at certain times and trying to remember what those were and how to get there. How hard it was to walk into a recreation room that buzzed with holiday gossip, the excitement of other people's reunions. The weight of the uniform, erasing all traces of who you were before. How aware you were of your knees.

Our parents were in Lagos, Hong Kong, Castlebar, Kilkenny ... Or else they were just down the road. At one extreme of the parental spectrum there were positions of influence that didn't allow for children, careers being pursued in places where there was war or the threat of war, or famine; at the other there could be separation in the air, whiffs of scandal, bailiffs, drink. Some of us were boarders because we were difficult, or because we had parents who were dead, or ill, unable or unwilling to deal with us. For us, the boarding school system was a middle-class alternative to foster care. Some of us realized that school offered some form of shelter and relief from the vagaries of adult life and were glad of it, but others raged against it. As a friend of mine says, no matter what the reason was, you felt dumped.

For every single thing you could say about boarding school, the opposite was also true. It was full of drama and boredom, both. We lived in buildings with graciously proportioned exteriors, surrounded by 'grounds' and high stone walls, but slept in poky dormitories with ancient plumbing. We studied in high-ceilinged, draughty rooms and moved through spacious, polished corridors and owned nothing, not even our time. We were surrounded by dubious, disturbing works of art and we were always hungry. We were dosed regularly against worms, checked for nits, supervised in the bath to make sure we didn't pay undue attention to our bodies. Our letters home were read.

Ask people what their strongest physical memory of boarding is and they will mention things like hunger, or cold, or chilblains – what's happened to chilblains? No one seems to get them any more. We used to cut the toes out of our socks and wear them as finger-less gloves to ease our cramping fingers through the winter. Meals were too far apart. We had to drink tepid water, developed a loathing for overcooked vegetables, stringy meat, tapioca; the smell of chalk and liquid gumption, cold water in narrow baths. At night you lay and listened to the school clock measure out each quarter of an hour and wondered how you would bear your hunger or, worse, your thirst until morning. We were surrounded by the sensual excesses of religion – the monstrance and the tabernacle, the sta-tions of the cross, the hypnotic rhythms and images of the litanies – *tower of ivory, star of the sea …* They used sacred music on us like a drug. But if we were easily seduced by the marble and the gold, the bells and the choral singing, the dizzyingly sweet incense that hung, visible, in the air, then the extreme hunger of our pre-com-munion fast and the shock of cold wood on bare knees brought us back to reality fast enough. Mass was often punctuated by a familiar *thwock* as a girl keeled over, faint, in those chill early mornings. We had a secret fascination with the ones who fell. Was it a mark of holiness or worldliness, strength or weakness? We were excessively and deliciously preoccupied with sin, with all its degrees and inflec-tions, all its ramifications. We were encouraged in this by the nuns, sin being a favoured topic of conversation. You could derail any class with a well-timed question, and with all those rules and regulations there was endless scope for misbehaviour.

Given the emphasis that was placed on the mortification of the flesh and perceiving our bodies as the enemy, it's hardly surprising that we used to put blotting paper in our shoes to try to induce those saintly faints, carried mercury in our pockets, stitched the palms of our hands together during needlework. We developed a repertoire of symptoms calculated to unnerve the infirmary nun so that she'd let us in for a day of tea and toast and reading the particular form of pornography that the lives of the saints represented. We pored over images of the martyrs, especially children like Maria Goretti, who met such interestingly grisly fates at the hands of pagans. The adults were interesting too: Agatha, presented with her severed breasts on a shield; Sebastian, pierced by a hundred arrows and looking like a tamer version of Cuchullain at the Ford. Some of us were destined to end up as pagans ourselves, we were warned. It was a sobering prospect, but more attractive than martyrdom.

There were signs that all was not well below the carefully regulated surface, signs that no one bothered to investigate, like the girls who walked in their sleep, or shouted wild words into the dark and denied them in the morning. There was the girl who cut herself with a nail scissors one night and felt nothing until another girl saw what she'd done and screamed, waking everyone up. A girl lost her memory on the stairs one day, as casually as if it had fallen out of her pocket; someone else was found trying to climb out through a third-storey window in the middle of the night, thinking that a helicopter had come to bring her home. There was the girl who picked a hole in her own forehead, slowly and determinedly, over the course of a winter term. It was as bad, or worse, for boys, like the one we heard about who pulled a knife on a priest. All the parents were aghast, but we were unimpressed by their expressions of shock – we all knew exactly why he'd done it. They'd been to school too, so why didn't they?

When your every waking moment is regulated, observed and accounted for, when your days are measured by rules and regulations, routines and rituals, you need all the lives you can get. I found mine in reading and in writing. Although the nuns distrusted books, they were never put out by the sight of a girl reading. If you had your head bent to a piece of paper, you could write your way out of – or into – anything. You could sit at a desk for hours with your head down and all they saw was that you were present, accounted for, quiet. They didn't seem to understand the osmotic process that drew you out of yourself, through the lines, into the world of the book – the one you were writing, or the one you were reading. And they never checked that the cover matched the book. When I discovered that the government, like the nuns, believed that books could be annulled by decree, it was a simple thing to glue the cover of a textbook over the spine of an O'Brien, say, or a McGahern, and read away.

Another escape was through letters. Most of us had a collection of correspondents, usually boys, in different schools around the country. Sometimes you wrote to people you barely knew and had little in common with besides your mutual incarceration during term-time, but that only made the correspondence sweeter. Letters offered proof that you were a person, that you had a life beyond the institution. We sent each other gossip and poems (our own and other people's), songs (likewise), diatribes against authority, quotes from inspirational and not so inspirational thinkers. I took to transcribing some of these into notebooks and leaving them where the nuns would find them – 'Those who can, do. Those who cannot, teach.' I was a fairly unbearable adolescent, even to myself. No wonder they kept suggesting I move elsewhere.

Those letters were a thrill to get, a challenge to write. How do you make school routine interesting? If a teacher was in the habit of flinging chalk around the room when provoked, then we provoked her, so that we could give a more accurate rendition of her temper; or if a particular nun had a habit of leading us out to the stairs to administer a scolding, because we were (all) so much taller than she was, then we looked for ways to make that scolding happen. Knowing the living death of boredom, the one thing we wanted to be on the page was entertaining.

It could backfire. I once wrote a letter to a new boyfriend who was a day-boy in a school across town. I racked my brains for something interesting to tell him and settled on a recent hockey match. Boys like sports, right? A complete construction suddenly appeared out of nowhere, the way they do when you're lucky, and I got carried away by the logic of sticks and balls, the excitement of an open net, the language of tackle and score – I described a game of hockey that was basically sex on the page. I was fourteen. I thought it would give him a laugh.

At last I got a reply. From his mother.

She advised me to stay well away from her son in the future. If he ever saw me again or made contact with me, she warned, or if I ever tried in any way to get in touch with him, she would send copies of the letter I had written, which had shocked her deeply and was incontrovertible evidence of my sluttish nature, to my mother and to the nuns and possibly to a solicitor. (I got an apologetic letter from the boy as well. She'd really do it, he said. He'd tried to get the letter back, but she had it locked away. He was sorry, but for both our sakes it was best to call it quits. I was sorry too. He was a lovely boy. Well brought up.)

Teenagers weren't supposed to know anything about sex in those days, never mind make jokes about it. But we handed round the more excessive pronouncements of older nuns as if they were chocolates, hooting with laughter at the stricture against patent leather shoes, or the injunction to spread a newspaper on a young man's lap if circumstances dictated that you absolutely *had* to sit there. (What on earth could such circumstances be, we wondered. And how would a newspaper protect you?) Despite our laughter, we inherited a kind of body-shame that went back to those early days when a silent nun would glide in and out of the bath cubicles to make sure that nothing untoward was going on. There was a belief that you lost your virginity through using tampons. Enraged by this nonsense, an unusually confident friend took it upon herself to instruct her classmates in the art of tampon use. She still dines out on her description of the scene: eight teenagers lined up in a row of toilet stalls behind closed doors, shrieking with consternation and hilarity, while she paced up and down outside, information leaflet in hand, calling out instructions that introduced them to their anatomy at a time when most girls couldn't find their way around their own bodies in the dark.

Boarding school can have a disruptive effect on your sense of who you are and where you belong, especially if you go to more than one of them, as I did. The tribal dimensions of your schooling come undone if you keep moving. It's like having layers of identity added and then stripped away again, but incompletely, before a new layer is applied. All those uniforms and school songs, the traditions and games, who you're supposed to be affiliated to and who you're not supposed to have anything at all to do with; who's better or worse than you at games and which games, whether or not you take part in the *feiseanna*, which boys' schools you have (the most abstract of) links with, whether or not you know anything about Gilbert and Sullivan.

For gregarious people, it could be a joy to be living in a herd of people your own age, with all the drama, tribal warfare, conflicting loyalties and codes of silence that went along with it. We comforted, amused, shocked, challenged, tortured and defended each other. There were stories after lights-out in the dormitories, whispered confessions, exaggerations, downright lies. For more sensitive souls, it could be agony. You didn't have to be six to be homesick, or to feel overwhelmed when you found yourself sleeping in a room with several bigger, more mature and knowing girls. It could be excruciating to enter and re-enter crowded rooms, to live and re-live that passage from door to far corner, pretending not to know that you were alone, or that you didn't care; the cliques and in-groups that all schools have are more intense when you're a boarder because there's no escape. There's no contact with a sensible adult or older sibling who could say, I know, it's hell, but it won't last for ever; or, better still, give you advice that you might act on. The boredom of daily routine could get so intense that we'd stir up any kind of trouble, just to have something to think about. If you were being bullied, there was no relief. If you were in a war with some other person or group, which was far more common than many outsiders realized, there was no cooling-off period. God help you if you were either an early or a late developer physically – you were condemned to stand out like some kind of freak and put up with whatever slagging came your way as a result.

But there were compensations in the fertile chaos of growing up en masse, with all the passionate argument and fervid speculation about life, careers and sex that living with so many older girls provided. What we lacked in hard information we made up for with invention. We went through fads and phases of this belief system, that diet or the other beauty product. We taught each other how to dance. Exam weather meant something different when you could climb up onto a roof (out of bounds, of course) to study, with sheets of tinfoil-covered cardboard angled so as to accelerate the rays of the sun more directly towards your already peeling face. We ironed each other's hair, squeezed each other's blackheads, applied undiluted peroxide and raw Dettol to our acne, confided in each other under cover of darkness and listened to Radio Caroline or Luxembourg on illegal radios, while a nun with raw hands and a sweet nature sat outside and pretended not to know what we were up to.

The pianos we had access to may have been badly out of tune, but they were pianos. Anyone with energy could spend hours playing tennis or hockey because the equipment, and the other players, were there. We learned the value of friendship, the small but precious courtesies and compromises of living with other people, how to be alone in a crowd. We learned the rhythms of time and separation and reunion. To distrust authority. The many forms of weakness. For clever girls in academic schools, there was the immeasurable benefit of the habit of study to bring to the university education that followed, if they were lucky.

My last year of school was spent in a part of the country so beautiful as to give me a fright every morning when I opened my eyes and those mountains were still there. Because it was so remote, we had more physical freedom than I had known anywhere else. During our free time we could go where we wanted, which gave rise to long walks in the rain, hours spent sitting beside streams or staring into the depths of a haunted lake. This is the sort of thing every teenager needs, and I was lucky to get it. When the swans came someone would die, or so the story went. And they came, and someone, an elderly nun most of us had never seen, did die and no one was surprised. The swans left the day after she was buried, their beating wings making a sound like doors.

I was in a state of adolescent shock during my year in this school and I practised being sullen and having no ambition or anything remotely resembling expectation while the universe ordered up a series of bizarre events to challenge me. It began with a visit from two of Ireland's finest, who went through my desk and ended up reading extracts from my diary to a pair of bewildered nuns. Something in my attitude, or maybe in what they'd read, really irritated those policemen, who came back every couple of months to remind me – and the nuns – that I'd never amount to anything. It's funny the way life will oblige people with justifications for this sort of carry-on, but I swear that the illegal substances found on the premises in that year did not belong to me; I was not the one who brought the two boys from Ennis (Hi Billy, hey Ned) back after Easter to camp in the grounds, although I may have contributed to the general depletion of convent stocks of bread rolls and blankets to help keep them there; and I really didn't start that chimney fire during the ESB strike when we all walked around the darkened school wrapped in our eiderdowns and clutching candles, while grates that hadn't seen use for forty years were pressed back into action. (Yes, I was one of the people who used to raid the ashtrays in the staff room for re-usable butts, but I never sold them on. Mine were for personal use.)

The question of my early departure from this school was broached several times, but in the end we agreed that we'd stick it out, these particular nuns and I. We'd see it through. They were sane, calm, generous women and I was grateful for them, even then. When I left, they told me that they expected to read all about themselves one day; they hoped they wouldn't have to wait too long. I forgot all about that conversation until now. I wish I'd remembered it sooner.

(Winter 2005–6)

The red and the green

ROY FOSTER

Grappling with the problem of representing the French Revolution in prose, Thomas Carlyle came to the conclusion that narrative was inescapably linear, whereas action was 'solid': textured, dense, multi-dimensional. Anyone trying to convey history 'as it was' comes up against the same problem. Film-makers might seem to possess a certain advantage, having access to stratagems that convey the many-faceted and contradictory perspectives of history on the hoof; but they have to want to use them. And while it may be difficult to reflect history accurately, it is an even more daunting task to convey a contested historiography – even in a film as long as Ken Loach's *The Wind that Shakes the Barley*.

This makes it all the stranger that he and his team chose to set their Anglo-Irish war drama in Cork, using Cork-accented actors, re-staging the Kilmichael ambush (with an important omission), and filming in the beautiful uplands near the Kerry border. This is, of course, the terrain over which wars have recently been fought all over again – since Peter Hart's books *The IRA and Its Enemies* and *The IRA at War*. With skill and empathy, Hart traced a picture which reproduces fault-lines of class resentment, religious and ethnic antipathy and local power-struggle, existing along with the more identifiable war of liberation against the traditional oppressor. He also (particularly in his portrait of guerrilla supremo Tom Barry) raised merry hell among local historians. His delineation of the rise of a revolutionary elite, and his anatomy of – for instance – the Hales family, suggests the material for a great novel. Or, perhaps, a film that reflects the forces of history as profoundly as Visconti's *The*

Leopard, Angelopoulos's *The Travelling Players*, the Taviani brothers' *Allonsanfan*, Bertolucci's *The Conformist*, Malle's *Lacombe Lucien*, or Mikhailov's *Burnt by the Sun*. Loach shares his Marxist credentials with many of these masters, but little else. Despite beautiful camerawork, marvellously realized production design (by Fergus Clegg), a good screenplay by Paul Laverty, and some fine performances (particularly in supporting parts), the director's hand lies heavy on *The Wind that Shakes the Barley*. It is over-long, and quickly abandons characterization for didactics. This sometimes works, when political argument is brought straight into the action (a Sinn Féin court-room, the Volunteers' debate over the Treaty, a priest's sermon condemning the anti-Treatyites to excommunication). And there are some brilliantly observed vignettes: a forgetful – and scene-stealing – messenger-boy, the rebels' first clumsy lessons in guerrilla tactics. But the film is oddly lacking in narrative drive or psychological punch. This is a pity, because it could have been an epic. Ernie O'Malley's masterpiece *On Another Man's Wound* is clearly a partial inspiration, but Loach only occasionally tries to convey the transformative power of the revolution, the lyricism of a life spent on 'raids and rallies', and the profound if solipsistic disillusionment – for those who had made this their life – of the Truce, which lead to the Treaty. The conclusion of O'Malley's book probably suggested that messenger-boy: reading it still brings a catch to the throat.

On the 9th of July, a Dublin boy, Paddy O'Connor, came to Mrs Quirke's whilst I was away. A dispatch-rider was sent for me. The boy would not tell his business to any other member of the staff. He handed me a typed order:

> In view of the conversations now being entered into by our Government with the Government of Great Britain, and in pursuance of mutual conversations, active operations by our troops will be suspended as from noon, Monday 11th July.
>
> RISTEARD UA MAOLCHATHA
> *Chief of Staff*

Two days from now, on the 11th of June at noon, we were to see that all officers and men in the Division observed the terms of the Truce which had been agreed to by the British. There was no intimation as to how long the Truce would last.

Con Moloney typed my orders to the five brigades. We sat down to talk about the news in wonder. What did it mean? And why had senior officers no other information than a bald message? Would the Truce last a week, or perhaps two weeks? We were willing to keep up the pressure which had been increasing steadily; soon, in a month or more, the Division would begin operations in the towns and use columns by sections. Bewildered, we waited for Micky Fitz, the quartermaster, to discuss the speeding up of 'cheddar' and 'war flour'.

And so ended for us what we called the scrap; the people later on, the trouble; and others, fond of labels, the Revolution.

The throat remains firmly uncaught throughout Loach's treatment of Damien O'Donovan, a young doctor who chooses to fight with the rebels against the Tans, is radicalized by a socialist comrade, opposes the Treaty, and is eventually executed by command of his own brother, Teddy (Padraic Delaney). Part of the reason for the watcher's detachment is that Damien is himself cast as observer as well as activist: his character is left little opportunity for development, or emotion. The camera lingers on Cillian Murphy's beautiful El Greco face, but it registers only three recurring expressions: he hoods his eyes, he sticks out his chin, he sucks an imaginary lemon. His companions in the struggle are realized even less distinctly; each time one of them is killed it takes some effort for the audience to sort out who it was. In any case, they are all clean-cut, handsome heroes with soft voices, while their opponents resemble Nazi storm troopers with Yorkshire and Geordie accents. This is fair enough: the atrocious actions of the Black and Tans are a matter of record, and their murderous saturnalia probably did more than anything else to turn public opinion against Britain's continuing rule in Ireland. But Loach's film, by beginning sharply in 1920 with no background information whatsoever, contrives to give a completely misleading idea of the historical situation in Ireland at the time.

The audience with whom I watched the film in a London cinema would have come away with two 'facts' that are presented in the film. First, that IRA resistance was created in response to the Black and Tan reign of terror. This is, of course, an exact reversal of chronology. The Anglo-Irish War began with the shooting of policemen in early 1919, a process escalated by the radical wing of the Volunteers and opposed by those in the movement called contemptuously 'the politicians'. After a year of inept counter-measures, Lloyd George's government embarked on the disastrous policy of recruiting mercenaries and, later, of 'reprisals'. (The best account is still Charles Townshend's brilliantly forensic analysis of the disconnections between government and military policies in *The British Campaign in Ireland 1919–21*, published over thirty years ago.) The second lesson slammed home by Loach is that those who opposed the Treaty did so for reasons of socialism, 'democracy' and anti-partitionism: the reasons articulated by Damien, his mentor Dan (Liam Cunningham), and his lover Sinead (Orla Fitzgerald) in a violent debate over accepting the 1921 terms. It is one of the best scenes in the film, but it is misleading nonetheless. Socialist politics had long since taken an acquiescent back seat, and it is significant that Dan and Damien talk reverently of Connolly's part in the 1913 lock-out and the Citizen Army, while Larkin (whose relationship to nationalism is much more problematic) is never mentioned.

Dan, it transpires, learned his politics in the Frongoch internment camp after 1916. This is almost the only reference to the events before 1920. That London audience was certainly not told of the cliff-hanging politics over the passing of the Home Rule bill before 1914, when that measure, supported by a parliamentary majority in Westminster, was held up and diluted by the Liberal government's dithering in the face of possible civil war threatened by the opposition of a million Ulster people (including a majority of the urban working class, though Ken Loach would not like to hear it). The impression created by this film is that Black and Tan rule was the general state of things in Ireland before independence, fully authorized and sanctioned by the authorities – which was not the case. Nor will those who watch this film knowing nothing of Irish history be given any clue that there was an Irish Home Rule party, and that the republicans were waging war against them with at least as much vigour as against the British army. There was another revolution within the revolution, and this has been engrossingly demonstrated by the growing number of local studies of the era since David Fitzpatrick's seminal work on Clare, such as Marie Coleman on Longford, Michael Wheatley on the north-west midlands, and Fergus Campbell on Galway and Mayo. Loach presents us with a single example of the local middle class, in the best scene of the film: a republican court, trying to mediate between a gombeen man and a widow paying exorbitant interest on her grocery bill. The gombeen man is backing the rebels, so Teddy disputes the court's decision when it rules against him. It is marvellously written and played: the Sinn Féin judge (a woman), the realpolitik of the Volunteers, the watchers in the court, the sense of two authority-structures at war. It is one of the few moments when *The Wind that Shakes the Barley* approaches the film it might have been.

Elsewhere, the historical picture is distinctly shaky. Loach is determined to portray Ireland as a country not only groaning under military dictatorship, but impoverished by centuries of exploitation. Several characters are illiterate: the socialist Dan even 'learned to read and write' at Frongoch, which must have made him the fastest learner in the West. The awful dirge which gives the film its title, mercifully sung only once (and then off-key), includes the lines 'But harder still to bear the shame / Of foreign chains around us.' The chains were fairly light by 1914. The politicized County Cork of the Anglo-Irish War was part of a polity that sent 103 MPs to Westminster, had an independent judiciary and openly recruited civil service, a broad and broadening distribution of landownership, a vibrant civil society, rapidly developing labour organizations, a notably advanced educational system and an exceptionally lively (and uncensored) press. Home Rule had, of course, passed through Westminster and an impatient Irish political elite was waiting to assume autonomous power. The war changed some of this, and 1916 transformed the nationalist consciousness. But the revolution, when it took hold, built on these pre-existing conditions too, and Loach's Cork has no room for them.

It is also (with the single exception of Sir John Hamilton, an aristocratic Big House owner) a Protestant-free zone, again in marked contrast to the world re-created by Hart. (To add to the irony, much of it was shot on location in the famously Protestant town of Bandon.) When the IRA execute 'informers' in the film, they are informers; according to Hart's version, they were as likely to be social undesirables, sexual deviants, and rival property-owners. In an essay accompanying the published screenplay,* Luke Gibbons insists 'there is clear evidence that the shooting of Protestants was motivated not by religion but by their activities as informers'. The 'evidence' remains unproduced, and this judgement would certainly not stand for the murder of, for instance, the Pearson brothers in Kinnitty, Co. Offaly, in June 1921, and the burning out of their house – the subject of a recent local study. Many of these incidents took place long after the Truce. Protestant small farmers like them were certainly targeted for reasons that went beyond 'informing' and tapped into far more ancient memories and antipathies. Usually, when Loach's revolutionaries inflict violence, they do so as a 'warning': the scene where they invade a police barracks and line up the RIC men simply in order to caution them may have had an occasional parallel in contemporary events, but it is certainly unrepresentative. Here, Paul Laverty's intention 'not to romanticize the inevitable violence' (as declared in the book of the screenplay) wears rather thin. A majority of those killed by the IRA were fellow Irish people, and usually their own neighbours, rather than heavily armed fiends in Crossley tenders. The lines between the opponents are, for all the film's ravishing outdoor colour and beautifully filmed indoor chiaroscuro, strictly black and white.

The film is far less crude than some other gung-ho treatises on national liberation that make clunky parallels with the present day (*Braveheart* comes to mind, or *Rebel Heart*); but it is still skewed. In interviews the director has referred to hurling being 'banned' in this era and the Irish being 'forbidden to speak their own language', apparently unaware of the imposition of Irish as a compulsory matriculation subject in the National University a decade before the film begins. In interviews, and in the screenplay book, Loach has also drawn sweeping parallels with the invasion of Iraq, which hardly fit the case – except for the inevitably counterproductive effects of imported soldiers put into 'peacekeeping' roles against guerrilla resistance. He inveighs against 'the cunning of people like Churchill, Lloyd George, Birkenhead et al.; when they were forced into a corner, when it wasn't really in their interests to keep denying independence, they sought to divide the country and give their support to those in the independence movement who were prepared to allow economic power to stay in the hands of people who, in the time-honoured phrase, "they could do business with"'. This interpretation would not stand up to the most cursory examination of the Treaty negotiations. The idea that de Valera, Childers, Cathal Brugha et al. were motivated by socialism is baroquely wishful thinking. The film's historical advisor, Donal Ó Drisceoil, gives a more accurate and judicious version in the same volume, referring to revolutionary socialism as 'a tendency within the national movement'; but it is Loach who gives the public interviews. He is far more interesting when he writes about his method of creating 'collective spirit' among his cast by rigorous 'basic training': this helps explain both the strengths of the film and its weaknesses.

Where there are nods towards the literature or memoir of the time, ambiguity and nuance are ironed out. The scene in which Sir John and his informer employee are taken to the hills and shot suggests another passage from O'Malley's book, or Frank O'Connor's *Guests of the Nation*, but without the tragic ambiguity beneath the surface. When Kilmichael is replayed, the controversial aftermath (were prisoners shot after surrendering?) is tactfully left out. The two-dimensional Damien O'Donovan is very far from his prototype medical-student-turned-revolutionary Ernie O'Malley, that violent, mercurial, quasi-nihilistic intellectual superbly portrayed in Richard English's biography. Repetitions of locale are used repeatedly – same place, similar atrocity, different perpetrators. This climaxes in the *Animal Farm* oppositions of Loach's last scenes, with the Staters indistinguishable from their Tan predecessors. It is in line with the strictly schematic representation, but would make far more sense if the audience had been given any sense of preceding tensions and fault-lines within the movement (it is only at this stage, for instance, that we learn anything of the strong-farmer background of the O'Donovan brothers).

None of this is likely to bother audiences much. The review-quote chosen for the film's publicity in Ireland stated didactically: '"Not to be missed by any citizen of the State" (*Irish Daily Star*)'. The citizenry duly turned out in large numbers to a film already garlanded by the Palme d'Or from Cannes and a useful outpouring of outrage from the right-wing press in Britain. There were only a handful of people in a Hampstead cinema when I saw it on a hot Friday night in June, but things were very different in Dublin, where the first two weeks were booked solid. *The Wind that Shakes the Barley* does not seem, however, to have ignited a phenomenon on the scale of Neil Jordan's *Michael Collins*. The Collins film conveyed the characterization, psychological dynamics, and sexual allure of its revolutionary heroes with more panache than Loach's; but it similarly simplified what they were fighting against. Both films have been readily attached to present-day political agendas, though very different ones. Jordan's was interpreted as an argument on behalf of revolutionaries abandoning the guns in order to pursue compromises that might give them, in the end, what a majority wants. *The Wind that Shakes the Barley* unequivocally comes down on the other side of the question; the condemned Damien writes in his farewell letter that when Teddy opted for the Treaty, he died inside. Given the current state of our own polities, north and south, and the credibility of our politicians, the Irish public's favourable reaction to Loach's representation of 1920–21 as an aborted socialist-nationalist revolution craving completion may be significant. But what they have been watching is an exercise in wish-fulfilment rather than history.

(Autumn 2006)

Fables of home

GEORGE SZIRTES

1

I was at a poetry festival recently as part of a panel discussing the relationship between poetry and song. Traditional song, I argued, lay at the heart of community, encapsulating its history and its longings, its triumphs, disasters and habits of mind. How could I help but be moved by song? At the same time, I added, it disturbed me in the way it both enfolded and excluded, in the simplified stories it told and the self-flattering emotions it engendered. This was, I admitted, as much a reflection on community as on song. 'Community?' the poet beside me shrugged and raised a quizzical eyebrow. 'What else is there?' he asked.

That's an awful question for a poet to answer. This essay is an attempt to explore it from the perspective of a Hungarian-born poet brought up mostly in England, one who, furthermore, was born into an atheistic family in which, he believed, the father was Jewish and the mother Lutheran by birth. After she died he discovered that she too was born Jewish. He, in the meantime, had undergone full-immersion baptism at the age of twenty. The story for him has moved on a little since, but that's another story. He, meaning I, is aware that these sound like a series of melodramatic twists from a soap opera, and would be glad to be rid of them, but for the fact that, to some extent, they are a condition of his life. Furthermore, he believes that there are many scattered people in analogous circumstances. He, meaning I, would therefore like to begin in Budapest, in personal prehistory.

John Lukacs, in his book about the Budapest of 1900, depicts the city as a romantic whirlwind of cafés, intrigues, adulterous assignations, vast commercial enterprise and immense personal energy. He also shows it to be deeply, if inadvertently, internationalist. A high proportion of the leading writers, critics, artists, scientists, engineers, lawyers, doctors and financiers were Jewish, and the Jewish population was essentially an immigrant population, but one that – in Budapest at least – had thrown itself into the project of being Hungarian. Jews Hungaricized their names, relaxed their religious practices and were often more overtly patriotic than the Hungarians themselves. They took on the country's literature, manners and customs, and embraced its causes, in what now seems like a fit of enthusiasm that succeeded in blanking out – for the time being at any rate – areas that were about to become problematic: the issues of blood, land, status, property and, ultimately, loyalty.

No social group is homogeneous, of course, and that same cosmopolitan yet Hungaricized population harboured revolutionaries, subversives and idealists of various hues. It made little difference. The multiple faces of assumed nationality were to overlap and become a blurred single mask for those who watched the immigrants' progress with various degrees of resentment. The identities of those who watched and resented were themselves complex. Their history had been the familiar shifting pattern of foreign occupation and intermarriage, but their status was underwritten by property and by land; by economic dependence, custom, nostalgia and antithesis. The honest, stable *rus* was pitted against a dubious, manipulative *urbs*. There was a clear and widening cultural split between the sleepy poor life of the country estates and the internationalist dynamic of the modernist city. Budapest, in other words, looked westward while the rest of the country, by contrast, became more aware of its Asiatic origins. This division bore fruit in the arts: in painting, poetry, fiction and music.

The First World War destroyed that version of Hungary. By the treaties of Versailles and Trianon, the country lost two thirds of its territory to other nationalities resident in the regions involved, nationalities Hungary had treated without any great respect. This two thirds included large areas where Hungarians were in a majority. It meant that one third of Hungarians suddenly had to get used to living abroad in hostile, often resentful countries. A landlocked country is always likely to find its borders shifting, but this was a savage and traumatic cut. The trauma is still there and strongly felt. Defeat in the war was followed by collapse: a socialist administration was followed by a Bolshevik one, neither of which lasted more than a few months. Admiral Horthy, admiral of the no-longer-relevant Hungarian navy, rode in to Budapest on a white horse to establish a right-wing authoritarian regime.

It was a regime with enormous nostalgia for the ceremonial side of rural life. The Bolshevik revolution that had preceded it, as it well knew, had been led mostly by intellectual urban Jews. The process of idealizing country life did not extend to improving the sorry condition of the peasants, who were often living in extreme poverty. The fancy-dress costumes and fairy-tale ceremonies of the nationalist regime referred to a vestigially feudal Hungary, to a supposed common interest between peasantry and gentry that would be pitched against the grubby hooked-nosed shopkeepers and urban intellectuals gathered in dubious cafés.

A new wave of rural writing appears in the thirties, a mixture of biography, fiction and sociological study, often conducted by educated writers of rural origin, such as the poet Gyula Illyés. The cultural divisions of the late nineteenth century constantly sharpen and blur and sharpen again in the twentieth. Urbanists and ruralists work side by side for a while, then, under the pressures of fascism, move apart. The most influential literary magazine of the inter-war years was called *Nyugat*, meaning West. Illyés himself published there. The name pointed to Dante, Goethe, Shakespeare and Baudelaire, but also to Freud and to Marx. It also said something about European integration at the level of the imagination, an issue that is still in the forefront of our minds.

Following the Second World War and the occupation by Soviet troops, with the imposition of a Moscow-based regime that followed, writers were expected to line up strictly behind the new ideology. Socialist realism was the line, and socialist realism had to be aware of its responsibilities. Its precise application led to interestingly iconographical and possibly proto-deconstructionist debates of Byzantine complexity. Which way is Comrade Lenin facing in the painting and what is the role of the shadow by his feet? What is the significance of the cut of that peasant's moustache? A number of the finest writers were imprisoned or prevented from publishing, and the most promising of the new magazines, *New Moon*, was banned and its editors and contributors charged with bourgeois individualism.

In 1953 Stalin died and early in 1956 Nikita Khrushchev made a speech to a closed session of the Party Congress denouncing him. News of this speech travelled by various means. I have a strong personal memory of the local Party cell visiting our flat in Budapest to announce the end of the Stalin cult. My mother – who had been excluded from the Party on account of her middle-class Transylvanian background, to say nothing of her inability to obey any Party *diktat* that conflicted with her conscience – held me up to the photograph of Stalin on our wall and told me to ignore these men and to continue to admire the genial-looking man in the picture.

The denunciation led directly to the revolution. The students of 1956 gathered by the statue of Petőfi, born Petrovics – the great youthful revolutionary and, above all, *nationalist* poet began life with a foreign name – and marched along the main road to the river. By the time they reached the statue of the Hungarian patriot General Bem – who was Polish – on the other side, the protest march had turned into revolution. After its defeat the authorities were very careful about Petőfi's statue. He remained a symbol of precisely what he said he wanted to represent: Hungarianness on the one hand and internationalist liberty on the other.

As late as 1988, a very good friend of mine, a woman I loved and admired, wanted to lay a few small flowers at Petőfi's statue on the anniversary of the 1848 revolution, but was brusquely turned away by the police. Others who tried to do the same were beaten up or given a night in prison. The following year, the year when I spent eight months in Hungary and watched everything change, there was another demonstration which sparked the new, quieter revolution. I was on that march myself, which started precisely where the earlier revolution started: by the statue of Petőfi. There I joined the mixed band of liberals, nationalists, environmentalists, urbanists and populists who set off to repeat the march of 1956. Once the march took place the regime was effectively doomed.

2

In his *Autobiography* the Scottish poet Edwin Muir makes a distinction between the story and the fable of his own life: the story, he says, is what he tells us, the fable is the sense he makes of it, its archaic echo with myth. There are a number of theoretical positions that hint at the same dual experience of narrative. The Russian Formalists' notion of *sjuzet* (the naked story in simple chronological order) and *fabula* (our telling of that story in the order our narrative sense demands) is an example. I am not going to make heavy weather of this beyond noting that all such binary systems are essentially conventions that are supposed to help us make sense of experience. I find they help me here.

Seamus Heaney, in one of his early poems, talked about 'the music of what happens'. For my purposes I want to think of Muir's original idea of the *story* as what more or less happens, and the *fable* as its music. I want to set the chaotic world of one damn thing after another against its shaping, editing and telling, which is our attempt to discover meaning in it. The fable is what fabulists, storytellers and poets are concerned with. Their job is to convince us and carry us away with them so we feel we're flying with a purpose towards our one true place. Conviction isn't necessarily truth, nor is there a simple distinction between truth and lies in literature. Instinctively, though, I resist the notion of poets as warty boys and liars. I am, of course, like all poets, fascinated and seduced by the music of what happens, but I want to retain the freedom to distrust the music a little.

Under every simple poem or story, to follow Muir, is a deeper myth of identity and history. I am therefore aware that when I offer elements of my personal journeys I am, for all my attempts at confining myself to story, bound to enter the realm of fable. The very term 'journey' tells you as much.

My own provenance is a confused one. My father's grandparents came out of Moravia and Bohemia, and my mother's family came from Transylvania. Moravia, or Slovakia, was once part of Hungary, and the capital of Slovakia, Bratislava, was once Pozsony, the capital of Hungary. Belgrade was once a major Hungarian city. My mother's name on her mother's side was Kardos, which is Hungarian enough, but on her father's side she was a Nussbacher, which suggests either that that side of her family came from German-Saxon stock, or that they adopted a German-Saxon identity, as some Jews did, for the purpose of assimilation (the German-Saxon community formed a significant if small part of the population of Romania). The city where my mother was born has been known by various names: as Kolozsvár in Hungarian, as Clausenburg in German and as Cluj in Romanian, a name that was dolled up by Ceaucescu to Cluj-Napoca in reference to the ancient Roman colony there: the name asserted the claim of Romanians to be descended from the Romans. Their ancient adversaries the Hungarians, meanwhile, tended to suggest that the name Romania was derived from the term *Romanies*, meaning Gypsies, and that the Romance language they spoke was a ragged remnant of that spoken by their Roman masters.

Transylvania contained some of the oldest Hungarian settlements, but at the time my mother was born it had become part of Romania as a result of the post-First World War settlement. For a few brief years of the Second World War it reverted to Hungary, and that was when my mother, at the age of sixteen, fired by a youthful enthusiasm to become a photographer, travelled to Budapest to apprentice herself to a splendid documentary photographer called Károly Escher. By the time she returned home from Ravensbruck, the concentration camp where she endured three months, Transylvania had been re-awarded to Romania and all her family, every one of them, was dead.

My father's family was of that group of liberal Jews who saw themselves as Hungarian. They were a mixture of working-class and lower-middle-class people. My father's father worked on the shop-floor of a shoe factory and was, it seems, a melancholy character who wrote plays that were never performed. He died before I was born. My father, who was a clever boy, was leaving school just as the first anti-Jewish laws were enacted. He couldn't go on to higher education, so he found office work. Another wave of legislation drove him out of the office and into a plumber's workshop, until he was called up into the army. As a Jew, he was not permitted to wear insignia or carry arms, so at first he was set to dig ditches, then later sent to do forced labour in a series of camps in the Ukraine. Only three people, my father and two companions, survived his last labour camp, and they did so by escaping on the route march to an extermination camp.

Returning after the war, my parents, like most Jews, were radicalized. They were essentially atheistic, potentially revolutionary, certainly left-wing. The surviving members of my father's branch of the family, whose name was Schwartz, immediately Hungaricized their names. My father became Szirtes, a name taken from a popular cinema actor; his cousin became Fekete, meaning 'black' as in Schwartz; and another cousin became Ráday for no better reason than that was the name of the street they lived in. My father returned to the plumber and my mother joined an evening newspaper as a photographer. She was supposed to be too frail to consider childbearing, but she bore two children all the same. Her view on their upbringing was quite clear: she was to defend them from the horrors she and her family had gone through. For that reason she chose to cut herself off from her Jewish past. Throughout her life she maintained the fiction that she came from a Lutheran background. Neither my brother nor I was circumcised. We received nothing of Jewish social culture, except the temperamental sort they unwittingly passed on to us.

My father in the meantime was being rapidly promoted through the ranks of the now ruling Communist Party, and before too long he became a department leader in the ministry of building and works.

This was the position when we left the country, illegally, on foot, on the night of my eighth birthday, 29 November 1956, and walked into Austria. The reason we left was not clear to me then. A lot of people left because the revolution, a brave and honourable affair for most if not every part, had been defeated. They fled from that form of communism. My parents, though, were fleeing from fascism. My mother in particular – and there were others like her – was afraid that fascist forces were still alive and stirring in Hungary. The prisons had been opened and it was only eleven years since the war had ended. It was also well known that all four leaders of the previous repressive Stalinist government had been Jewish, though not one of them bore a Jewish name. This was grist to the anti-Semitic mill. There was a small anti-Semitic element in the streets during the uprising, though it had not infiltrated the revolutionary government. The revolution was suppressed on 4 November and so were the few overt fascists who had taken part in it. We left over three weeks later. What she had heard of the streets had frightened my mother. I think she feared too much, but then she knew far more clearly than I did, or do, what there was to fear.

We travelled to England, meaning to go on to Australia. Being thwarted in that desire, we were taken first to the seaside, and then in March moved to London, where my parents found jobs and my brother and I grew up. As my father was the only one with any command of English it was necessary to go on a domestic crash course, so we spoke only English at home.

We were very warmly and efficiently received in England, we moved around London as circumstances and money allowed, and by the time my brother and I went on to higher education – art college in my case, music academy in my brother's – we were living in a lower-middle-class suburb of London, close to Wembley Stadium.

My mother, though, had been through terrible problems with her heart. She had several unsuccessful operations and her spirits, which were often fiery, would increasingly be very low. She made a number of attempts on her own life, and one day, after I had graduated and married, she succeeded in killing herself. She was fifty-one. It was not that we were specifically isolated as a family, nor that there was no support, for there was, but the combination of pain, fear and, in the end, I believe, a cultural vacancy, told on her. But this marks the end of her conscious journey and of my parents' journey as a couple and as a family. For me it is semi-conscious only. I am not in control of any part of it.

3

The first of the two personal journeys I shall describe here was my return to Hungary, as a visitor and occasional part-time resident, starting in the mid-1980s. This journey was driven by curiosity about my mother's past. It began nine years after her death, by which time I had written three well-received books of poetry in English; I felt ever more intensely that I needed her past to help me advance into the nature of things as I instinctively felt them to be.

I travelled to Hungary on an Arts Council prize in 1984. Even before then I had begun to read Hungarian history and Hungarian literature in English translation – I had not used the Hungarian language for twenty-eight years and it was very rusty – and after my mother died, I spent years talking to my father on tape, about his life, and about hers, of which I knew little as she was not in the habit of speaking about it.

Returning was a marvellous and disorienting experience. It was strange to hear Hungarian spoken everywhere but, more than anything, it was place and space that hit me. Our early life imprints a kind of map on our reflexes. The shape and sound of things was deeply moving – I often wept – and if I think of the notion of home, I think of this love of landmarks – streets, courtyards, stairways, in my case – their spatial punctuation and their sensual coding. The first place is the most real place, which does not mean it has to be a good place: it is simply a place that equips you with notions of reality.

I was fortunate with my meetings in Hungary. The literary people I found myself among were curious and enthusiastic. They hadn't expected to find an English poet who happened to be Hungarian. Very soon they were introducing me to the literary structures and ambitions of the place.

Since the Second World War the party-state had run everything. All publishing was in its hands, although by the mid-eighties it operated partly through the relatively benign patronage of the ministry of culture (but the patronage could be withdrawn), and partly through the hidden iron hand of censorship (you could, if it came to it, be arrested). Editorial offices were in effect political offices, but, by this time, only lightly-lightly. Certain subjects were not to be mentioned – the Russian military presence, the revolution of 1956, homelessness, unemployment, the terrible tensions with Romania and other border states about the Hungarian ethnic minorities – but it was perfectly possible to write brilliant books without those points of reference, and people did write brilliant books. On the other hand they learned to censor themselves and were well rewarded for it by the usual system of honours and sinecures. Beyond all this both the state and individual writers were deeply concerned that Hungarian authors should be read in other languages. For the writers, to be read elsewhere, in the West chiefly, was to get out, gain independence and authority, and possibly to have a foreign bank account. They would also be escaping a double prison: 'the velvet prison', as the sociologist Miklos Haraszti called it, of a compromised state, and the narrow cell of a wonderfully supple but minor language that nobody read. The state encouraged the foreign translation of its leading authors because this reflected well on its own health, much as the prowess of footballers or athletes did. The anthologies produced had to encourage this endeavour without seeming too jingoistic or pushy. Under the façade, neither author nor state had any faith left in the system. The shrug of opposition united almost everyone. This odd complicity could work to the advantage of writing. If nothing else, it heated the language and spiced it with complex irony.

After 1989 this all changed rapidly. By this time I was visiting Hungary every year, sometimes for months; in 1989, by coincidence, I spent almost the entire year there. The year was marked by great demonstrations and meetings. I went along to these, as a captivated observer rather than a full participant, but when someone offered me a red-white-green rosette I took it and wore it with pride. In revolutionary moments such gestures are great uniters of people and serve as sources of a heady comradeliness. I have only to remember how the first few days of the 1956 revolution involved no looting and how people could leave money in boxes on the street for the wounded or sick to use. On 15 March 1989, on the anniversary of the 1848 revolution, a huge crowd of us, about 200,000, swept down the main street following precisely the route of the 1956 demonstration, starting from the statue of Petőfi, born Petrovics. There were tears and laughter. Mass happiness is unforgettable.

But I could not continue the entire length of the march. As we moved on I felt ever more keenly that I had no real right to be in the crowd: their fate, whatever it was to be, would not be mine. Even close Hungarian friends, friends who had been anxious about what might happen, not just on the march but long after it, had, in that atmosphere, let me know that I was not part of the endeavour, that I was not in a position to understand the issues. And they were right: how could I understand as they did, they who lived there? But how I wished the crowd well, these people who had not been their own masters for more then thirty-odd years in the last five hundred.

I continued to return to Hungary. In October 1995 I arrived with a BBC producer to make a radio programme about the commemorations of the 1956 revolution. It was a Sunday and we were advised by a Hungarian journalist to go straight down to the remnants of an evening rally organized by a right-wing party, MIÉP (the Party of Hungarian Health and Justice), which was led by an ex-dissident, fiercely nationalist, writer of comic short stories. The huge square before parliament contained only straggly groups by the time we arrived, one of skinheads, the other of middle-aged respectable-looking people. My producer took out his microphone and we were immediately besieged by the respectable ones. We barely escaped the scene without a thorough beating.

The next day we attended the memorial service at the grave of Imre Nagy, the martyred prime minister of 1956. As we were returning from the cemetery we passed a procession of blackshirts on the ring-road. They bore a placard that showed a villain with a hooked nose. There were about eighty of them, with a retinue of a hundred or so. The producer and I parted, then met later for another political rally organized by a more respectable right-wing party around the statue of Jozsef Bem, the Polish general. The main figure here was the leader of the minority Smallholders' Party, Jozsef Torgyán. But first we had other speakers, some moving traditional music about the tragedies of the defeated revolution of 1848, and an actor reciting the best-known poem of the first great patriotic poet of the romantic period, Mihály Vörösmarty. The poem is called 'Szózat', meaning call, or appeal. This is how it begins in an old translation by Watson Kirconnell:

> Oh, Magyar, keep immovably
> Your native country's trust,
> For it has borne you, and at death
> Will consecrate your dust! ...

Alas, how pale that sounds. The Hungarian, as below, should be imagined snarling, choking, pensive, mournful and furious by turns.

> Hazádnak rendületlenül
> Légy híve, ó magyar;
> Bölcsöd az s majdan sírod is,
> Mely ápol s eltakar ...

It made a ferocious music. Someone then made a long speech in the course of which he listed the members of the then current government (and I should add that though nominally socialist, and led by major figures from the pre-1989 regime, I would have placed the government slightly to the right of Tony Blair). At one point, a man in a pastoral Hungarian costume called out at one of the names: 'Ez nem egy magyar ember' – 'That man is not Hungarian'; the cry was then picked up by others for more of the names. There were several of them, it seemed. Of course the people mentioned were Hungarians, but they were not to be regarded as such (because they were Jewish, or because their parents had been communists, who knows why?). Under the circumstances it was clear that I was not a Hungarian of any description. And almost at that precise moment the blackshirts, continuing their circuit of the city, were popping up on the nearest ring-road, just to my right.

I do not want to suggest that the 'nation' had reverted to fascism; I do not believe that for a moment. But the rhetoric of nationhood – the essentially xenophobic music of what was happening, the reliance on the fable of ourselves – seemed perfectly at home here. The song and the community were fully employed in the business of enfolding and excluding, so much so that the greatest degree of enfolding seemed instinctively to entail the greatest degree of excluding. Community? What else is there? Outer darkness.

4

The journey to Hungary was on the back of my mother. Everything I wrote involved her in some way, as a ghost, as a figure to consult, confront and address. My second journey, or its fable, is the journey to England, which began forty-five years ago and continues to this day. This journey, symmetrically enough, is on the back of my father, who, twenty-five years after the death of my mother, is still alive and living in London.

We arrived, precisely to the week, at the breaking point of modern British history: the Suez crisis. I have said we were received with kindness; we were also received with diffidence. Diffidence then was a blessing to my parents. After fifteen years of having to declare an identity, to be made to inform on other people and to be constantly asked questions about themselves, it was a relief to be able to settle in, to disappear. No one enquired about our religion. We carried no ID or party card. We were odd, but interesting, and my parents were nicely enlivening for those who liked being enlivened. I went through school, and my journey continued through the language, which was and remains an immense enigma and delight. England was a rich, safe haven, walled in by a sublime sea and, out beyond the sea, by other large bits of reassuring pink on the map. I met with little vaingloriousness on this account as I moved my way through the intricate levels of the working and lower-middle classes. There was a mildness and irony about the climate after Suez and we were, or had become, British citizens. Of course we would never be English, because that term was to do with nation, with blood and land, but Britishness, the baggy Britishness of which Tom Paulin has been so contemptuous, could include us.

About a year ago the Jewish English humourist Howard Jacobson wrote about his sense of nationality in *The Independent*. I quote him:

> It is often argued that English culture is the rich thing it is because of the contributions made by those from outside, from elsewhere, from the margins. I agree with this, as how could I not, but you cannot have a margin unless you have a page. Nor can you contribute to a void.
>
> The Polish-born novelist Joseph Conrad chose to write in English (though his second language was, in fact, French) and thereby put something not English forever into English culture. But it was an idea of Englishness, even an idealisation of Englishness, a devotion to what he understood to be its moral and psychological complexion, no less than its linguistic resources, that induced him to write in English in the first place.

I recognize this feeling, though I cannot be quite in Jacobson's place. It is sometimes painful to be 'en Angleterre, mais pas anglais'.

Sometimes, however, I feel as free as a bird. Sometimes I think I am a herald of the world to come, and that we are beginning to see the end of national states, watching instead waves of people and fragmentary cultures swirling around in an economically determined amplitude that stretches over specific areas of the earth. Being without a home does not have to mean being without history or without human passions. I am all too full of both, I fear.

I have been recounting a little group of stories, no more than anecdotes perhaps. I have tried to tell them, not *slant*, as Emily Dickinson advises poets to do, but as straight as I can. But some of these stories I have told before, and I am aware, every time I tell them, every time I get the shape of them just a little better, that they are becoming my personal fable, or the fable of the Jews, or the fable of the Uprooted, of the British Immigrant. And I fear that, at the point they do so, some important truth will have leaked away. Something will have been lost to pure music. My feelings will have become more absolute in the process, and though absoluteness means perfection, it is the perfection of the full myth, the closed system, that I most fear. I want to believe in a poetry that is not pure music, or pure anything, but includes those things that horrify and move me by their strange, unclassifiable intransigence.

Having lived in England for so long, it is another true place to me, the place of a second birth, full of voices, shapes and places that move me. Like Hungary, like my mother and father, indeed like any experience, it is a complex and broken thing I want to mend, a journey I want to make in ways I believe in – between story and fable, touching and feeling both in my hands.

The chief obsession of any artist is to make something lasting in which they recognize the world in its full nature. Many years ago I was reading at Winchester for students, invited by the Anglo-Welsh poet Jeremy Hooker. We were looking at one of the windows in the cathedral, which had been smashed and reassembled, with some white panes fitted where they could not locate the original shards. I could see that this patchwork thing was not quite what people want a window to be, but I found it moving precisely because it had been broken. Because those brightly coloured and fragmented figures with their archetypal narratives seemed ever more part of the world. I see them everywhere now, and detect them even under masks of family, nation, race and tribe. I suspect these figures are where many of us are, what we face when we look at our reflections in the mirror in the morning. All those dreams and anxieties left crumpled in the sheets, between the covers.

My dreams are most disturbed when they concern the death of someone I love. There is a terrible tightness in my chest and I usually wake and can't go to sleep again for a few hours. The tightness in my chest is real. We do die, sometimes together, sometimes in great numbers. Below us the nation of the dead lives in our imagination by rules we cannot guess. Some, like Hamlet's father, call out for revenge. History, in one guise, *is* Hamlet's father: and immediately one thinks of Polonius, Ophelia, Laertes, Gertrude, Claudius and of course the prince himself, all dead by the end. And, lest we should forget, Tom Stoppard reminds us that those bit players, Rosencrantz and Guildenstern, are dead too. Eight for one. That's a lot of dead bodies, not all of them murderers themselves. Even Claudius, you think, must have had something going for him. Gertrude certainly thought so; after all she was a queen when Hamlet senior was alive and she was still a queen when he was dead. And I wonder whether things between her and Hamlet's father were quite as rosy as Hamlet imagines.

(Winter 2001–2)

If a guy doesn't think this is fun ...

MOLLY McCLOSKEY

1

In June, I spent four days in the seaside town of Herceg Novi, in
Montenegro. One morning I walked up to the town centre to get
cash. At the bank, I discovered I'd forgotten my passport. The teller
helpfully suggested that I might 'remember' my passport number. I
made a show of thinking hard about this, then said, 'Yes! I do
remember,' and scribbled some numbers. She smiled, pleased with
me for having played my part in our harmless collusion, and passed
me on to a colleague who counted out my money, smiling just as
warmly. Everyone in Herceg Novi was almost preternaturally pleasant, much more so than in Belgrade where, when I'd mentioned I
was going to Montenegro, the locals had warned me of how terribly
rude the Montenegrins were.

Having pocketed the money, I wandered through the laneways
and up and down the steps of Herceg Novi, until I happened upon a
small asphalt basketball court banked by cascading scarlet flowers.
Ten young boys were practising under the supervision of a coach,
running through a medley of drills before breaking into teams for a
game of five-on-five. I paused to watch them, leaning on the low
wall, and began to weep.

I was in Herceg Novi as part of a wedding party: an old friend
who now lives in Kosovo had married a local woman. The last time
I saw the groom was in 1987, when he was working for the Jesuits
in Honduras and I hitched with my best friend (his ex-girlfriend) to
visit him. Although life is far better for me these days than it was

then, seeing him reminded me that there was a lot less of it ahead of us now. Also, I was exhausted. And I had the simmering anxiety that comes with being separated from one's belongings: I'd arrived on Friday and it was now Monday and Lufthansa still had no idea where my luggage was.

But mostly it was basketball that was making me cry. There is something uncannily familiar in the scuff of sneakers on blacktop and the sight of bodies rolling off each other in particular ways, with particular ends in mind; in the precise angles at which cuts are made; in the loose wrist of a pure shooter and the quick jerk of a head fake. I watched the boys in Herceg Novi, and their repertoire of movements was as known to me as an old family recipe.

I stayed for fifteen minutes or so, by the end of which I was no longer really following the game, or inhabiting the bittersweetness of whatever recollections it had spawned, but was instead developing a theory as to why I was crying based on a combination of Henry James, Plato, and my father. I was thinking about the gift of ignorance, that sometimes shameful possession of the traveller.

James wrote, 'It is the privilege and presumption of the tourist to take in the human misadventures of a foreign scene with the indifferent frivolity of a play-goer.' Standing courtside, I felt neither indifferent nor frivolous, and the boys didn't look like they were suffering any misadventures. This being the Balkans, one assumes they had seen more than their share already, but I was spared any knowledge of their stories. All I saw was ten kids at play. I was even spared the understanding of what their coach was yelling at them (to me it sounded like encouragement but, if he was anything like the coach my brothers had as boys, it might well have been the Serbian equivalent of *C'mon you goddamn pansies!*). So I was free to enjoy the Form, the Platonic basketball is-ness of the moment: boys on a sunny day in shiny jerseys, all elbows and knees, shoulder blades jutting like boomerangs, and all of life ahead of them. And then there was my father, who has spent his life doing just what I was doing then: watching boys – and young men – in various corners of the world (as well as in many derelict corners of America) play basketball.

Most of what I know about my father's career comes from a book by Cameron Stauth called *The Franchise: Building a Winner with the World Champion Detroit Pistons, Basketball's Bad Boys*. The book was published in 1990, but I have only just read it, not having known about its existence until a couple of years ago when I saw it on my father's shelf, then having left it untouched on my own shelf until recently, not realizing that it was, largely, a book about my father.

In the early 1950s, my father played professional basketball for the Sunbury Mercuries, a Pennsylvania team in the Eastern League, which was a precursor of the National Basketball Association (where the Bad Boys would later materialize). The Mercuries played thirty-five games a season, each player collecting a small fee after each game. In a good year, my father, who was twice Most Valuable Player of the league, made $1,500 – what a poorly paid NBA player now makes in a day.

Meanwhile, he and my mother were having babies, six in total, and all of us took up the game as soon as we could hold a ball. My first hoop was an iron pot atop the coffee table in the rec room (there is a newspaper photo of my entire family seated round the table as I waddle toward the iron pot with a ball that is nearly bigger than I am). My debut, at the age of six, was with the California Fancies, an imaginary dream team concocted by my eight-year-old brother. He was Mike Jetson, star centre, and I was guard Kip Reynolds, a good solid player but not quite in the same league as Mike. My mother cheered us through the season, despite the fact that between my father – now coaching at Wake Forest University, in North Carolina – and my older siblings, she was already attending several real games each week. My brother 'Mike' kept detailed statistics for the Fancies on his special clipboard, including the stats of our make-believe teammates, all of whom, like Mike and Kip, had names straight out of the Hardy Boys, our principal reading material of the time. 'Mike', being the older of us and the boy, not to mention the stat-keeper, naturally got to be the top scorer every game.

Sometime in the midst of my California Fancies career, I got my photo in the paper again, not as second-leading scorer Kip Reynolds, but as myself, fast asleep during the biggest win of my father's career to date, an overtime upset of the University of North Carolina. The stands have emptied around me. The headline reads: DADDY'S DEACONS NIP TARHEELS WHILE LITTLE MOLLY SLEEPS.

Despite our youthful fervour for the game, none of us kids panned out. My eldest brother got on the freshman team at Duke. Then he grew his hair long and did a lot of acid and nothing was ever the same again. The next brother got a basketball scholarship to Virginia Tech; halfway through he stopped playing and became team manager, a role much better suited to the drinking life he had by then begun to lead. Ten years later, I got a basketball scholarship to St Joseph's University, in Philadelphia. My education, housing, and books were free; in exchange I had to attend practice and play games, the latter often involving travelling and being excused from classes. None of these things was terrible. But two years into the scholarship, I quit the team. The next day, when the news had gone round, a rotund and intensely irritating little Irish-American named Murph said, 'Oh, good. Now you can just get drunk all the time.'

You're beginning to see the pattern.

On the phone, as I'd deliberated over throwing away thousands of dollars a year worth of freebies, my father had said to me, 'Well, if it isn't fun anymore ...' (At the time, the comment seemed disingenuous, totally at odds with his No Pain, No Gain life philosophy. But apparently not; fun is as essential as pain. In the heat of the most nerve-racking series of his NBA career to date – the 1989 Eastern Conference finals which pitted the Bad Boys against the Michael Jordan-led Chicago Bulls – he told Cameron Stauth: 'If a guy doesn't think this is fun, he's in the wrong business.')

My father's fortunes, meanwhile, were improving, though he too had his ups and downs. Stauth uses a quote from him as an epigraph to *The Franchise*: 'Winners are losers who just won't quit!' This is a man who knows. Having cracked the big time in 1972 with his first head coaching job in the NBA (for the Portland Trailblazers), he was fired two years later for clashing with the star player and for not winning enough games. My outstanding memory of the third grade is of my male classmates, after yet another Trailblazer loss, saying to me: *Your dad sucks!* (Which is perhaps not as bad as what a friend of mine told me: when he was a boy and his father was coaching at a major college in the midwest, they used to wake up after losses to find FOR SALE signs on their front lawn.)

After a year or two in the wilderness selling time-share, my father found his way back to the NBA as an assistant coach with the Los Angeles Lakers. By that time my parents had separated, and I stayed in Portland with my mother, but I visited my father in L.A. I liked going to games there; the Lakers had Hollywood stars for fans. Once, between quarters, I followed Jack Nicholson into a deserted corridor of the Forum, where he was putting some substance up his nose, and asked him for his autograph. I was thirteen; he was remarkably pleasant.

Thank you, I said.

Thank *you*, he said.

But after a couple of years my father was out of work again. A brief stint with the dismal Indiana Pacers followed, before, finally, at the age of fifty-three, he took on one of the least coveted jobs in the league, General Manager of the Detroit Pistons, the team Stauth calls 'the ultimate loser franchise'.

The season he took over, 1980–81, the Pistons won 16 games and lost 66, which was not an unusual showing for them. But within a few years, my father – through a series of clever and controversial trades (his nickname was Trader Jack) and draft picks – had turned the team into contenders. He'd also rescued himself from the brink of NBA oblivion, the realm of scouts, assistant coaches and other lesser beings. In 1989, the team won the first of its back-to-back NBA championships. By then, the Pistons had adopted the sobriquet 'Bad Boys' because they played in a manner that was, depending on your point of view, either tough and aggressive or just plain dirty. Stauth calls it Coalminer Style, in reference to my father's roots. My father's father worked in the mines in upstate Pennsylvania all his life. He died of emphysema and pneumoconiosis (otherwise known as black lung). According to Stauth, my grandfather took my father down into the mines just once. It had what I presume was the desired effect.

Before I ever read Stauth's book, I had given some thought to my father's path. When I saw him in a tastefully swanky suit or thought of him on the Pistons' private jet (they were the only team in the league then to have one), getting six figures to do something he loved, something fun, that didn't involve being underground, in the dark, inhaling coal dust all day, and surrounded by younger guys in even more expensive suits, who came from far rougher places than he did, I'd think how bizarre, how arbitrary, the American dream can be.

3

During the 1989 Eastern Conference series against the Bulls, my father dreamt he was guarding Michael Jordan, an anxiety dream I suspect many men in America have had, whether they work in the NBA or not.

I have two recurring basketball dreams, one of failure, one of redemption. In the first I have stolen the ball and am going for a breakaway lay-up at the opposite end. There's nobody near me. Nothing could be easier, but of course I miss. Then I get the rebound – there's still nobody near me – and I miss again. Same again, and again, and again. The dream-message is clear:

YOU ARE A FUCK-UP

In the second dream, I'm in my final year of college and return to play on the team as a walk-on, which means someone with no scholarship who is on the team for the love of being on the team and who hardly ever gets any game-time. I have reinvented myself as a responsible person who is making amends for having reneged on her commitment, for having thrown away a coveted scholarship I felt I hardly deserved. I am proving I can show up every day, on time, sober, like a good girl. I like this idea, both in the dream and in waking life, that I would forego the money and come back an unheralded grunt.

I did resurface, but I didn't achieve redemption. Instead, I watched history repeat itself, in slightly more farcical form. Around 1990, while living in the West of Ireland, I discovered there was a 'Ladies' team right there in Sligo. Despite initial reservations prompted by the term 'Ladies', I signed up.

We were the All-Stars, and our coach was a towering, balding, pear-shaped Englishman named Mike, or Miy-uk, as we called him, mimicking his accent. Miy-uk's primary piece of advice to us seemed to be: *Breathe through your noses, girls! Through your noses!* But I liked Miy-uk, and Miy-uk liked me. I saw his eyes light up when he heard my American accent, and light up even brighter after he'd seen me play. It's not that I was great. Even back in 1982, in the bloom of youth and with a full scholarship, I could've foreseen my own obsolescence. The women's game was improving much faster than I was. I was not a good enough ball handler, I couldn't jump that high, my shooting was inconsistent, I played (according to my brother) 'matador defence'. And, I was never hungry enough, probably because deep down, I didn't really care. I thought basketball was beautiful – I loved the aesthetics of the game, the fluidity, I loved executing my trademark move: head fake right, quick first step left, one dribble, off the glass and in – but winning had always been more a pleasure than a need. Still, relative to the other Sligo Ladies All-Stars, who hadn't the benefit of my training and pedigree, I was pretty good.

We played against teams in Gort, Ballyhaunis, Ballina, Castlebar, Bunnanadden, and Ballaghaderreen. We won some tournaments and some league titles and had some rather enjoyable drinking sessions. Though I hadn't touched a ball in eight years, the game was buried instinct and my body remembered everything almost immediately. The pick 'n' roll, the post-up, the baseline bounce pass, my twee habit of yelling *Let's talk!* to get my team-mates communicating on defence. I slipped back into the rhythms of the game the way you slip back into a second language when in a place it's spoken, surprising yourself with your fluency.

I played with the All-Stars for about six years, though I hardly recall anything from our games. It's the weirder stuff I remember. Like the day I posted up against a girl with a very soft and flabby midsection, poking her gently and bringing my hand back up to my face to find my ring finger shooting out at a forty-five-degree angle. The tiny point guard of our team, who was also a nurse, yelled *Stand back!*, then took hold of my dislocated finger and, bracing herself as though she were engaged in an almighty tug-of-war, yanked my finger out so that it could plock back into place.

I remember the guy from the men's team and the way he spoke of our dangerous mutual attraction as 'the unforbidden fruit'.

And I remember the Three Sisters of Ballina (though not their names). The Three Sisters could shoot the lights out and they scurried around on defence like animals driven demented by a threat only they could perceive. Despite being about four feet tall, they scared me. They were hungrier than I was, and meaner and earthier; they looked like they'd just come in from birthing calves in the field. And, to paraphrase my third-grade classmates, their gym sucked. When it was cold (which it always is in winter in Ballina), condensation would form on the gym floor. It was like playing atop banana skins. After yet another slide, I would call over to Miy-uk: *This is crazy!* I felt we shouldn't have to play there at all. But everybody else just shrugged. The Three Sisters, along with the rest of the Ballina team, knew the secret of sprinting downcourt without losing their footing. As for the All-Stars, except for me they were Irish, and so didn't complain, at least not about the things I thought they should complain about, the small and rectifiable injustices.

Still, there was a charm to it, to the cold slippery gyms in the middle of nowhere and to the fact that we travelled to them through the dark winter nights purely for the love of the game. (My father's first coaching job in the fifties was at Germantown Academy in Philadelphia, where they had no gym at all; he found an unheated barn with a leaky roof, and allowed the boys to wear gloves during practice). It was almost like being in the early days of something, before money had spoiled us, before we got all the free Adidas we wanted and were put up in four-star hotels (perks I enjoyed at St Joseph's). I could almost believe we were headed for bigger and better things, instead of just towards middle age.

For me, there was the added charm of getting to be, once more and for the last time, The Star. I hadn't been The Star since high school, when The Sted and I led our team to the state quarterfinals before choking against an inner-city school that had the kind of player I'd always found disproportionately intimidating: a black player. In real life, The Sted and I had nothing to say to each other, but on court we enjoyed an intuitive and productive symbiosis. I would lob it in to her for the inside shot – The Sted was 6'2" – or, if the defence collapsed on her in the key, she would pass it back out to me for the jump shot. She was also good on defensive rebounds, flinging the outlet pass to me as I sprinted downcourt calling for the ball in hopes of an easy breakaway basket. (Shamefully, or shamelessly, I always kept a mental tally of my points-so-far.) Our successful plays invariably culminated in a high five, executed on the run and feeling to me, every time, both instinctive and ridiculous.

Like college and professional players, we girls, in between games, were made to watch films of ourselves in other games, so that we could spot our weaknesses and correct them. When we won the league title, The Sted and I were interviewed for the Portland TV news. We spouted what Cameron Stauth calls 'mantalk'. We said things like, *Well, we really went out there and played our game tonight … we really took it to them …*

All those years later, in Sligo, I knew I was slumming it, out there in the arsehole of the back of beyond of what is simply not a basketball country, but I took an unashamed pleasure in the limelight, dim as it was. Kip Reynolds was finally having his day in the sun.

But eventually, during the 1995–96 season, my lifestyle caught up with me again. After a particularly heavy few days and nights of carousing in the licensed establishments of north Sligo, I was giving a friend of mine a lift into town on my way to a game. She looked

at me with a sort of worried amazement. 'You're playing in a basketball game tonight?' she said. 'You must have an incredible
metabolism.'

I smiled, nervously. I was nervous a lot back then.

That night I had an out-of-body experience on the free-throw
line. Standing there feeling both intensely anxious and disconcert-
ingly detached from the anxiety, I thought: *What am I doing here?*

I did not have an incredible metabolism, and I was sick of playing
with a hangover. The worrying slosh in my belly, the way exertion
worsened the shakes, the hot pounding headaches. I had to give up
one of two things and, as before, the answer was self-evident. I gave
up basketball.

5

In Sligo, I used to see the Americans around the gym, one or two
guys every year who hadn't been good enough to get drafted by the
NBA – by the likes of my father – but weren't quite ready to give up
the dream and get a real job, so were playing in Europe for a paltry
salary. They tended to be six-foot-something and black and so stood
out around town. When I saw them, I felt I'd rejected them by association.

But they also reminded me of something nicer: of the guys who
used to come to our house in North Carolina when I was small,
good college players who would eventually disappear into civilian
life. Every year while my father was at Wake Forest, my parents had
a Sunday afternoon party before the season began and the house
would fill with twelve gigantic young men – the black ones seeming
even more gigantic because of their afros. (During those years,
according to Stauth, my father got letters calling him 'nigger-lover'
for having too many black players on his team. When a reporter
remarked to him on the exact number, he said, 'Is that so? I hadn't
been counting.') There in the rec room (what would later be the
home court of the California Fancies), they would scoop me up – I

was blonde and four years old – and hold me high above their heads. They seemed to me both benevolent and thrilling. The imaginary friend of my girlhood was named Walker, after a Wake Forest player named Dicky Walker.

In Portland, I never got scooped up. I was a bit bigger by then and the players weren't often in a good mood. I remember following my parents down the long concrete corridor outside the Trailblazers' dressing room as they walked arm-in-arm ahead of my brother and me, my father's head down, my mother appearing to support him, after another loss. Afterwards, we often stopped for a late-night snack on the way home at a diner called Sambo's. There were pictures of a little black sambo adorning the walls and nobody thought twice about it, any more than we did about the figure of Aunt Jemima on the maple syrup bottle. We'd sit around a semi-circular table in the fluorescently lighted Sambo's, my parents morose, I morose for reasons of my own (imagining the next day's chorus of *Your dad sucks!*). But even with the losses, it was still cool having my dad for my dad, and his having the job that he did. I got to go out all the time on school nights. The waitresses at Sambo's knew who he was and treated him with a certain deference (even if he did suck), just as the people at our tennis club did, and the guys at the gas station. In fact, wherever we went in Portland, people knew him, because his picture was always in the sports section, and this glint of recognition in people's eyes made me think *I'm with someone important*, just as the fact that he ducked reporters who phoned him at home made him seem important. Never mind that they were calling to harass him about why the team was losing; the point was that he had to avoid the media, swatting them away like flies, like lesser mortals. Being famous, I thought, is cool.

6

My father's competitiveness is legendary in my family. He once visited me at MacDowell, the artists' colony in New Hampshire where they have a pool table in the front room. I am a halfway decent, if wildly inconsistent, pool player, and I beat my father (who probably hadn't played in twenty years) the first game.

Damn! he said, then proceeded to hammer me fourteen straight times.

Besides his obsession with winning, one of my father's other strengths as a General Manager was, as Stauth says, 'finding diamonds in the rough', kids in tiny colleges that were getting overlooked by everybody else. Players with unpronounceable names in funny parts of the world. Places like Herceg Novi, for instance. I don't know if he's ever scouted in the Balkans. I can't get an answer out of him.

(Autumn 2004)

The view from street level

CATRIONA CROWE

1

'It is a street,' writes Maeve Brennan in 'A Snowy Night on West Forty-Ninth Street', a 1967 piece for *The New Yorker*, 'of restaurants, bars, cheap hotels, rooming houses, garages, all-night coffee shops, quick-lunch counters, delicatessens, short-lived travel agencies and sight-seeing buses, and there are a quick dry-cleaning place, a liquor store, a Chinese laundry, a record shop, a dubious movie house, a young imperturbable gypsy who shifts her fortune-telling parlour from one doorway to another up and down the street, and a souvenir shop.'

This is a description of the kind of city street that would have met with the approval of Jane Jacobs, the visionary analyst of city life and planning who died in April of this year, aged eighty-nine. Diversity of use, she believed, was essential for vibrancy in urban neighbourhoods, and yet it was under attack by urban planners, architects and city officials. Her first and most influential book, *The Death and Life of Great American Cities*, published in 1961, accused planners of destroying perfectly sound city districts with their well-meaning but ill-informed strategies.

Jacobs anticipated many of the themes that have become foundations for contemporary social analysis – complex adaptive systems, emergence, social capital and social networks, among others. Her conception of the city began with its inhabitants, rather than with buildings, and emphasized the value of streets and sidewalks as against the unspecified open spaces surrounding monumental housing projects that were then in vogue as an alternative to 'slums'. She argued that, given certain conditions, which could be enhanced by good planning, the people of the city would make it thrive, make it safe and make it interesting.

She believed that many of the followers of Le Corbusier and Lewis Mumford, two of the most influential contemporary urban thinkers, actively hated cities as manifestations of chaos, and wished to create regimented, income-sorted, inward-looking settlements that lacked the vibrancy, innovation and diversity of the great urban neighbourhoods she loved. Jacobs appreciated and trusted the complex organic structure of the traditional city, and believed that, left mostly to its own devices, it would flourish.

More fundamentally, she believed that most people were capable of engaging in the complex and delicate social networks necessary to sustain a city, because she observed them in action every day. It is her highly empirical take on the operation of the city, beginning with her own perceptions of Hudson Street in Greenwich Village, where she lived in the 1950s and '60s, that makes her so readable and so convincing. She shows how a simple transaction, like arranging to leave one's house keys in the local delicatessen to be collected by a visitor, stands for a whole series of relationships that promote sociability, safeguard privacy and allow favours to be done.

2

I first read *The Death and Life of Great American Cities* in the early 1980s, when I was living in Mountjoy Square in Dublin's north inner city. The area had just experienced one of the last clearances of Georgian 'slums', in Summerhill and Gardiner Street, clearances which local protests, in which I participated, had failed to prevent. Hundreds of people were more or less forcibly moved to the new suburb of Blanchardstown, away from facilities and networks that had sustained them even in poor housing conditions. One of the saddest sights I remember from that time was the wrecker's ball smashing into the huge houses on Summerhill, exposing layers of wallpaper and random abandoned objects and furniture, the detritus of so many lives. Sean O'Casey's Dublin was biting the dust.

Although Dublin is not a great city, but a small one, characterized by collections of villages that command fierce loyalty from their denizens, Jacobs's observations about how successful streets worked resonated with me. The Georgian houses on Summerhill and Gardiner Street had been outward looking: the front doors were usually open; children played on the footpaths and on the famous twenty-seven steps leading from Summerhill to the Gloucester Diamond; people sat on their front doorsteps in good weather; social interaction was frequent and vibrant; the pubs on what used to be called 'the four corners of hell', the junction of Gardiner Street, Summerhill and Parnell Street, were patronized almost exclusively by locals; the shops in Parnell Street likewise. There were many 'eyes on the street', one of Jacobs's prerequisites for a safe and successful city neighbourhood.

While the people of this part of Dublin had their problems, most of them caused by extremely high unemployment, they comprised a close-knit, functioning community. Those of us who supported their resistance to being forcibly evicted argued that this should be taken into account by Dublin Corporation in their plans for redevelopment, but it cut no ice with the city officials. The 'slums' were cleared. Within a couple of years, the core of community leadership in the area had vanished. In 1982, when our newly elected independent TD, Tony Gregory, found himself in the miraculous position of holding the balance of power in the Dáil, he cut a deal to provide housing which brought some people back into the area; but when the government collapsed in November of that year, the housing programme stopped.

Some parts of the north inner city had 70 per cent unemployment in those years, largely because of the advent of containerization at the docks and the flight to brownfield sites of major employers like Goulding's fertilizers. A fairly thriving black economy sprang up, with people doing ingenious things like selling ice on Dollymount Strand on hot days, and the traditional street-trading sector was swelled by new workers peddling fruit, vegetables, jewellery, fireworks (illegal) and novelties like monkeys on a stick and disco-boppers. But these stopgaps could not reverse the destruction of the fabric of the neighbourhood. Heroin was starting to make its way onto the streets; some young people with no apparent prospects were starting to shoot up, and others were alerted to the huge money-making potential of this new market.

While there was a perception among outsiders that the north inner city was dangerous in the late seventies and early eighties, it didn't feel like that to those who lived there. I regularly walked home across the city after midnight in those years. But after heroin took hold in the mid eighties the community (and strangers in the area) became vulnerable to theft, intimidation, extortion and violence on an unprecedented scale. Street corners and parks that had been innocent and useful gathering places became drug supermarkets, often in full view of the police.

Some of the land formerly occupied by tenement houses in Summerhill and Gardiner Street was turned into a park. This park was not patronized by the locals, who already had a park in Mountjoy Square and another in Foley Street. (Jacobs is brilliant on the evils of unwanted parks.) Many protests against the futility of this park, which rendered one side of Gardiner Street dangerously empty, were ignored. The net result of the Corporation's efforts was to make a once welcoming, open, albeit run-down street closed, intimidating and unattractive to pedestrians.

It took many more years, and vigorous activity on the part of what remained of the local community, to convince the Corporation that they should work with the people, rather than, at best, on their behalf, or at worst, actively against them. The programme of public housing regeneration spearheaded during John Fitzgerald's term of office as City Manager has made a huge difference to the fabric of the area, both physical and social. Sadly, it came too late for Gardiner Street, now lined with mean-spirited

Georgian pastiche apartment blocks that are oriented away from the street, towards their internal courtyards and parking garages, and have no discernible community spirit. The street is much less safe now than it was in the late 1970s.

Interestingly, the most vibrant recent development in the area has happened without benefit of planners at all, namely, the transformation of Parnell Street into a multicultural enclave, with Chinese, Korean, Nigerian and Polish restaurants, bars, groceries, hairdressers and internet cafes, and lively street life. As Jacobs points out, areas where rents are cheap will regenerate spontaneously given the right conditions, and the city authorities' job should be to help create and sustain those conditions.

This is as true today as it was in the 1960s, and as true in Dublin as in New York. Happily, much of the thinking that so enraged Jacobs when she wrote *Death and Life* has now been rejected. The Ballymun towers, Ireland's single experiment in high-rise 'project building', are currently being demolished and replaced by high-density (but not high-rise) local authority and private housing, with community, cultural and commercial facilities to serve the residents. Ballymun, first tenanted in 1967, exemplified all of the faults of project building identified by Jacobs in *Death and Life*, consisting as it did of massive single-use, income-sorted, undifferentiated buildings surrounded by undesignated green space. The community-led process which fought for the changes now taking place was influenced by Jacobs's ideas, although many of its activists had never heard of her.

3

Jane Butzner was born in 1916 in Scranton, Pennsylvania, the daughter of a doctor and a former schoolteacher and nurse. After graduating from high school, she took an unpaid position as the assistant to the women's page editor at the *Scranton Tribune*. In 1934, in the middle of the Great Depression, she followed her sister to

New York City. The two young women used to play a game called 'Messages', which entailed imagining how to transmit a message from, say, a New Guinea tribesman to their local grocer in Greenwich Village – a version of the 'six degrees of separation' idea, and a useful way of thinking about interlinked systems.

During her first years in the city she held a variety of jobs, working mainly as a stenographer and freelance writer, often writing about working districts in the city. These experiences, she writes, gave her 'a notion of what was going on in the city and what business was like, what work was like'. While working for the Office of War Information she met an architect named Robert Hyde Jacobs, and married him in 1944. They had three children, whom they raised in, and on, Hudson Street. She and her family emigrated to Toronto in 1969, when her sons were threatened by the draft.

Jacobs never had a formal third-level education, although she attended classes at Columbia and Barnard, particularly in science subjects, during her early years in New York. While some of her critics questioned her qualifications to comment on planning issues, she had a healthy disrespect for what she called 'credentialism'. She thoroughly enjoyed her a la carte sampling of what universities had to offer and felt that taking a prescribed course would have wasted her time. She was immensely well-read, as likely to quote from Shakespeare, Jefferson or T.S. Eliot as from planning or architectural experts. She liked to demystify planning theory: 'The processes that occur in our cities are not arcane, capable of being understood only by experts. They can be understood by almost anybody. Many ordinary people already understand this; they simply have not considered that by understanding these ordinary arrangements of cause and effect, we can also direct them if we want to.'

In 1952 she joined the staff of the journal *Architectural Forum*, and in the following years she became involved in campaigns against two proposed developments: the attempt by Robert Moses, the New York City road and bridge supremo, to build a freeway through Washington Square; and the construction of the East Harlem Housing Project, with its consequent demolition of over a thousand dwellings and major human displacement. She and her supporters defeated Moses's plan for Washington Square by dint of petitions, street protests and astute lobbying, and thus saved a very beautiful and historic park from destruction. It was not easy: Jacobs was arrested twice during this campaign, and Moses described the campaigners as 'nothing but a bunch of mothers'. The East Harlem project, however, went ahead, and its dreadful effects on its tenants and surrounding neighbourhood provided Jacobs with powerful evidence of the dangers of untrammelled utopian planning, imposed by people who regarded ordinary city streets as chaotic and wanted citizens to live in regimented, ordered buildings surrounded by acres of open space.

4

The Death and Life of Great American Cities sets out the conditions that allow cities to thrive. Diversity, Jacobs says, is the key to development, interest and pleasure. There are four requirements for the generation of diversity, all of which must operate together:

1. 'The district, and as many of its internal parts as possible, must serve more than one primary function; preferably more than two.' These functions must ensure the presence of people outdoors at different times of the day, and for different purposes. Thus, residential, retail and work functions will bring people to the streets right through the day, while cultural, entertainment and catering functions will bring them there at night. Streets with only office blocks, or only apartment blocks, will be empty – and thus dull, dangerous, or both – at crucial times of the day or night.

2. 'Most blocks must be short; that is, streets and opportunities to turn corners must be frequent.' Jacobs gives the example of West 88th Street in New York, a long street running between Central Park at one end and Columbus Avenue at the other. Its residents never have any reason to pass through West 87th Street or West 89th Street, since these streets are not on their way to anywhere. A street

bisecting these streets, parallel to Columbus, would literally open up the area to those who live there, giving them multiple options for reaching their destinations, and creating the opportunity for services and businesses to establish themselves on new corners.

3. 'The district must mingle buildings that vary in age and condition, including a good proportion of old ones, so that they vary in the economic yield they must produce. This mingling must be fairly close-grained.' Only rich organizations can afford the rents required for newly constructed premises. Thus, a district can end up with only banks, chain stores and chain restaurants, and other high-end users, with no space for the small enterprises or specialist shops that generate diversity and innovation. These users generally flourish in older building stock where rents are lower.

4. 'There must be a sufficiently dense concentration of people, for whatever purposes they may be there. This includes dense concentrations of residents.' Jacobs's figures on residential density in cities reveal that high-density areas are often healthier, less crime-ridden and more enjoyable to live in than low-density areas. Planners tended to confuse high density with overcrowding, and thus insisted on disastrous low-density, suburban-type schemes.

Jacobs' street-level perspective on the life of cities is truly revelatory. Her beautiful description of the 'ballet' of Hudson Street is worth quoting at length, because it conveys nearly everything she wants to say about successful streets:

The stretch of Hudson Street where I live is each day the scene of an intricate sidewalk ballet. I make my own first entrance into it a little after eight when I put out the garbage can, surely a prosaic occupation, but I enjoy my part, my little clang, as the droves of junior high school students walk by the center of the stage dropping candy wrappers. (How do they eat so much candy so early in the mornings?)

While I sweep up the wrappers I watch the other rituals of morning: Mr. Halpert unlocking the laundry's handcart from its mooring to a cellar door, Joe Cornacchia's son-in-law stacking out the empty crates from the delicatessen, the barber bringing out his sidewalk folding chair, Mr. Goldstein arranging the coils of wire which proclaim the hardware store is open, the wife of the tenement's superintendent depositing her chunky three-year-old with a toy mandolin on the stoop, the vantage point from which he is learning the English his mother cannot speak.

Now the primary children, heading for St. Luke's, dribble through to the south; the children for St. Veronica's cross, heading to the west, and the children for P.S. 41, heading toward the east. Two new entrances are being made from the wings: well-dressed and even elegant women and men with briefcases emerge from doorways and side streets. Most of these are heading for the bus and subway, but some hover on the curbs, stopping taxis which miraculously appear at the right moment, for the taxis are part of a wider morning ritual: having dropped passengers from midtown in the downtown financial district, they are now bringing downtowners up to midtown. Simultaneously, numbers of women in housedresses have emerged and as they crisscross with one another they pause for quick conversations that sound with either laughter or joint indignation, never, it seems, anything in between.

It is time for me to hurry to work too, and I exchange my ritual farewell with Mr. Lofaro, the short, thick-bodied, white-aproned fruit man who stands outside his doorway a little up the street, his arms folded, his feet planted, looking as solid as earth itself. We nod; we each glance quickly up and down the street, then look back to each other and smile. We have done this many a morning for more than ten years, and we both know what it means: All is well.

This account of Greenwich Village in the 1950s seems like another world now; Manhattan is no longer a place where low-income families can live and thrive, due to its sky-high rents and property prices. But even if the description is archival, the richness outlined deserved to be recorded for its own sake.

When I get home after work, the ballet is reaching its crescendo. This is the time of roller skates and stilts and tricycles, and games in the lee of the stoop with bottletops and plastic cowboys; this is the time of bundles and packages, zigzagging from the drug store to the fruit stand and back over to the butcher's; this is the time when teenagers, all dressed up, are pausing to ask if their slips show or their collars look right; this is the time when beautiful girls get out of MGs; this is the time when fire engines go through; this is the time when anybody you know around Hudson Street will go by.

The sequence, full of rhythm and cadence, captures the pure pleasure of living in the middle of a city, if one is interested in other people and the intricate systems that underlie our daily lives.

I walk to work along South Great Georges's Street and Aungier Street. The short stretch of Aungier Street from Stephen Street to York Street would please Jane Jacobs: it contains, on one side, three restaurants, including Darwin's (slogan: 'serving evolutionary food'), four pubs (including the very beautiful and unreconstructed Swan Bar), a shop selling old-fashioned sweets like clove drops, bon bons, bull's eyes and liquorice allsorts; Bogart's, a second-hand men's clothes shop (slogan: 'wear it again, Sam'), a shop specializing in images of angels, a posh handbag shop, an 'adult' store (currently advertising an erotic rabbit for € 49.99), a bookmakers, a letting agent, a jeweller, an internet café, a bed-and-breakfast, a business school, a bridal-wear shop, a Chinese herbalist and a madrasa. Coyle's hatters, where the man in charge could guess your hat size just by looking at you, is sadly closed, as is Star CDs, a small second-hand music shop whose kindly proprietor was brutally murdered about a year ago. There is not a Spar or Centra in sight.

On the other side of the street, and further up beyond York Street, there are modern, fairly high-density apartments. York Street itself has two large local authority flat complexes. The Dublin Institute of Technology, the Carmelite church and Bishop's Square office complex all attract people at different times of the day to occupy the street. If Aungier Street is left alone, it will continue to be satisfying to its residents, to visiting strangers and to habitual passers-through like me.

Jacobs was no romantic about cities. She accepted that they could contain troublesome areas and individuals, that even the most successful districts contained within them the seeds of their own decline, that there are cycles of growth and decay in every city, and that unpredictable financial conditions, both public and private, can fundamentally change the balance in a district. But while accepting that there are things beyond the control of the planners, she can point to things well within their control, which seem to be wilfully ignored.

She was critical of the US city planners' passion for accommo-dating the automobile, through the contruction of expressways that cut through neighbourhoods and the widening and straightening of streets. Such measures brought about the destruction of sidewalk space and buildings that got in the way, separated naturally linked areas, brought about huge increases in traffic and danger to pedes-trians, and fed the proliferation of parking lots and filling stations on city streets.

In her chapter on 'the curse of border vacuums', she brilliantly analyzes the troubles that befall districts at the edge – near water-fronts, expressways, railroad tracks, edges of parks, etc. Such districts, because not on the way to anywhere, can fall stagnant very easily. Her solution is to make them destinations in themselves, like the waterfront in San Francisco, or to encourage cross-fertilization. Border vacuums can occur even in the heart of a city: Jacobs denounces the carousel in Central Park for being too far into the interior of the park, instead of at the edge, where the adjoining streets could feed into it and from it.

Many of Jacobs's ideas are now accepted as conventional, so much so that the architectural correspondent of the *New York Times*, in his tribute to her after her death, cavilled at her lack of interest in large infrastructure, and proclaimed the beauties of the Los Angeles freeway system. It's getting fashionable to criticize her again, just as Lewis Mumford and others did when *Death and Life* was first published. (Mumford's review of the book in the *New Yorker* appeared under the heading 'Mother Jacobs' Home Remedies for Urban Cancer'.) But this is a reflection of her great influence. Within a decade of publication, *Death and Life* was on university architecture and planning curricula. In 1975, the American Institute of Architects recognized her as 'one of the earliest liberal opponents of such gen-erally accepted liberal programs as urban renewal and city planning'. The American Planning Association has instituted an Innovation in Neighborhood Planning Award in her honour.

Jacobs, who turned down almost all of the awards offered to her, was probably happier on the outside than in the mainstream. There is a lovely photograph of her, on the cover of the first paperback edition of *Death and Life*, sitting in her local bar, the famous White Horse Tavern, with a beer in one hand and a cigarette in the other, looking as if she's having a great deal of fun, and ready to argue with anyone up for it.

5

The Death and Life of Great American Cities was followed by six more books, two of which expanded her ideas on cities. *The Economy of Cities* (1969) proclaims the city, not agriculture, as the foundation of civilization, and posits the engine of import replacement as the driving force behind city development and growth. She illustrates this with an account of the beginnings of industrial life in Japan. Starting in the late 1800s, Japan imported bicycles. Repair shops sprang up in Tokyo, at first cannibalizing broken bicycles for parts. When enough of these existed, workshops started producing some of the most-used parts locally. More and more parts were made, until ultimately Tokyo could produce its own bicycles and export them to other Japanese cities, where the whole process began again. This process not only creates work, it creates expertise and innovation: cities learn how to solve problems in new ways, and transfer the experience of building one thing to another. And it creates wealth: with import replacement, the city becomes richer, because it not only still has what it used to import (bicycles, in Tokyo), but it can now afford new, pricier imports.

Cities and the Wealth of Nations takes issue with Adam Smith's *Wealth of Nations*, arguing that nations aren't the proper unit of macroeconomic analysis; cities are. Thinking in terms of national economies obscures the truth that the world consists not of developed and poor nations, but of dynamic and poor regions. One of the great advantages of this point of view is that it helps us to see how the backward regions in the First World follow the same dynamics as the Third World. These days such regions may be comfortable enough due to transfer payments from richer regions, but they are economically passive nonetheless.

Jacobs's body of work – which also includes books that range widely through social systems, economics and culture – represents a sustained and evolving reflection on the ways in which we live our lives. She is a classic reformer, not a revolutionary: she sees much that is good in our current structures, but has myriad ideas as to how they can be improved. She is constitutionally against unnecessary destruction, and a passionate believer in human ingenuity.

6

I was fortunate enough to meet Jane Jacobs in 2002, when *New York Review of Books* editor Barbara Epstein, who sadly also died this year, arranged for me to visit her in her modest and beautiful house at 69 Albany Avenue in Toronto. A large woman with lovely white hair and shrewd blue eyes, she was quite slow on her feet, but otherwise in good health. She had bought Guinness for me because she thought I might like it, which I did, very much. We sat in her large plain kitchen and talked for about two hours.

She was pessimistic about the future, but still hopeful that human responsibility and ingenuity would eventually triumph over the apathy she discerned as the greatest threat to the kind of harmonious, vibrant, creative society she cherished. She was very interested in an organization in Dublin with which I am connected, the SAOL project for women with addiction problems, based in Dublin's north inner city. The project's principles of rehabilitation through education and empowerment rather than medical intervention appealed to her.

I was interested in her opinions about Canada, her adopted country – she took citizenship in 1974. She had fought successfully against a destructive freeway through Toronto, just as she had forty years earlier in Greenwich Village, and had considerable influence on the regeneration of the St Lawrence neighbourhood, a successful housing project. She praised Canada's overt efforts to combat racism and to foster intercultural respect, and its profound divergence from the United States in matters of world hegemony. But she felt that Canada was going the same way as the US as regards state abdication of social responsibility and unthinking worship of the free market, and this saddened her.

I left her house with the sense of having met someone calm, powerfully effective and immensely articulate, but with no interest in power for its own sake. She was deeply impressive precisely because of her belief that ordinary people can, and should, change their environments for the better by intelligent use of the systems, some formal, most not, which surround us. She possessed that rare capacity to inspire continued efforts, perhaps doomed but always interesting, to change the world.

(Autumn 2006)

Sixth sense, seventh heaven

SEAMUS HEANEY

I'm interested in what happens when a poem manages to get up on its own legs, so to speak – how it develops its own capacity to move itself along and what then are its means of movement. In the happiest writing experiences, a state occurs in the writer and the material when, to quote the words of Robert Frost, 'the wonder of unexpected supply keeps growing'. Which is to say a sixth sense of possibility grows into a gleeful seventh heaven of reward. Or to put it in the terms used by William Wordsworth, in his sober but lucid account of the same phenomenon written two hundred years ago for the 1802 preface to *Lyrical Ballads*:

I have said that poetry is the spontaneous overflow of powerful feelings: it takes its origin from emotion recollected in tranquillity: the emotion is contemplated till by a species of reaction the tranquillity gradually disappears, and an emotion, kindred to that which was before the subject of contemplation, is gradually produced, and does itself actually exist in the mind. In this mood successful composition generally begins, and in a mood similar to this it is carried on ...

What Wordsworth is describing is a process that has three stages or levels of operation. First, there is the lived experience that precedes the business of writing: 'the emotion', as he calls it, whatever has gathered up in the poet's mind and body and assumed an unaccounted-for significance, the whole complex that produces a sense that there's something in there needing expression, ready to reveal itself as something else. Or you could think of the emotion as the poet's 'me-ness', and say that the 'me-ness' wants to get turned into an 'it-ness', that the poet wants to know what he's all about, wants the inchoate psychic matter to come forth as a contemplatable shape. And at that stage of wanting, of sensing a need for expression, the second stage has already been reached: the mind is becoming active in itself, the process of searching for equivalence is under way, and whatever happened in actual life to prompt the process takes second place to the writerly appetites it has prompted in the poet.

All of this is covered by Wordsworth's succinct account: 'the emotion is contemplated till by a species of reaction the tranquillity gradually disappears, and an emotion, kindred to that which was before the subject of contemplation, is gradually produced, and does itself actually exist in the mind'. And so to the third stage, the actual writing, because, as Wordsworth adds, 'In this mood, successful composition generally begins, and in a mood similar to this it is carried on.' The actual writing is the simplest stage of the process, because once there is verbal purchase on the emotion, as Wordsworth calls it, or the dark embryo, as Eliot calls it, or the inspiration, as it has been traditionally called, the poem has established its biological right to life and will be seeking compulsively to flesh itself out in words.

These various stabs at saying what happens are made by poets, more or less off the cuff, but they echo and correspond to a more systematic, more philosophically worded account of the process by Jacques Maritain in his 1953 book *Creative Intuition in Art and Poetry*. In a chapter entitled 'The Three Epiphanies of Creative Intuition' Maritain proposes the following names for the three constituent movements of the whole business: first, he suggests, there is discovered a Poetic Sense or Inner Melody, and then this inclination or potential coalesces into Action and Theme, which result in, thirdly, the actual writing, what he chooses to call Number or Harmonic Expansion. Maritain, however, seems to be most concerned, as I am, with the second stage of his adumbrated process, the emanation of the action and theme from the original 'poetic sense'. 'A poem', he declares (and one does not need to be a Thomist to agree), 'has no will of its own, unless metaphorically. But in things which have no will of their own ... there is a property that corresponds to what the will is in voluntary agents – namely, action.'

The action, Maritain insists, is not the servant of anything outside itself, not the vehicle of a pre-existent, paraphrasable meaning, and yet it is still hungry for theme, which he conceives of not as a topic or a subject to be addressed but as a potentiality discovered within the material:

The action and the theme are complements or objective reflections of the poetic sense: if they are not in consonance and unity with it, they mar the poem. They originate in creative emotion: without it they have no poetic existence. The idea of a theme can present itself to the mind independently of creative emotion: [but] it gives nothing if it does not pass through creative emotion; the theme itself, the meaning of the action, exercises its function in the poem only by virtue of creative emotion.

The last thing to be said about all this, but a vastly important thing, is that the three steps which for the sake of clarity are outlined here as a sequence probably occur within the poet as a simultaneity, an awakening of nerve ends and word-slips. Maritain calls this third part of the process 'harmonic expansion', and it's the part we can actually trace in poets' manuscripts, the trial-and-error word-search. Admittedly, this is bound to be a slower activity than the conceptual rush and flash of the moment when the unforeseen presents itself as the vividly attractive; and yet even in the 'harmonic expansion', there can be unexpectedly swift leaps and crystallizations.

The poem, in other words, must be all of a piece, must grow its own legs, arise, take up its bed, and walk. Ideally, it will have that element of surprised arrival. But where will it have arrived from? From the poet's reading? Yes. From the forgotten experience, whispering its tale, like Wordsworth's 'emotion recollected in tranquillity'? Yes. From a deliberate exercise of verse-craft, like the Anglo-Saxon poet unlocking his word hoard? Yes. From spiritual journeying, like

Emily Dickinson's? Yes. From exaltation, like Yeats writing 'The Cold Heaven'? Yes. From exhaustion, like Eliot writing 'The Waste Land'? Yes.

Here, for example, is a poem that arrived unexpectedly from all those things and from God knows what else. It has gone through a certain amount of Maritain's 'harmonic expansion', in that I know I made several revisions, but I also know from the drafts that the action and theme derived from a sixth sense of a subject, from what Maritain would have called the 'poetic sense'. The words that arrived on the page came from a potential discovered in the given material. I had no plans for the poem, no designs on the reader, nothing to go on except a supply of images from the inner frond-forest. From the start, and out of the blue, there was a picture of a beggar at the threshold of a roofless cottage, a puddle of rain-water in the hearth, and a high cold sky with moving clouds. There was also an understanding that this was an image of the soul being called to judgement on the brink of eternity, what I had once learned to call 'the particular judgement' – as opposed to that final, general judgement in the Valley of Jehoshaphat. The particular judgement was a far lonelier affair, and the prospect of it both expanded and bewildered the consciousness of the child who was taught to expect it. And it is that sense of expansion and bewilderment and solitude that found its way into the poem.

> Shifting brilliancies. Then winter light
> In a doorway, and on the stone doorstep
> A beggar shivering in silhouette.
>
> So the particular judgement might be set:
> Bare wallstead and a cold hearth rained into –
> Bright puddle where the soul-free cloud-life roams.
>
> And after the commanded journey, what?
> Nothing magnificent, nothing unknown.
> A gazing out from far away, alone.

And it is not particular at all,
Just old truth dawning: there is no next-time-round.
Unroofed scope. Knowledge-freshening wind.

Remembered and unremembered reading, long forgotten but suddenly recovered places, an unexpected sureness of voice – all worked together here. The first draft was written down in the Reading Room of the National Library in Dublin on an afternoon in August 1988, on the day I completed the long task of annotating a selection of Yeats's poems for *The Field Day Anthology of Irish Writing*. I may not have been exhausted, but there was a definite sense of release, of a pressure lifted, a light let in, and I'm sure that had something to do with the given-ness of the lines. A great sense too of the dimensions of Yeats's achievement, the boldness of his imagining, the extravagance of his concerns with life after death, with the adventures of the soul when it leaves the body, with its 'shiftings', as he calls it one place.

At that time, I was more conscious of what spirit meant, since I had recently stood at the deathbeds of my mother and father and witnessed the pure change, simple, momentous, and mysterious, that happens at such moments. I had taken to saying that I felt my head was now bare to the universe, that the roof of childhood had been removed. And clearly, this new emotion and way of figuring had also entered the poem. I was aware when I was writing it, for example, that I was drawing at a great distance upon the medieval morality play *Everyman*, in which Death visits Everyman and commands him to take a long journey, but what I was not aware of was my unconscious dialogue with Yeats and the poem of his I mentioned earlier, 'The Cold Heaven'.

Yeats introduced this poem on BBC Radio some time in the 1930s and the simplicity of what he said in the studio had made a deep impression on me. I had copied the words out of A.N. Jeffares's *Commentary on the Collected Poems* and appended them to the poem in my Field Day selection. 'The Cold Heaven', according to its author, was his attempt to describe the feeling roused in him by the cold detached sky in winter. Which is one way of putting it, and a totally convincing way, but the poem has extra and inestimable dimensions:

> Suddenly I saw the cold and rook-delighting heaven
> That seemed as though ice burned and was but the more ice,
> And thereupon imagination and heart were driven
> So wild that every casual thought of that and this
> Vanished, and left but memories, that should be out of season
> With the hot blood of youth, of love crossed long ago;
> And I took all the blame out of all sense and reason,
> Until I cried and trembled and rocked to and fro,
> Riddled with light. Ah! When the ghost begins to quicken,
> Confusion of the death-bed over, is it sent
> Out naked on the roads, as the books say, and stricken
> By the injustice of the skies for punishment?

Who could be surprised if gleams of unextinguished thought from that poem broke into another poet's mind? The earliest draft I can find of my own winter sky poem begins:

> The particular judgement. Winter light
> Hard in a doorway, and on the stone doorstep
> A beggar shivering in silhouette.
> Great brilliant speed, greater unchangeableness.
> Nothing magnificent, nothing unknown,
> The not-me gazing out of the me-alone.

And then the next draft:

> Brilliant tourbillons. Winter light
> In a doorway, and on the stone doorstep
> A beggar shivering in silhouette.
>
> Not entered yet and yet having arrived.
> A wallstead and a bare hearth rained into,
> Soul-puddle where the slow bright world-clouds move.

And above this version I had written as a possible title the word 'Shiftings', the word which also features in Yeats's occult vocabulary, and reappears in the final version of the first line:

> Shifting brilliancies. Then winter light
> In a doorway, and on the stone doorstep
> A beggar shivering in silhouette.

The fact that two and a half lines of this first stanza remained constant throughout all the revisions is testimony, of course, to their rhythmical and phonetic rightness, and this rightness of the thing in the ear is in the end what poetry is all about. It's what I love to attend to when I read and analyze poems by other poets, but when it comes to one's own poems, it's a job that should be done by somebody else.

The job I can do is to dig around the roots of memory and throw up some of the stuff that turned into images in the poem. In this case, a memory of myself at the age of three or four, standing on the doorstep of an old wallstead in the middle of the fields, looking at ragwort and grass-seed sprouting up between the broken flagstones of the floor, the piles of fallen-in rafters and thatch in the corners, a puddle on the hearthstone, and so on, with the big sky moving overhead. Feeling exposed, wide open, unprotected, windswept, and, if it is permitted to say so, riddled with light. As Robert Frost puts it in his vivid essay 'The Figure a Poem Makes', 'The impressions most useful to my purpose seem always those I was unaware of and so made no note of at the time when taken, and the conclusion is come to that like giants we are always hurling experience ahead of us to pave the future with against the day when we may want to strike a line of purpose across it for somewhere.'

The great thing about the twelve lines I've been discussing is that they felt both finished and ready to be expanded upon. And by good luck I was in a position to dwell with them and let them suggest the next move. For if Maritain was right to say that a poem doesn't have a will of its own, except metaphorically, he was also right to claim that it is instinct with a capacity for action, all set to be dictated to by its own inner workings. Happily, then, what was dictated to me by the unroofed wallstead was a second poem about being roofed

in. That summer of 1988 I was blessed to be able to re-enter a house
that had been precious when I moved into it with my wife and family sixteen years before. We had left Belfast and gone to live in the
country south of Dublin, in Glanmore Cottage, from 1972 until 1976
– four years which marked a crucially important period of my life.
Now, by the good grace of the former owner, Professor Ann
Saddlemyer, I was able to purchase the cottage and repossess it as a
place of writing, and those days of late summer and early autumn of
1988 were days of return to another precious energy source. Equally
importantly, they were days when I had time to myself – I was just
at the beginning of a sabbatical year from Harvard – and when I
retreated under the slate roof and behind the stone walls of the cottage, it became a listening post where I could hear down into the
very foundations of my sixth-sensed self. And so, on 11 September
1988, a second poem arrived, also twelve lines long, a kind of
antiphonal response, really, to the line with which the first poem
ended: 'Unroofed scope. Knowledge-freshening wind.' This second
one came quickly and needed very few changes:

> Roof it again. Batten down. Dig in.
> Drink out of tin. Know the scullery cold,
> A latch, a door-bar, forged tongs and a grate.
>
> Touch the cross-beam, drive iron in a wall.
> Hang a line to verify the plumb
> From lintel, coping-stone and chimney-breast.
>
> Relocate the bedrock in the threshold.
> Take squarings from the recessed gable pane.
> Make your study the unregarded floor.
>
> Sink every impulse like a bolt. Secure
> The bastion of sensation. Do not waver
> Into language. Do not waver in it.

The final line and a half were both utterly unforeseen and
utterly called for. There was a certain frolicsomeness in the oppos-

ing imperatives; they felt like a conundrum rather than a contradiction: 'Do not waver / Into language. Do not waver in it.' At any rate, the sportiveness of the thing brought me alive and all of a sudden it was clear that the diptych was itching to become a triptych. And the bit of language that offered a way ahead was the word 'squarings' in line 8, a childhood word that had presented itself unthinkingly, but that now seemed to require a gloss. 'Taking squarings' was schoolboy-speak for aligning oneself in a game of marbles, getting ready to take aim either at another marble or at one of the marble-holes, as described in the following lines:

> Squarings? In the game of marbles, squarings
> Were all those anglings, aimings, feints and squints
> You were allowed before you'd shoot, all those
>
> Hunkerings, tensings, pressures of the thumb,
> Test-outs and pull-backs, re-envisagings,
> All the ways your arms kept hoping towards
>
> Blind certainties that were going to prevail
> Beyond the one-off moment of the pitch.
> A million million accuracies passed
>
> Between your muscles' outreach and that space
> Marked with three round holes and a drawn line.
> You squinted out from a skylight of the world.

So there it was. I had my triptych, but I had been roused into new possibility. There was no pre-existing design, but the given materials were stirring; the word 'squarings', for example, now suggested that I might try to do twelve of these twelve-liners, and since that didn't seem impossible, I decided to try it. (The sequence would eventually grow to comprise four groups of twelve twelve-liners.) I sensed I was at last working in accordance with advice I had earlier given myself. In 1982 I had been bold enough to put the ghost of James Joyce into a poem called 'Station Island' and had written lines

for him that were meant as 'apt admonishment' for myself: 'Let fly',
Joyce counsels, 'keep at a tangent,'

swim

out on your own and fill the element
with signatures on your own frequency,
echo-soundings, searches, probes, allurements,

elver-gleams in the dark of the whole sea.

Joyce's urging came at the conclusion of a poem where other
shades had very different things to tell the protagonist. Several of
the speakers had died in the course of the Northern Ireland troubles, including an IRA hunger-striker and two Catholics who had
been victims of random sectarian assassinations. It was hard in
those conditions to give oneself up to the frolicsome and the
sportive, and the dialogues with the dead in 'Station Island'
amounted to a questioning of poetry's right to take pleasure in itself
in such a dire situation. But the question had been worked through
and the reward came with the plunge into subjectivity which the
twelve-line poems effected. A great deal of their insouciance arises
from their having escaped the shackles of the civic.

Put it like this: the poems I was now being given to write were
turning out to be the poems that the Joyce-shade had been wanting
me to write, so for a few months it was all go. I began to treat the
twelve-line form as a sprint, to give myself a couple of hours to
breast the tape. I thought of them in terms of speed and chance. I
imagined the twelve poems being linked the way twelve splashes
would be linked by a skimming stone hitting the surface of the
water twelve times. I tried to make myself wide open to whim; for
example, after the 'squarings' section, I started off another section
with an image of three marble holes that an uncle of mine had
thumbed into the wet concrete of a road when it was being constructed in the 1920s. He had done this the night before he sailed for
Australia, and once the concrete hardened the thumb-marks were

there to stay, and were still there when I was a youngster, little dark-eyed peepholes to the other side of the earth. 'Three stops,' as the poem called them, 'to play / The music of the arbitrary on.' And as it turned out, that phrase, 'the music of the arbitrary,' characterized the freedom and opportunism of the whole undertaking.

(Autumn 2002)

Writing against the writing on the wall

GLENN PATTERSON

The following is an edited version of a lecture delivered on 12 December 2003 to the European Federation of Associations and Centres of Irish Studies conference on 'Representation and Responsibility' in Braga, Portugal.

'When we try to translate truth out of one sphere into another,' E.M. Forster writes, 'whether from life into books, or from books into lectures, something happens to truth: it goes wrong, not suddenly, when it might be detected, but slowly.'

Forster likens this process to the divergence between a bird and its shadow as it takes flight. I am mindful that today I am most often going to be trying to leap straight from life into lecture, using books only as occasional boosters, so who knows how far the shadow of what I do say will end from the substance of what I intended.

1

Many of you, I'm sure, will be aware that we recently underwent – the democrat in me stops short, just, of saying *suffered* – elections in Northern Ireland. You will forgive me, I hope, if my deliberations on the theme of this conference have been a little coloured by the results. For those of you who don't know the precise outcome – and let's face it, why should you? – the two most successful parties were the Democratic Unionists, led by the Reverend Ian Paisley, and Sinn Féin, led by Gerry Adams. The Belfast or Good Friday Agreement, which was intended to strengthen the middle ground of Northern

Irish politics, represented by the nationalist Social Democratic and Labour Party and the Ulster Unionist Party, appears to have driven voters away from the centre towards the extremes. The upshot is that for the foreseeable future our Assembly will exist in name only and responsibility for the day-to-day running of Northern Ireland will remain with London and, to a much, much lesser extent, Dublin.

Only five years ago Paisley and his DUP appeared to be in the political wilderness. In the run-up to the 1998 referendum that endorsed the Good Friday Agreement, graffiti appeared on the walls of east Belfast where I live: 'Defeat the DUP–LVF treachery: vote Yes!' – the LVF being the Loyalist Volunteer Force, a particularly vicious breakaway from what we have come to refer to as the *mainstream* loyalist paramilitary organizations.

I should say before I go on that there is little of what you might call freelance political graffiti in Belfast. It is not unusual to see walls that haven't yet been painted on reserved by one or other of the paramilitary organizations for future use.

In 1998, the walls were saying that mainstream loyalists – the adjective is no more convincing in the repeating – saw themselves as the moderates, the DUP as the extremists. Five years later – five years, numerous bloody feuds and breaches of ceasefire, for which read sectarian murders, later – loyalist paramilitary support for the Agreement has all but disappeared; the Progressive Unionist Party, which, as we are careful to say, 'has previously predicted the mood of' the Ulster Volunteer Force, saw its representation in the notional Assembly reduced from two to one. The writing on the east Belfast walls last year was 'No Short Strand Taigs here: enter at your own risk', a chilling reference to the small Catholic enclave just on the east side of the river Lagan from the city's Central railway station.

It is easy to lose a sense of perspective when confronted by what is written and, even more so, by what is painted on Belfast's walls. Like cinema screens, walls magnify often to the point of distortion. Take the organization known as the Red Hand Commando. (Somebody, please, take the organization known as the Red Hand Commando.) The Red Hand Commando is so small as to have appeared for long stretches of its history to have no existence independent of the larger UVF to which it is allied. Of the fifteen murders for which it is thought to have been responsible in the last three decades, as many as a third were claimed by a single man called Frankie Curry, himself since murdered, and seem to have sprung from nothing more strategic than the desire to 'get a taig', or settle a score. Bars appear to have featured heavily in the planning. Yet within a one-mile radius of my house there are at least three murals depicting the Red Hand Commando as soldiers in uniform. I have often wondered, given the size of the organization, whether there wasn't a mural for every Red Hand Commando member in Belfast.

A few years ago I was doing an interview for a London-based television company. They proposed starting the interview with a slow pan from an enormous UVF mural ('Still Undefeated', it said) on to my face. I pointed out to them that more or less every interview I had ever done for London-based television companies started with a slow pan from an enormous UVF mural on to my face. I pointed out a wall directly across the road from this particular enormous mural. Here a short time before someone had scrawled the words 'Big Norman is Gilbert the German' and 'Neil Barrie eats pies'. Someone else – the city council perhaps, but more likely one of those organizations who had already reserved the wall – had whitewashed the words, only for the graffiti artist to come back with the triumphant statement, 'Neil Barrie <u>still</u> eats pies!' Of Big Norman, aka Gilbert the German, there was sadly no further word.

To the television company the UVF mural represented Belfast, 'let viewers know where they were'; to me it represented only the UVF. It is anyone's guess what the Neil Barrie graffito represented: a slur on Neil Barrie, a simple celebration of his appetite for pies. Nor can I say for certain what it was about it that appealed to me so much: its slight surrealism, or the small defiance of its reappearance – its temporary reappearance, I should say, because a matter of weeks after we finished filming it had been whitewashed again, this time for good.

Italo Calvino, in a paper delivered in the mid 1970s at a symposium entitled 'Right and Wrong Political Uses of Literature', says that 'Politics, like literature, must above all know itself and distrust itself.' If I have one overarching complaint about the murals of Belfast it is not that they are kitsch in Milan Kundera's definition of the word as that which denies the existence of shit, in this case the shit of murder at the dead of night (though deny it they undoubtedly do); nor that they are badly executed (though badly executed in most cases they are); but that as propaganda, politics in primary colours, they brook no argument. Not even the argument by proximity of Neil Barrie and his pies.

Following that rash of virulently sectarian graffiti last summer there has been something of a rethink in how east Belfast represents itself. It has been decided – presumably by the paramilitary organizations in the area – not just to remove the offensive graffiti, but also to replace some of the more militaristic images with murals celebrating east Belfast's cultural heritage. So, as well as depictions of the shipyards there have recently appeared wall-sized portraits of the east's most famous sons: George Best, Van Morrison, and – how many of you would have known this? – C.S. Lewis.

Lewis was born just a few hundred yards from where I'm currently living. Outside the local library there is a sculpture of him, one hand on the handle of an open wardrobe door, the wardrobe of course being the portal to the fantastical world of Narnia in his most famous series of books, beginning with *The Lion, the Witch and the Wardrobe*. Frankly, given some of the things that have gone on in the east of the city in recent years I have half expected some mornings to drive by and find the wardrobe door shut and Lewis gone once and for all to the other side.

2

On the Saturday before our recent election I attended an event developed and produced by Tinderbox Theatre Company: *Vote! Vote!*

Vote!, subtitled 'An Alternative Assembly of Artists', for which thirteen writers – I was one – had written short election-related dramas.

Tinderbox have in recent years made a name for themselves as producers of site-specific and site-significant theatre. *Convictions*, another multi-authored piece, was performed in the courtroom, holding cells, judges' chambers and visitors' gallery of the now derelict Crumlin Road Court House. Before that, and coinciding with the two hundredth anniversary of the United Irishmen's rebellion, they staged a stirring production of Stewart Parker's *Northern Star*, directed by Stephen Rea, in Rosemary Street Presbyterian Church, where William Drennan, a leading light of the United Irishmen, used to preach.

Vote! Vote! Vote!, like the elections it was intended to comment on, had been postponed from May. It opened in the old Belfast Assembly Rooms – another link with Belfast's radical Presbyterian past – then played a night in Newry and one in Derry before returning, on the night I saw it, to the Council Chamber of Belfast City Hall. The audience sat in the seats normally occupied by the city's elected representatives, or at least occupied by them when they're not walking out, or being thrown out for intemperate language. The four actors, who shared the roles in all thirteen playlets, used every other available space: the floor of the chamber, the public gallery, the Lord Mayor's chair.

I can't say I had been looking forward to the evening, given that my own contribution was the last but one to be performed, that I don't have a theatrical bone in my body, and that I knew in advance from my wife, who had seen the piece in the Assembly Rooms, that the one prop I had insisted on in the script – a wheelie bin, from the inside of which were to be read articles of the United Nations Charter for Human Rights – had not been included.

In fact, though the quality of the pieces varied, and though I spent most of the five minutes of my own piece thinking that whatever the drawbacks for the novelist of never knowing who, if anyone, is reading your work, they were a damned sight better than sitting in the same room as them, I have to say it was difficult not to get caught up in the occasion. There were present at least one outgoing member of the Northern Ireland Assembly and one serving city councillor – sitting, I was told afterwards, exactly where he sat for council meetings. There was present also a woman who in the 1970s had once protested at proposals to withdraw free milk from Belfast schoolchildren by leading a cow to the doors of the City Hall. She, like most of the rest of the audience, me included, had never set foot in this the focal point of local democracy. The stairs, she said, would have been too difficult for the cow.

The performance was followed by a discussion, or at least by an uncomfortable five minutes of silence before the director, Dan Gordon, broke the ice by reading out some of the entries to a joke competition Tinderbox had been running throughout the week: 'What's the difference between the *Titanic* and the Northern Ireland Assembly?'

It might still be possible to raise the *Titanic*.

There's only one tit in *Titanic*.

Or, my personal favourite: There's no chance of anyone going down on the Northern Ireland Assembly – and for the truth of that one I refer you to the mug shots of the candidates still looking out from lampposts across Belfast two days after they were supposed to have been removed.

Whether it was the quality of the jokes or not, eventually we started to talk. We complained about the decline in doorstep canvassing; we questioned the efficacy in this day and age of mug shots on lampposts. We speculated a lot about what something called the electorate, which did not seem to include us, wanted. One person spoke to say she had nothing particular to say, she just didn't know when she'd ever get another chance to say it in the council chamber.

At length the playwright Damian Gorman asked a pertinent question: what, fundamentally, does an Assembly of Artists, or more specifically writers, have to offer the political process?

Well, based on the evidence of *Vote! Vote! Vote!*, writers are, you will probably not be surprised to learn, better at pointing up folly than at offering programmes for parties to follow.

Damian Gorman's own contribution to *Vote! Vote! Vote!*, 'Smear Campaign', was a case in point – presented as a press conference to announce the one issue on which, after weeks of negotiations on the Caribbean island of St Kitts, all the Northern Irish pro-Agreement parties have finally been able to agree. There are speeches by the luxuriously bearded Proinsias Mac Giolla-Cuddy of Sinn Féin and Sir John Todd of the Ulster Unionist Party, and then a banner is unfurled announcing in three languages 'More Comfortable Smear Testing for Women', which in the Ulster-Scots comes out as 'Heedin' Tae A Mair Comfy Tippin' O' Weemin'. In a particularly nice touch the actresses on stage, playing members of the SDLP (Bobbi Bradley) and the Women's Coalition (Concertina D'Arcy) don't get to speak, but simply to unfurl the banner, twirling Busby Berkeley style.

Answering his own question – and referring beyond 'Smear Campaign' – Damian Gorman stated that his responsibility as a writer was to the story. I was reminded of the introduction to Kurt Vonnegut's collection *Bagombo Snuff-Box and Other Stories*, in which the author refers to a creative-writing course he once taught. The first of its eight rules as listed by Vonnegut reads, 'Use the time of a total stranger in such a way that he or she will not feel the time was wasted.' When it comes to responsibility I suspect that this is as much as most writers will recognize.

Damian Gorman went further, however, and said that the responsibility to story is not merely a question of aesthetics, or consideration to the reader: his stories, he hoped, might encourage other people to tell their stories, or simply highlight the fact that there are other stories to be told. Italo Calvino, in the paper I quoted from earlier, says much the same thing when he states: 'Literature is necessary to politics above all when it gives a voice to whatever is without a voice.'

It is interesting how words and phrases enter into the political idiom. In recent years in Northern Ireland everyone has begun to talk not of peace, pure and simple, but of *a just and lasting peace*. We all recognize the phrase *take the gun out of Irish politics*. A lot of this can be explained by the truism that if you want people to accept your arguments you must first get them to speak your language, but there is also a sort of inflationary pressure on language whereby two words are considered to carry more weight than one, three words more weight than two. One of my current favourite formulations is *the reality is*, which is what you get when you subject *I think* to 50 per cent inflation. On a pre-election TV debate I heard the phrase four times from the representatives of four different parties. In its manifesto form at least, party politics speaks the language of an absolute truth which art long ago ceased to believe in. Calvino again: 'literature does not recognize Reality as such, only levels'.

Party politics says this is the way things are; the writer, responsible to story in the sense that Damian Gorman intends it, says, 'And like this, and like this, and like this ...' multiplied by as many times as there are people in the jurisdiction ... the world ... the course of human history.

It is perhaps inevitable that when we talk about voices even a novelist such as myself should as readily light on examples from the stage as from the page. One of the more enjoyable contributions to *Vote! Vote! Vote!* was 'Blank Canvas', by the Voices Women's Group from Turf Lodge. I don't know if this group is connected by more than geography to the JustUs Community Theatre Company who in 1997 collaborated with Dubbeljoint Theatre Company on *Binlids*, a play that sought to redress the negative and stereotyped representations of west Belfast's nationalist, or more specifically republican, community. *Binlids* made particular use of the voices of its large, mostly non-professional cast, creating a chorus of the phrases 'that's not us' and 'ask us'. Much of the play had been devised and there is no doubt that it allowed voices – stories – to be heard that had not previously been heard on the Belfast stage, or any other stage, for that matter, certainly not New York's, where the play eventually toured. Unfortunately for a play that set such store by the correction of false, or partial, impressions, it also used a pretty broad brush to portray some of the other characters: unionists, the English, even the SDLP. The group of friends with whom I went to see it, the majority of them Catholic, for what that matters, were united in feeling excluded from the experience.

This raises the question – not just of *Binlids* – of how far our responsibility in regard to character extends. Is it enough for us all merely to be saying 'this is us', in hopes that everyone else will tell us who they are?

The Belfast novelist Robert McLiam Wilson has memorably referred to the novel as 'shoe-swapping on the grand scale', and it is the never-ceasing wonder of literature down the ages that it invites us to imagine what it is to be someone other than ourselves. This is surely as true for the writer as for the reader: self-expression is part of the endeavour, but so too are exploration and empathy.

For years I used to liken the relationship between the writer and his characters to the relationship between the lawyer and his clients: you're not obliged to like them, I used to say, only to represent them as fairly as you can. I stress *used to liken, used to say*. When I went to write it again for this lecture I was troubled again by Forster's bird of truth: is that really what I think, is that really what I *do* myself?

3

Last Thursday, while wrestling with thoughts like these, I took some time out to go and hear John Banville read at Queen's University. (I am sure John Banville would be amused to hear himself portrayed as a little light relief.) It had been in my mind when it came to questions and answers to ask him, as a joke, if he had anything to say on the subject of representation and responsibility so that I could quote him here. In the end I didn't have to bother. Practically the first question he was asked – by a student of mine, as it happens – was how much he knew of his characters' lives when he started a novel. Banville looked slightly nonplussed. (Banville does nonplussed better than just about anyone I know.) Characters are not real people, he said. They are constructs of language. They don't have a future or past, they exist in the sentences.

He felt his technique might explain or be explained by his preference for Sienese over Florentine Renaissance painting: the Sienese, as he helpfully explained, being less given to foregrounding the human form, rendering it instead as part of the landscape, a mere note in the harmony of the picture. And there is a part of me that believes that too: the writer's responsibility is to the sentence, the *composition*. The larger part of me, however, like the larger part of the larger number of writers at work in Ireland north and south at present, is, I would hazard, according to John Banville's definition, by instinct more Florentine than Sienese, though we should not make the mistake of treating character as always and ever synonymous with human being.

My own last novel, *Number 5*, took its name from the door of the house, on a 1950s housing estate, in which, over the forty years of the novel's duration, five different families set up home. Each family's story is introduced by a brief estate agent's description of the house, which is not only shaped by the people who live in it, but also helps to shape them. To this extent the house itself is the book's central character. This thought in turn influenced my decision to write the entire book without using any street names, without even using the name Belfast. One Irish critic picking up on this said he didn't know what bit of Belfast it was set in, but he knew if it had been west Belfast it would have been a different novel. To which the answer is, well, yes.

I know it is bad form to talk about your own reviews, even negative reviews, like the one I'm referring to. What interested me about it, however, was less the fact that it seemed to suggest that one experience – one level of reality – had greater validity than another, or that each book ought to contain within it an acknowledgement of all the books it is not, than that it was the reverse of a question more often asked of writers, namely by what authority they write of matters of which they themselves have no direct experience.

The novel I have just finished, in contrast to *Number 5*, is set in a topographically specific east Belfast. It is tied to a series of events in the year 2000: the Bloody Sunday inquiry, then just getting underway in Derry; the opening of a new arena, the Odyssey, on land once used for shipbuilding; the feud between the UVF and UDA; the visits to Belfast of the Dalai Lama and Bill Clinton.

There are certain risks inherent in setting a book in the recent past. Nothing dates as fast as the year before last. Novels are not newspapers, of course. If you're lucky you will finish your novel within two years of the idea for it first coming to you, will see it in print nine months after that. All the same, my new novel includes the line, which I did not expect to see so soon contradicted, 'summertime is marching time, the time of Bonfires planned and improvised and of confrontations along (a popular summer term) the sectarian interfaces'. Yet last summer was almost free of major sectarian incident. On the July day that I sent the typescript to my publishers a sculpture was unveiled at one of the east Belfast interfaces: a short wall mounted with the bronzed face masks of Protestant and Catholic primary school children spelling out the word HOPE.

The novel's central character is a Presbyterian minister and its title, *That Which Was*, is taken from the Bible, the book of Judges: 'In those days there was no king in Israel, and each man did that which was right in his own eyes.' It was intended to refer to the difficulties of interpreting the past, or of reconciling our different interpretations, but I wondered for a time whether unwittingly it had summed up the book's own belatedness.

I was particularly concerned about this with *That Which Was* because as well as being tied to certain documented events, the book is informed by something far less provable: a mood of uncertainty in sections of the Protestant community. This mood is manifest at times as dejection, at other times as paranoia: the belief that there exists a conspiracy against their interests, summed up in phrases such as 'the peace process is all one way' and 'they've got everything, we've got nothing'.

I'll admit that I was troubled at times when I was writing by questions related to the title of this conference. How do you ensure that in attempting to express a mood you don't end up endorsing it, on the one hand, or reinforcing it on the other? And then too I am conscious of the fact that though my upbringing in the 1960s and 1970s was typically Belfast working-class Protestant, my profession, and, yes, my income – to say nothing of personal politics – have to an extent removed me from that background.

In the early summer of 1996, some friends and I collaborated on a documentary for Channel 4. The documentary was called *Baseball in Irish History*, a title derived from the great socialist tract of Irish republicanism, *Labour in Irish History*, by James Connolly. Belfast, in 1996, had one baseball team. There was, however, a flourishing trade in baseball bats in the city's sports shops. Scores, perhaps hundreds, of people were being beaten with these bats, many of which were customized with nails. (The term 'puncture wounds' had already become colourless with overuse.) A great many of these beatings were being administered by organizations who would profess socialist politics. Their victims were in the main young working-class men accused of 'anti-social behaviour'. The point of the documentary's title was that, to our minds, there was about as much socialism as baseball being practised in Northern Ireland in 1996.

Incidentally around this time there was a notable campaign of guerrilla graffiti against Sinn Féin-sponsored murals by relatives of Malachy Clark, a teenage glue-sniffer and victim of an IRA punishment squad who had subsequently hanged himself. Stop the Beatings, the graffiti said, over and over and over.

Nevertheless my friends and I were accused afterwards of not understanding what it was like to live in a district terrorized by thugs – the thugs referred to being not the perpetrators of the beatings, but their victims. If we knew what they had done, it was suggested, we wouldn't be so quick to condemn.

Our thesis, however, was that even if these young men were guilty of the 'anti-social' behaviour of which they were accused, they were granted no defence representation, no appeal of mitigating circumstances. Worse still, there were clear indications that the paramilitaries' concept of anti-social behaviour extended far beyond stealing cars or breaking and entering. I had first been spurred to write the proposal for *Baseball in Irish History* after a woman was beaten up by five men in her home, close to where I grew up. The woman was a lesbian. She had already been burned out of a previous flat. One of the people we interviewed was an SDLP councillor from a large housing estate in west Belfast who had been beaten after speaking out against an earlier incident in which two of his constituents had been beaten and expelled from their homes. (The same fate had befallen another SDLP councillor, two years previously, after he too spoke out against attacks on his constituents. That councillor, John Fee, lost his seat to Sinn Féin in the recent Assembly election.) The night that the documentary went out, the councillor we interviewed had his house attacked with breeze blocks.

Our conclusion was that if we turned a blind eye to the beating of 'bad boys' we relinquished the right to protest when our own habits and inclinations provoked the ire of the paramilitaries; that when they came to beat us, as the saying might have gone, there would be no one left to speak out.

At the time I began writing *That Which Was* the beatings – and worse – were still numerous enough that I kept a diary of them:

> 21.04.01: Waterside, Derry. Man murdered by up to four gunmen, one possibly carrying a long-barrelled gun. Suspected victim of DAAD. [That's Direct Action Against Drugs, a cover name for the IRA.]
> Vulcan Street, Mountpottinger. Thirty-five-year-old man shot in feet, hands and elbows.

> 22.04.01: Fifteen-year-old taken from his home to Westrock park, where he was beaten by two men, suffering fractures to his hand and bruising.

> 02.05.01: Young man abducted and beaten in the Whiteabbey area. Severe injuries to arms and legs.

04.05.01: Thirty-eight-year-old murdered leaving sister's house in Stephen Street (off Library Street), a couple of hundred yards from Royal Avenue.

07.05.01: Thirty-seven-year-old man shot in both legs in an attack (at 10.30 a.m.) at his home in Malvern Way.

09.05.01: Man admitted to hospital with gunshot wound to right leg after a shooting incident in the Taughmonagh area.

17.05.01: Sixteen-year-old boy shot in both ankles in a house in Parkhead Crescent, Newry.

21.05.01: Nineteen-year-old found with gunshot wounds to both ankles in Edgar Street, east Belfast, shortly after 9 p.m.

23.05.01: *Irish Times* report of Newry beating six days earlier: 'Eight masked men shot the teenager with a low-calibre weapon and hit him on the head with a hatchet.'

So numerous were the attacks at this time that the novel's working title was *Punishment* (a title which I considered also encompassed the climate of inquiry exemplified by the Bloody Sunday tribunal). One of the storylines running through the novel is of a young man beaten by men wielding bats and – for reasons which my minister speculates might be related to his alleged crime – a wheel brace. The punishers have at times been positively Taliban-esque in the literalness of their punishments.

By the time the novel was finished, the punishment attacks had diminished considerably in number. There had always been an argument that they only existed in any case because of a failure of policing: once all sections of our community could give their allegiance and their trust to the police service there would be no need for the men with bats.

There is a contrary argument, however, which says that for as long as the organizations to which the men with bats belong continue to exist, there will exist too the potential for their freelance version of justice. As Sinn Féin edges closer to endorsing policing arrangements and the majority of unionists, despite the posturing of the DUP, are at the very least resigned to them, the question has to be asked, who is still to be appealed to? The batmen? Do we just want to get rid of one lot of human-rights abusers in order to replace them with another?

Because – whether it is connected to the end of the election campaigns, or whether these things are simply seasonal, dark nights providing better cover – the beatings and shootings are on the increase again.

The most recent writing on the wall where I live went up about a fortnight ago. Mark McClure, it says, shot for housebreaking. When I read this on one wall I thought maybe it was a complaint, an expression of outrage. When I read it on a second, I thought maybe it was the equivalent of a newspaper headline, a matter of grim fact. When I read it on a third, then a fourth, I realized that it was both a justification and a warning to other budding Mark McClures: if we can do this to him we can do it to anyone.

To adapt, or rather mangle, Flaubert – Mark McClure, shot for housebreaking, *c'est toi.*

You'd be hard pressed not to conclude that the mural makeover intended to present a kinder face of east Belfast loyalist paramilitarism was as much a fantasy as anything in C.S. Lewis's works.

4

Feed the words 'bird' and 'shadow' into your computer search engines and you might find, as I did, a Tibetan Buddhist saying that curiously complements the E.M. Forster analogy with which I began:

When the eagle soars up, high above the earth
Its shadow for the while is nowhere to be seen;
Yet bird and shadow are still linked. So too our actions:
When conditions come together their effects are clearly seen.

One of the best passages of writing by any Northern Irish writer in the last several decades is in *Ripley Bogle* by a writer I have already mentioned, Robert McLiam Wilson:

Think about killing someone. Go on. Some guy. Some poor sorry sod. Anyone. Think about killing him. Take your time. Think about it. Think about his life, his mom and dad. Think about his children. Think about all the boffing he's done, the breasts he's kissed, the thighs he's creased, all that kind of thing. Think about his toothaches, his constipation, his beerbelly. Think about the books he hasn't read, the people he hasn't met and the places he hasn't seen. Think about his vanity and ignorance, his greed and selfishness. Think about his industry and his kindness, his clemency and tenderness. Think about him buying his unfashionable shoes and his painfully vulgar jackets. Think about his bad jokes and embarrassments. Think about his baby talk and teeth, his flask and sandwiches, his favourite meals, his cigarettes, his football team, his dirty socks, his face and his span of years. Think about him. Think about his life.
Think about killing him. Think about that.
What's worth that, eh? Who needs that?

Almost fifteen years after that was published there is still a crying need for writing that will deconstruct the lethal one-liners and the self-aggrandizing myths of the muralists, that will invite readers, by identification with invented characters, to think about the link between the bird and the shadow, between action and effect, between what is portrayed and the cost in human terms of what is actually done.

(Spring 2004)

'She's live, she's modern ...'

ANN MARIE HOURIHANE

1

Thérèse Martin believed in relics. In 1887, on a pilgrimage to Rome with her father and sister, she stopped in Padua to venerate the tongue of St Anthony. The tongue was a first-class relic: that is, a body part of a deceased saint. (Second-class relics are objects that have been in close physical contact with the flesh of a deceased saint; third-class relics include cloth that has touched a first- or second-class relic.) In May 1925, twenty-eight years after her death, Thérèse Martin's own bones were divided, a consequence of her canonization that year. Some of the bones were taken from Lisieux, in Normandy, where she had been a Carmelite nun, to the Pope in Rome. Her sternum was placed in a reclining wax figure representing her last sleep. The rest were placed in a luxurious reliquary, paid for by 'the people of Brazil' under the guidance of a French missionary priest. Later, Pope Pius XI requested that Thérèse's right hand and right arm, which had written the book *Story of a Soul*, be placed in a separate reliquary. In 1997, the centenary of her death, Thérèse's bones were divided again. A new reliquary, a replica of the first, was built. It too had been paid for by Brazilian devotees, and it is known as the Centenary Reliquary. A portion of the bones was placed inside it, within a silver case that had been dipped in gold. The Centenary Reliquary weighs four hundred pounds and is protected by a perspex shell. This is the reliquary that toured Ireland between 15 April and 2 July 2001.

There have always been plenty of relics of St Thérèse of Lisieux.

Even before her death, in 1897, her sisters were harvesting her hair, her handkerchiefs, her fingernail clippings. In the infirmary of the Carmelite convent at Lisieux, Thérèse told her fellow nuns to save the petals of a rose 'because they will help you to give pleasure later on. Do not lose one of them.' After her death the floorboards of her convent cell and the wooden slats of her bed were broken up and distributed amongst the faithful. The convent began mass-producing relics of Thérèse. Her sister Céline (Mother Geneviève of the Holy Face), who kept a record of these things, was amazed to find that in the twelve months from July 1909, 183,348 little pictures and 36,612 small relics had been sent out, on request.

The pictures produced in Lisieux by Céline at that time were issued when there were good photographs of Thérèse available, some of them dating from her time in the convent (we see her as Joan of Arc in a dramatic production by the novices), some of them taken by Céline herself. Céline had even taken photographs of Thérèse's corpse. It seems that a decision had been made to paint an amalgam of 'the best expressive elements contained in various photographs'. Production of relics and pictures had started ahead of time: in other words before Thérèse's cause for canonization had been launched on an unsuspecting, but ultimately enthusiastic, Catholic Church. The pictures were in such poor taste that they turned Thérèse, long before her canonization, into the patron saint of kitsch, a position that she could be said to occupy to this day. As Ida Friederike Görres, in her 1959 book *The Hidden Face: A Study of St Thérèse of Lisieux*, put it: 'These pictures enjoyed enormous popularity among simple souls – and caused aesthetic shudders among the less simple. Probably they were instrumental in erecting the stoutest wall between more intellectual Catholics and a deeper knowledge of the saint.' To the middle classes, taste is everything. To the devout and to the Church authorities, it is nothing.

The visit of this saint's corporeal remains to Ireland in 2001 – they toured the country in a specially adapted Mercedes called the Thérèsemobile – inspired devotion and discomfort in almost equal measure. Three million people are said to have visited the reliquary, to have been wheeled towards it, to have kissed it, to have laid their comatose children beside it, to have placed a rose (Thérèse's flower) on it. The *Sunday Business Post* called it the biggest mass movement Ireland had ever seen. As Thérèse's reliquary was given a military escort from the Rosslare ferry, some muttered not so much about state religion as state voodoo; for them, displays of Catholic enthusiasm in Ireland today are, as it were, too close to the bone. During the visit of Pope John Paul II in 1979, the pontiff was flanked in the Popemobile by Bishop Eamon Casey and Father Michael Cleary, both of whom, we later learned, had fathered sons. In the nineties, revelations of institutionalized physical and sexual abuse of children in the care of religious personnel made Casey and Cleary look merely hypocritical. St Thérèse was a reminder of a type of innocent devotion, and perhaps a type of gullibility, that a lot of people wanted to forget.

'We had thought this type of thing was dying out. ... did not such a figure as Thérèse, and the host of her venerators and proclaimers, embody the very type of bourgeois Christianity which we were resisting, which in our youth we had fought to overcome[?]' That was Ida Friederike Görres in 1959. In 2001 Bishop Brendan Comiskey, chairperson of the Relics Visit Organising Committee, dismissed the superior carping of what he called 'self-styled intellectuals' with regard to the religious activities of what he called 'the peasantry' – the Bishop being a member of the peasantry, naturally. Right on cue Kevin Myers, in the *Irish Times*, asked if the spectacle of Irish soldiers acting as 'pallbearers' for 'an expensive catafalque' came from 1951, the darkest days of an authoritarian Church in Ireland. Myers cited the defeat of the Mother and Child health-care scheme in that year, when the government had capitulated to the Catholic hierarchy. 'Those days are over, we have been repeatedly assured: so if that is the case, why are the soldiers of this Republic, in full ceremonial dress, parading a Catholic ossuary through Rosslare town in the year 2001?' It's a good question.

Thérèse Martin had three blood sisters amongst the Carmelite community at Lisieux: Pauline, Marie and Céline. (A fourth sister, Léonie, the outsider of the family, joined another order of nuns.) The Martin sisters came from a family obsessed with religion. At the diocesan tribunal inquiring into Thérèse's life and virtues, a preliminary to canonization, her sisters testified to the devout nature of their household. Marie described the family home as a place where 'detachment from the good things of the world' was encouraged.

Thérèse had a horrible death at the age of twenty-four. She died of what was then called galloping consumption, tuberculosis that had attacked not just her lungs but her intestines. She was unable to receive communion for the last six weeks of her life, because she was vomiting so much. A nun whom Thérèse had supervised as assistant novice mistress left the deathbed, because she could not bear to witness such agony; the prioress had refused to allow a doctor to administer morphine. Thérèse was remarkably brave. As an even younger woman she had prayed, 'Take me before I can commit the slightest voluntary fault.' (This was part of the prayer that she had pinned over her heart the day of her profession.) Later, in the third section of *Story of a Soul*, which she wrote when she was already ill: 'I never did ask God for the favour of dying young, but I always hoped that this would be His will for me.' When she started to cough blood one Good Friday night, she later wrote, 'It was like the sweet and distant murmur that announced the Bridegroom's arrival.'

She was buried not in the convent grounds but in the town graveyard. A recent law forbade interment in private graveyards, and the Martins' maternal uncle Isidore Guérin had bought a plot specially for the Carmelite nuns. Thérèse was the first nun to be buried there. She was buried deep, because the grave was intended to hold four corpses. Before she died one of her fellow nuns had said to Thérèse that her physical remains might remain incorrupt – a sure sign of sanctity. But Thérèse had said she'd rather decompose like everyone else.

Her sisters prevailed on their prioress to erect a special headstone on Thérèse's grave, bearing a saying of hers which endures as one of her slogans to this day: 'I will spend my heaven doing good on earth.' No other Carmelite nun in the graveyard was to get such an unusual memorial. The headstone made the grave easier to find. The fact that Thérèse was buried in a public graveyard meant that members of the public could visit, as they soon did in enormous numbers.

The main reason for the visitors, and for Thérèse's vertiginous rise to sainthood, was *Story of a Soul*. The book, which appeared on the first anniversary of her death, was the result of assiduous work by her blood sisters within the convent. They can be said to have commissioned it, edited it, and censored it, to have distributed it and championed it. In this the three Martin sisters who remained at the Lisieux Carmel were extraordinarily prescient. They were public-relations geniuses at a time when public relations had yet to be invented. Like many geniuses they used events over which they had no control – the expansion of the missions, the First World War – as fuel for their own project. Their project was Thérèse.

She had been a precocious child. At eight she was in a class of fourteen-year-olds. Like many gifted children she was bullied there. She was withdrawn from the school by her devoted father and so, although she was bright, she was essentially uneducated. After she left school she studied history and science, but 'I confined myself to a certain number of hours, unwilling to go beyond in order to mortify my intense desire to know things.' Talking one day in the convent with Pauline and Marie, Thérèse was reminiscing about her childhood. Marie, the eldest sister, asked her to write down what she remembered. The first part of *Story of a Soul* was addressed to Pauline, the second part to Marie, and the third and final part to the convent prioress, Mother Mary Gonzague.

When a Carmelite nun dies it is customary to circulate a short obituary notice to other convents, so that her soul will be prayed for. It was the Martin sisters' intention that *Story of a Soul* should be circulated in this way after Thérèse's death. They also wanted it published in book form. Their uncle Isidore Guérin paid for the publication of the first 2,000 copies. The only snag was that Mother Mary Gonzague – of whom one cannot help feeling rather fond – insisted 'for the sake of uniformity' that all three sections of the book now be addressed to her. The Martin sisters bitterly resented this, and never forgave her. But they were playing the long game.

In 1910 Thérèse's body was exhumed for the first time and it was found to have decomposed, although her outsize Carmelite habit (she had virtually starved to death) was almost intact. The bones, which were said by some witnesses to exude a sweet fragrance, were placed in a coffin of oak and lead and re-interred in an individual grave in the same Carmelite plot in the town cemetery. In 1917 the remains were exhumed again so that a church tribunal could examine Thérèse's bones. Her sister Céline – tough girl – was one of the nuns from the convent who cleansed the bones and wrapped them in fine linen. The bones were placed in an oak casket, inside a lead coffin, inside a rosewood sarcophagus, and interred again in a brick-lined grave. As Thérèse moved nearer and nearer to sainthood her bones became more and more valuable. The third exhumation was in 1923. This time her body was to be interred within the convent walls. Devotion to Thérèse had grown in the intervening years and a crowd of thousands followed the new lead coffin to the convent, reciting the Rosary. There were no hymns or music, because Thérèse was not yet a saint. It was said that when the grave was opened there was a smell of roses, and a paralyzed little girl was cured; in the Carmel chapel a young blind girl was said to have been cured.

3

'One of the things I noticed from the Thérèsemobile', says Father J. Linus Ryan, a Carmelite priest at Terenure College in Dublin and the national co-ordinator of the tour of St Thérèse's relics, 'was lots and lots of little altars. With pictures and statues on them which weren't the best in art, and that were chipped and old looking. And I

thought to myself, "That's in that family for fifty or sixty years."'
Father Ryan remembers his own family's picture of St Thérèse, at
his childhood home in Kildare town. 'It was a gooey kind of one, all
sequins. I remember running up and down the hallway, trying to
hide from her eyes.'

Father Ryan organized the first 'Eurovision' televised Mass,
which was broadcast from the Carmelite church in Whitefriars
Street, Dublin. In 1973, on the centenary of St Thérèse's birth, he
organized the celebration there. He has no doubt as to why St
Thérèse has been so popular in modern Ireland. 'She's live, she's
modern, there are pictures of her as a little girl. Both houses that
she lived in as a child are still standing. She played on a swing, the
swing is still there.'

As leader of the Carmelite community in Kildare, where his family is from, Father Ryan had tried re-launch St Brigid, the greatest
female figure of early Christian Ireland, as a saint for modern times.
'But it's a bit contrived,' he says. 'You're trying all the time.' He
remembers a colleague of his, who had done a lot of research on
Brigid, talking enthusiastically about how the saint would travel
across the plains of Kildare, with her blonde hair streaming in the
wind. 'I said to him, Brian, she was a brunette. Brian was bringing
his own image to it, you see. With Thérèse you're all working from
the same sources.'

At the turn of the century, according to Mary Kenny in her book
Goodbye to Catholic Ireland, the devotion of ordinary Irish people was
'very particularly centred on pious French women'. She names St
Bernadette, St Thérèse, St Catherine Labouré (foundress of the
Miraculous Medal), St Margaret Mary Alacogue (foundress of the cult
of the Sacred Heart), and St Louise de Marillac. 'People say the Irish
are more inclined to worship foreigners,' says Father Ryan. The Irish
saints are 'too far back', he says. 'Then you have Thérèse and her
golden ringlets.' In other words, it is an unequal contest.

Pilgrimages, outdoor devotions and night vigils, such as those
that marked the tour of the relics of St Thérèse, have a long history
in Ireland. The traditional climb of Croagh Patrick takes place at

night. To the old Irish, says John J. O'Riordan in his book *Irish Catholics: Tradition and Transition*, 'it was always sweeter to make a pilgrimage than to say one's prayers at home'. That is still true, as the keepers of Lough Derg, Croagh Patrick and Knock well know. To this day Croagh Patrick is a secular devotion. It was never particularly supported by the Church authorities, who at one point during the nineteenth century prohibited the vigil Mass.

Along with these grand penances voluntarily undertaken, there was an intimacy about the older Church. As part of the custom of 'holding stations' in an area, Mass would often be heard in private houses. With its love of diminutives, the Irish language made things – at least things it loved – small. St Ide's poem is addressed to Íosagán (Little Jesus). According to O'Riordan, Jesus was often addressed in this way, or as Son of Mary, in familiar and intimate style. Religious poems would be spontaneously recited by Massgoers. It was not unusual for Jesus to be addressed as a brother or a neighbour would be. This was a Church, then, that was locally based and communal. It was not the sacramental, Mass-going church that we are familiar with, but parts of its legacy have been silently maintained.

The reliquary of St Thérèse visited every one of the twenty-six dioceses in the island of Ireland, coming to rest in the cathedral of each diocese and in whatever Carmelite community was in the vicinity. It flew to Lough Derg by helicopter. It entered Mountjoy prison. It went into Northern Ireland and was protected by the RUC. Once he had obtained the bishops' approval for the visit, Father Ryan dealt with the administrators of the diocesan cathedrals. He won't exactly say that he met with resistance. 'I've led the national pilgrimage to Lisieux for the last forty years,' he says. 'Thérèse kept at them. I felt if we were going to bring the spirituality of St Thérèse then we should bring it to the people.' A mobile library of religious books was part of the cortège. The retrofitting of the Thérèsemobile was paid for by what Father Ryan calls 'a family of means'. He doesn't know how much it cost. Hotel accommodation for Father Ryan and the drivers was paid for by another sponsor. 'They just gave me the credit card. And we got another £3,000 for diesel.'

Some things about the visit of the reliquary did not surprise him at all. National co-ordinators of tours in other countries had told him, 'Think big, and it will be even bigger than you think.' Also, 'Be ready for the confessions; there will be enormous numbers, and the quality will be high.' He told Don Mullan, author of *A Gift of Roses: Memories of the Visit to Ireland of St Thérèse*, that when he was reporting on the visit to the Lisieux authorities, he had emphasized the success of the night vigils around the reliquary. 'The Irish are natural night-owls, in contrast to the people of France who go to bed shortly after seven o'clock in the rural areas. I said people who came back from work had time to shower and dress up and have their evening meal, and hadn't the constraint of trying to beat a church closing deadline; they knew that, no matter what time they arrived in the evening or into the small hours of the morning, they would find the church open.'

Mullan's book contains a remarkable anecdote related by the main driver of the Thérèsemobile, Pat Sweeney, a retired Irish army regimental sergeant major. (Of the complaints about the army escort for the reliquary, Pat Sweeney told Don Mullan: 'What a lot of these people would want to realize is that we prided ourselves on being Catholic.') Pat Sweeney also told Don Mullan:

> In Doneraile I saw a woman running along the side of the street, and I thought she had two heads. She heard that the relics were coming and she picked up her sister, who had no use of her limbs, and she threw her over her shoulder. She was running along the road and from behind you would think she had two heads … there were beads of sweat on her. I said, 'My God, do you not have a wheelchair?' She said, 'No, I hadn't time. I thought I was going to miss the relics and it's very important to my sister.'

Father Ryan produced information sheets, a website, press packs, a souvenir brochure that contained a 'vision statement', and countless leaflets. He agreed to the making of a video of the visit which became the surprise best-seller of the subsequent Christmas. Father

Ryan got a People of the Year Award, the Kildare Man of the Year Award, and a special medal from the Papal Nuncio on behalf of the Pope. He deserves it all, tough and clear-sighted as he is in his small rooms at the end of a long corridor in Terenure College. He hands me a brown envelope to hold all the printed material he is giving me. He has heard me on the radio talking about the St Thérèse video, and he's a realist. 'I don't mind a bit of satire,' he says.

4

St Thérèse was not a great mystic or reformer, like her fellow Carmelites St John of the Cross or St Teresa of Avilà. She was not a theologian. She was too sickly to be a missionary. Her social work seems to have consisted of helping an elderly nun to the refectory, and of smiling at another nun whom she did not like. Both events were minutely recorded.

The very narrowness of her experience is at the heart of her appeal. She inspires love rather than awe. Everything about 'the Little Flower', as St Thérèse called herself, has been made to seem small. She has been loved for this reason. Her life was a relentless effort to make herself small, like Alice in Wonderland. 'Yet I feel within me other vocations,' she wrote. 'THE PRIEST, THE APOSTLE, THE DOCTOR, THE MARTYR.' (Thérèse loved capital letters.) She narrates her time in the convent in Lisieux as a catalogue of petty triumphs and defeats, and of female masochism, which will be familiar to even the most amnesiac convent girl. (But the intensity of her language can be startling: 'One day when I particularly desired to be humiliated, a novice took it upon herself to satisfy me and she did it so well that I was immediately reminded of Shimei cursing David. ... And my soul enjoyed the bitter food served up to it in such abundance.') She may have been a lion, but she amputated parts of herself to become a lamb. Her emotional reach only came back to her when she suffered her crisis of faith, which she recorded.

St Thérèse was cut to fit the Catholic Church's image of virtuous females. As Ida Friederike Görres points out, old editions of *Story of a Soul* contain the following description of her: 'She was tall of figure. She had blonde hair, grey-green eyes, a small mouth, fine and regular features. Her countenance, the colour of the lily, was harmoniously carved, well-proportioned, always sweetly serene, as if stamped with heavenly peace. Her carriage was full of dignity, at once simple and graceful.'

The physical description is demonstrably false – those photos again – but it shows that women could work as hard as men to present a saccharine fairytale of female sanctity, even women as tough, as determined and as able as Thérèse's older sisters. Thérèse had to win every contest of femininity, including the physical beauty contest, and then reject beauty's snare. Thus on her visit to Rome she is supposed to have been courted by a young man who found her physically attractive. He was gently rebuffed by the fourteen-year-old Thérèse, who, after all, had gone to Rome to plead with the Holy Father for permission to enter a convent at the precocious age of fifteen.

It was also on this visit to Rome, apparently, that Thérèse first looked critically at priests. Unsurprisingly, her parents had an inordinate respect for the clergy. Céline Martin later said of her parents' attitude, 'I have never seen the like of it. I remember as a child considering priests something like gods, so accustomed was I to seeing them placed altogether beyond ordinary mortals.' We do not know in any detail what Thérèse witnessed on the family pilgrimage to Rome (her father and Céline were with her). 'It was then', Pauline told the beatification hearing, 'that she saw what weak and frail men priests were, in spite of the dignity that raised them above the very angels.' Or, as the Reverend Vernon Johnson has it in his horrible Catholic Truth Society pamphlet *St Teresa of Lisieux*, 'They were not wholly freed from every weakness of human nature.' He continues, 'Above all her help was lavished on priests.' Indeed, the male clergy seem to have been relieved to have a female saint of their own. Who knows what loneliness and guilt they shared with her?

'Pray to her,' said Pope Benedict XV. 'It is her vocation to teach priests to love Jesus Christ.' A remarkable statement. In 1915, a full decade before her canonization, Benedict had had a special medal of Thérèse struck for the French soldiers in the trenches. Thus Thérèse was promoted, or simply adopted, as a figure for male devotion. Father Ryan flatly denies my suggestion that she is a women's saint. He says that *Story of a Soul* 'is very sugary and off-putting, even for a woman', but he understands Pauline's enthusiasm for it. 'She knew it was a marvellous work, a little gem, a spiritual hit,' he says. According to Rev. Johnson, Pope Pius XI, who canonized her, viewed Thérèse as 'the beloved star of his pontificate' and 'his consoling angel in all his trials', and had a statue of her erected in his garden in Rome.

5

Thérèse's father, Louis Martin, was a gentle, shy man who had tried to join a monastery but was refused because he did not have Latin. Thérèse's mother, Zélie, a more dynamic character, tried to join a convent but was refused for reasons not recorded. Both Louis's and Zélie's fathers had been soldiers.

Louis became a watchmaker, and was so rarely seen in female company that neighbours assumed he had taken a vow of celibacy. Zélie started a lace-making business, which she ran with such flair that later Louis would give up his own business to work in it. (In most literature about Thérèse her mother's profession is given, misleadingly, as 'lacemaker'.) Thérèse grew up in a prosperous household, with maids and private lessons – Céline, for example, had painting lessons. When Thérèse entered the convent she was completely ignorant of housework.

It is possible that Zélie had started the lace business in order to provide herself with a dowry. She seems to have selected Louis, with his mother's co-operation, as her husband. At first Louis wanted what was known as a Josephite marriage – that is, a marriage without sex. It took ten months for Zélie, or perhaps a confessor, to persuade him otherwise. They went on to have nine children. Zélie and Louis attended five-thirty Mass each morning – 'the poor people's Mass', as they called it. Zélie also observed every religious fast, whether pregnant or not. Both Martins performed regular acts of charity. Zélie wrote to Pauline – her favourite daughter, and the one who was said to resemble her most – 'how dreadful death is in a house where there is no religion'. Her own faith was so perfect that her neighbours said she did not grieve even when her children died; she lost four, two girls and two boys, one little girl at the age of five. Zélie frankly admitted that one of her ambitions was to see some of her surviving daughters enter the religious life.

Monsieur Martin gave some of his daughters nicknames associated with his trade – Pauline was Little Pearl, for example – but Thérèse was always Little Queen, something that was later to disturb the canonization authorities greatly, as they thought this would have made a girl-child uppity. But her sisters were ready for this. Although Thérèse was their father's favourite, they said, he was always careful not to have the child praised to her face, and once upbraided a passer-by for giving Thérèse a compliment. As Pauline later told the hearings, 'When she was a child we took great care to train her in humility and carefully avoided praising her.'

When Thérèse was four and a half, Zélie Martin died of breast cancer at the age of forty-six. Thérèse had been the only one of her children she had been unable to breast-feed, and she had probably had the tumour for years. Like her daughter twenty years later, Zélie in her final illness moved to a room at some distance from the others, so that her cries would not disturb them. Her daughters saw her, white and sweating, kneeling to say her rosary. Her pain was so intense that she could not lie prostrate for more than fifteen minutes at a time.

After Zélie's death Pauline took over the rearing of Thérèse, punishing her by forbidding her to take her afternoon walk with their father, even though she knew that this would upset their father more than it upset the preternaturally obedient Thérèse. When Pauline entered the Carmelite convent, Thérèse seems to have experienced some sort of nervous collapse. She was ten years old. She had already experienced visions, despite Pauline's later declarations that as a child Thérèse was 'not a bit imaginative'. In a vision she had seen her father, older and more stooped, with a veil over his head. Later on Louis Martin had several strokes and went mad with what his daughters called cerebral paralysis. The poor man covered his head with a towel, or handkerchief, perhaps from shame. Neighbours said his insanity had been triggered by the fact that four of his five daughters had entered a convent, a sort of punishment for his pious hopes coming true. It is said that one of the photographs of Thérèse in the convent, as a plump sixteen-year-old novice, was taken purely to console M. Martin. It was taken by a priest, presumably with the permission of the prioress. But Louis Martin's daughters, together in the convent parlour, stoutly denied that their vocations had brought about his collapse. They were much embarrassed and distraught at their father's madness, but Thérèse was the most low-key, talking about it the least. Louis was hospitalized and only emerged when he became too weak to be disruptive. At that time he was released into Céline's care. Céline joined her sisters in the Lisieux Carmel just two months after he died.

Louis and Zélie Martin have stout supporters in the cause of their own canonization. In 1994 they achieved venerable status on the ladder to sainthood. 'The Pope was hoping that during the Year of the Family they'd produce a first-class miracle,' says Father Ryan. 'But it was not to be.' You can't help hoping that the Martins will make it, partly because they suffered so much for their religious faith, and partly because you can imagine them enjoying sainthood enormously, it being perhaps one of the few things they never prayed for.

6

'"O Little Flower, in this hour show your power." Say this sixteen times and St Thérèse will locate a lost object for you.' So began a report on the visit of St Thérèse in the *Irish Times* of 1 May 2001. The narrative of Thérèse's visit is a litany of these magical prayers – almost spells – and of spectacular religious faith. Thérèse promised that when she died she would let fall a shower of roses, and roses were everywhere. The scent of roses is taken to indicate her presence. Don Mullan smelled it in his car on the way from escorting the reliquary back to France. In his book many people testify to having smelled it. Nuns smelled it in the convent in Lisieux after Thérèse's death. Her sister Pauline hard-headed as ever, told the canonization hearings: 'I was afraid of illusions, and anyway as prioress, I felt it my duty to pay little attention to what the sisters were telling me.'

In her final weeks Thérèse had said: 'Pray for those who are sick and dying, little sisters. If you only knew what goes on! How little it takes to lose control of oneself! I would not have believed it before.' The sick came, or were brought, in great numbers to see her reliquary when it toured Ireland. The video of the visit contains footage of Mrs Anne Joyce bringing her comatose son Christy to the reliquary. Mrs Joyce tells the cameras, 'Where there's hope there's life.' She is a Traveller. Christy had been catatonic and physically disabled since contracting meningitis. Some months after the visit, the boy died.

One woman told Don Mullan that she was cured of a cancerous mole on her face having touched it with a petal of a rose that had brushed the perspex shell encasing the reliquary. Her doctor said, 'These things happen.'

Works discussed in this essay
IDA FRIEDERIKE GÖRRES, *The Hidden Face: A Study of St Thérèse of Lisieux*, London: Burns & Oates, 1959.
REV. VERNON JOHNSON, *St Teresa of Lisieux*, Catholic Truth Society, n.d.
CHRISTOPHER O'MAHONY, ed. and trs., *St Thérèse of Lisieux, by those who knew her: Testimonies from the Process of Beatification*, Dublin: Veritas, 1975.
JOHN J. O'RIORDAN, *Irish Catholics: Tradition and Transition*, Dublin: Veritas, 1980.

ST THÉRÈSE OF LISIEUX, *Story of a Soul: The Autobiography of St Thérèse of Lisieux*, trs. John Clarke, 3rd. edn, Washington, DC: ICS Publications, 1996.

AUDREY HEALY and EUGENE MCCAFFREY, *St Thérèse in Ireland*, Dublin: Columba, 2001.

DON MULLAN, *A Gift of Roses: Memories of the Visit to Ireland of St Thérèse*, Dublin: Wolfhound, 2001.

(Spring 2002)

Barcelona, 1975

COLM TÓIBÍN *Colm Tóibín*

At first there were two. They watched me easily, nonchalantly. They were good-looking and, like actors, utterly alert to themselves, dressed I remember now – and I may be wrong about some of these details – in black and white, one with a waistcoat, the other with a granddad shirt. One was taller; both were thin and lithe. The taller one was hungrier-looking, cheekier; the other seemed content to wallow in his own sallow beauty. They were watching me now and they wanted something from me and I was not sure what that was.

I was twenty then. I had left Dublin the day after my final exams, taken the boat first to Holyhead and then the night train to London and then the plane – my first plane journey – to Barcelona. I was raw and unhappy and I missed home. Sometimes in those early days in the city I stayed in bed all day, listening to the strange sounds – metal blinds being pulled up and down, motorbikes, voices – wishing I was back in my old bed in Hatch Street with everything familiar and easy. I dreamed one night that I found a great balloon to take me over the Pyrenees and the Bay of Biscay to the familiar comfort of Dublin. I dreamed of watching all the kingdoms of the world from this great height, all made golden by the prospect of abandoning the daily ordeal and the constant excitement of being in a great city alone for an indeterminate time without a word of the language.

The two of them were watching me still. To make sure I was not imagining that they were somehow in pursuit, I stood up from the seat and moved slowly down the Ramblas towards the port. They stood up from the seat opposite and, when I looked behind, I saw that they were following. I sat down again on another seat and they sat brazenly opposite me. When one of them smiled, I returned the smile. They were not threatening me; they were not frightening; and they were not going to go away. By now I was not sure, in any case, that I wanted them to.

The taller one walked over and sat beside me. Soon we discovered we had a problem. I had no Spanish and he had no English. When I spoke in faltering school French, he shook his head and pointed to his friend and called him over. His friend had no English either, but he spoke fluent French. Soon a number of facts had become clear: they lived nearby in Plaza Real; one was a painter; the other, the smaller one, was studying literature. They were not surprised when I said that I was alone in the city and was living in a *pensión* nearby and looking for work as a teacher. They spoke to me like they would never let me go.

We must have had a drink, or spoken at greater length. But it is also possible that, trusting and needy, we made our way quickly to the apartment on the top floor of a corner building on Plaza Real, an apartment that had within it, like a maze, other smaller apartments and locked rooms, one of which was owned by the painter. The student of literature's room, which had its own bathroom as well, was across the badly lit and dingy corridor.

I did not know what we were going to do when we went back. Talk some more, I suppose. Have a drink, perhaps. But I must have really known. I was not that innocent, even though I had never done anything like this before. I suppose what I really did not know is how or when or in what combination it would be done. I know that I eventually spent time naked with a bed with both of them separately, but I am unclear now about the order or the precise circumstances.

I know that we were in the painter's room. I thought his paintings were bad, too literal and crude, but the room itself was wonderful, laden with strange objects, prints and posters and funny ornaments. There was a small stereo and one classical record, among the collection of jazz and rock and old Spanish songs. It was

Beethoven's Triple Concerto. I asked them to put it on and it became the theme music for my visits to that room over the subsequent months, the only music I heard at that time. The lovely cello coming in last was more than an aspect of the pleasure I felt and the things I learned in that room; it stands in for them now, its chords and cadences and sudden shifts are enough to conjure up the scene in all its newness and excitement and glory.

The painter's room comes to me in two guises. It was a small, intimate, lamp-lit room, dominated by a large bed; it was also a large room where many people could happily sleep. I don't know how it could have been both. That first night it was a small room. There may have been a chair. The music was on. One of us was sitting on the bed. The painter was moving in and out of the room as the other, the one interested in literature, moved towards me and began to kiss me. There was a smell from his breath as powerful as the Triple Concerto. It was a smell I had never encountered before – the smell of garlic – and even now, were I to smell it from someone's breath, it would carry an erotic charge with it, a sense of pure easy pleasure, beautiful lips and tongues and teeth, and the promise of soft warm skin and sex.

I was unhappy that the painter might return and find us kissing, and when he did, I moved away, as though we had been caught by a parent or a teacher. This amused them. Barcelona in 1975 was a foreign country, I soon learned, they did things differently there. I tried to work out the rules. These two young men were friends, not lovers. They seemed to have followed me without discussing which of them might entertain me when we got home. They had no interest in being together with me, but they were not embarrassed at being watched by the other in this, the preliminary stage.

So we kissed again, this time as though it did not matter who was watching. I do not know if that was the night we made love – I think we made love only once – or if it was some other night. I do not know if that same night I ended up in another room, a much smaller room, with the painter, and watched him growing bored with me, having begun with an immense and all-governing passion, kissing me, holding me, running his hands over me. I do not know if we even came to orgasm together, but if we did, it was the very end of our sexual time together. The passion we had was a small game and we ended it soon after it began.

That night, or some night soon afterwards, I fucked the literary guy on the painter's bed. He was by far the more beautiful of the two when he was naked; he was smoother, more feminine, with a much thinner waist and beautiful long legs. His arse was hairless, almost fleshy. He kissed with slow passion and responded slowly, carefully and deliberately to every movement. His lips and his breath were what I loved most.

In a drawer on the right-hand side of the bed he found the jar of vaseline and he rubbed it on his arsehole and on my dick and then he turned away from me, face down, his arms stretched out in front of him, his head to the side. I had only done this once before. I presumed it was easy. I lay on top of him and shoved my dick in hard, with an aggression he might not have seen in me before. He screamed and turned, yelling at me in French to take it out, take it out, I was hurting him. When he was free of me, he turned away, holding himself and moaning. The idea that I had hurt him made me excited, but I was also alarmed that he would not speak to me or turn towards me. I did not think that I had done anything wrong.

Somehow, over the next few minutes, the French language ceased to work for us. He had to make sounds and gesture with his hands to emphasize that I had pushed in too suddenly, too fast and too hard and I must go in more slowly, gradually and gently. All of these instructions took time. It did not occur to me that I could lose interest in finishing what I had begun. I remained eager, ready to be educated, longing to fuck him some more. I was thus ready to start again and do as he said as he turned once more and put more vaseline on his arsehole. He wanted to be fucked again and I knew now that he did not want to be hurt. In trying to oblige, I nontheless made him wince as I put my dick inside him as fully as I could and began as slowly as possible to fuck him, trying to keep going and going until he seemed to be both hurt and happy at the same time.

As the old dictator began to die, we three tried to meet again. A few times I turned up at the apartment and rang the various bells and was let in by an electronic switch, only to find a stranger on the top floor. A few times I left a note. Once, the guy I had fucked turned up at my *pensión* and left a note for me. My landlady was curious about him, made nods and gestures as if to say that a strange and interesting man had called for me. Once I met the painter on the Ramblas; he signalled that he was in a hurry but would see me at the apartment later.

I wonder if the next time I found my friends in residence was the first night of the orgy. In any case, in my memory now the painter's room expands and there are suddenly other beds and mattresses on the floor and maybe twenty young guys. No one that night was drunk and there was no alcohol in the flat, which surprised me. In Ireland, were an orgy to take place – and this was unimaginable in 1975 – then everyone would have had to get drunk first and begin by pretending it was not happening. In this orgy, in the corner flat on the top floor of the building in Plaza Real, the twenty of us were very quickly and rampantly naked. There were no drugs; there was a great deal of easy laughter. In my innocence, I believed that there were no rules in an orgy. You took who you liked for as long as you liked and then discarded him when you liked and then you took someone else, or indeed several someone elses at the same time, if the occasion should arise.

I took the first guy who came towards me. He was friendly and large-framed, with brown eyes and soft skin. As soon as I touched him, his dick was erect. We found a bed to the side of the big bed and began to play. Soon a set of rules began to emerge. No one in the room fucked or sucked cock. Everyone kissed and fondled each other. It was as though a strange modesty had broken out. Everyone was in a couple; no one disturbed another couple, or moved from the guy of their choice to another guy of their newer or greater choice. After half an hour of pleasurable monogamy, I realised that I had misunderstood everything. I should have waited. I had made a big mistake.

That mistake was smiling at me now as we kissed. I smiled back. He was a nice guy. But across the room, alone, was another guy who was even nicer. He was watching the orgy with considerable interest but he was still wearing his underpants. He noticed me watching him. He was not tall, but he was strong without being too muscular. He could have been a runner or a swimmer. He had shiny brown hair which hung around his head untidily, and dark eyes, but he did not look Spanish. He could have easily been Dutch or from Eastern Europe. He had an almost feral look, like someone quietly ready to spring. I wished I had waited for him and slowly it became clear that he wished I had too. The problem was how to get away from the guy I was with, who was increasingly passionate and eager.

If I made the guy come, I wondered, would I then be free? But he did not want to come, nor did anyone else in the room, it seemed. This was another of the secret rules. That loss of serenity, as the Pope once called it, was not part of this orgy. Coming would be a moment of self-exposure and no one wanted to do it in public. I would have to wait. It took time before my loss of interest became clear to my partner. He was good-humoured about it. He stood up and walked out of the room, signalling that he would be back soon. I realized that there were other rooms off the corridor with other beds. I followed him to find the toilet. As I passed the guy whose underpants were still on, I nodded to him and he nodded back. I soon found an empty room and an empty bed and I waited.

The new guy was shy and hesitant when he came into the room. He sat on the edge of the bed and looked at me. He already knew that I was Irish, someone had told him. He spoke very good English, but often waited between sentences and phrases to think. I noticed how smooth his body was, how tightly packed and coiled he seemed. I wondered what he wanted and I wondered what it would be like to kiss him. He made clear, however, in the way he sat and spoke, that I would have no permission to try. There was something almost remote about him. His sexuality was more hidden, more cared for than that of the other guys in the room. He held himself apart. I knew that it would not matter to him if he left here without lying down with anyone. I found that almost impossible to imagine.

Suddenly, without warning or excuse, I put my hand on his chest. He looked at me gravely, remaining still. Before this, he had smiled as he spoke, and a few times as he grew silent we had smiled at each other. Now this was too serious for smiling. He sat and looked at me. It was as though his blood were changing its colour or its nature and it was going to take time. He could do nothing until that was completed. For five minutes then we were like statues. But I knew that it would have to end in him coming towards me, and once I knew that I was happy to watch him as he prepared himself for it.

I stroked his back and his chest as he lay down. He touched me as though every touch would be remembered and would come to mean something. He left his underpants on. I judged that as a reticence which mattered to him, so I did not touch him there. He kissed with an astonishing intensity. Soon we were joined in the room by the guy I had been with earlier and the painter, who was, I suppose, the host of this event. The painter was now dressed up with a mantilla on his head and a brassiere on his chest and nothing below. He was wearing make-up. Both of them were brazenly discussing my brazenness, my nerve at having moved so quickly from one guy to another. My new friend translated for me, and we both laughed, but I realized that I had broken a rule and that this was a house of rules, even though it did not seem like one.

I don't know when I first let my new friend fuck me. I had been fucked for a few seconds a year before, but it was so painful I had made the guy take his dick out forthwith and keep it out. Another guy, the summer before I left Ireland, had tried more successfully, but it was better when I fucked him. So when my new friend asked me if I liked fucking or being fucked, I said I liked fucking. He said he did too, and in fact he hated being fucked and couldn't do it. He was shy about saying all of this, but still he left me in no doubt. We had a problem. So I gave in.

We would never have done it while others could come in and

out of the room. I think we waited until the early hours when there was peace in the apartment and most people had gone home and the rest were sleeping. I was nervous. He had a way of suggesting an immense inner life in which outward actions were considered first as theory and then slowly and deliberately put into action. His dick took time to harden and then it stayed hard. It was very beautiful. Long and lovely to hold and not too thick or unwieldy.

I began to wish to be fucked by him as he held me and kissed me, assuring me that there was no hurry, we could do it another time. But I knew he wanted to do it now and for me in those years there was never another time. I wanted everything now. So in the night in this strange room, I turned around, my face down, and he moved with his mysterious slowness, touching my shoulders, turning my head around so he could kiss me and then slowly moving his hand down to my arse and testing my arsehole with his finger, probing it slowly. I could hear him breathing hard, as though this action, more than any other – and we had done many things in the previous two hours – had made him very excited. I was excited too, but I was tense. The thought of being fucked was much sweeter than the awkward, fumbling and painful mechanics of really taking another guy's dick right up inside your arse.

At first it was panic. I thought I was going to shit and I wanted to warn him. He had put his hands under my shoulders and was gripping me tight by the shoulders, not moving or thrusting, just letting his dick slide in further. I could not hear his breathing. He was absolutely still, and holding me still too, calming my panic with a fierce and stable energy. Slowly, I began to relax and, having wanted to make him take it out, I now began to want it there. Slowly, he began to fuck me.

The poet Don Paterson, in *The Book of Shadows*, a collection of aphorisms, writes: 'Anal sex has one serious advantage: there are few cinematic precedents that instruct either party how they should look.' My friend looked, as far as I could imagine, as though the mysteries of the universe were close to being solved by him. I imagine he closed his eyes a lot. He fucked slowly. At times he would turn my head and we would kiss as passionately as we could, considering the angles. It was awkward. When he came, he held me for a long time without moving. Then he put all his energy into making me come. On a later occasion, when his dick slipped out five or ten minutes after he had come, he said 'Goodbye', but I don't think that happened the first time.

The city was a vast distraction. I found a restaurant I liked; a few bars; a few English-speaking friends. I got some hours teaching. I signed up for Spanish classes. Like everyone else, I followed closely the news about the failing health of the old dictator. And now and then over those months, a crucial time in the history of Spain, I noticed how generally indifferent people were to anything except the private realm, which was inhabited by the young with great intensity. The books you read, the friends you met, the lovers you slept with, the music you listened to, the new identities you took on, these were the things that mattered in that autumn in Barcelona. The slow disintegration of the old man and his regime were like an invisible undertow. The surface of life was too exciting for anyone to do more than shrug at the possibility that this undertow would slowly begin to pull us elsewhere.

I called around to Plaza Real whenever I felt horny. Sometimes, my friend was there and we would make love. We would arrange to meet and make love again, often in different bedrooms in buildings elsewhere in the city that were owned by friends of his. I never introduced him to anyone I knew. I never told anyone about this secret life. A few times, when I called and he was not there, I stayed if there was a party. The parties were good. I realized that the painter, with his elaborate mantillas and constumes and fans, was slowly becoming a personage in the city. He moved up and down the street, cheeky, full of mockery and wit, with one or two friends, dressed like a young Spanish girl at a fair or a religious ceremony, but wearing two or three days' stubble.

He was, I realized one night, very funny. I had stayed over in his room, sleeping with some others on a mattress on the floor. Early in the morning he began a monologue, imitating accents, putting on voices. I had no idea what he was talking about, but everyone in the room was howling with laughter. It might have been that morning, or maybe it was another, when a woman, who seemed to have a room in the warren of rooms on that floor, arrived with her child, a little boy less than a year old, who could crawl but not walk. She left him with us, twenty half-naked, half-sleeping men. Our friend the painter set about entertaining the child, and we all joined in. Everyone was jealous of whoever had the child's attention. The baby crawled on top of us all, laughing and making us laugh. We made faces, did voices, played in whatever way we could with the little boy, until his mother came back. The baby cried at being taken away from us.

I discovered that my lover could read English with astonishing ease and fluency. When he spoke he was hesitant, but then I realized that he was also hesitant in Spanish and in Catalan. A few times at night I lay beside him and watched him reading late Henry James novels, amazed at his sharp grasp of the most complex sentences. Once, when the painter was out, and my friend had a key to his door, or it had been left open, we made love on his bed. I knew where the vaseline was kept. It was the first time that he fucked me from the front, my legs spread out, my ankles on his shoulders. At first, this was even more painful and strange than before, but soon it was easy. I loved looking at his face as he fucked, his eyes shut, his skin so smooth, and then his eyes opening and looking at me so intensely, as though he might eat me.

When the painter came back and saw us on the bed and the vaseline on the table beside the bed, he put his hands on his head and said: 'Por favor!'

My lover was not there the evening the dictator died, nor was I. He later told me that the party that night was the best of all. Outrage after outrage was committed, and, I supposed, many new strange and unwritten rules were devised. I was sorry I had missed it. I was drifting away. The painter had got tired of me sitting on his bed listening to the Triple Concerto. I was very interested in those years in taking my clothes off; dressing up as a *señorita* was not my style. So I did not go to the opening of Ventura Pons's film about the painter in the Cine Maldà. I read about it on the newpaper. By this time, the painter's name, Manuel Ocaña, was a byword for the new freedom and all the public outrages that came in its name.

I stopped seeing my lover. Six months later, however, when I got a flat around the corner from Plaza Real, I discovered that he had moved to another flat on the same floor of the same building. If he was home, the lights were visible from one of the streets between Escudellers and the Plaza Real. Sometimes when I walked home I would check the light and if I was feeling in the right mood I would go and ring the bell. He would come down, disturbed from his reading, and we would go up the stairs together. He would play his old game of talking and listening as though there was no sexual charge between us. And then I would move towards him and touch him, and, just like the first time, he would remain still, in his lovely old trance. This transformation from the social to the sexual, which I could do in a split second, took him time. And then he was ready. All these years later, I can still take pleasure in the tight, hard shape of him, his eager tongue, the shiny knob of his dick, the glitter in his eyes, his shy smile. I always knew that if I did not keep him, he would go. Someone else would claim him. One night, towards the end of my time in the city, he hesitated for even longer than usual when I touched him and then he told me that he could not make love with me. Someone else had come along and wanted him, and he could not fuck anyone else. He was, he said, sorry. I nodded. It was my own fault. I should not have wandered away like I did, coming to him only when I felt too horny to keep away. I walked down the stairs of that flat in the Plaza Real for the last time and into the shining city. I was ready, once more, for anything.

(Spring 2005)

These derelict fields

SELINA GUINNESS

1

The first night, it was raining so hard that I had to pull in on the Featherbed and wait for it to ease off, even though I was already late and not at all sure how I would find Glenasmole Community Centre in the warren of roads that lay below me in the dark. Yet as I crawled down the flooded boreen, grateful for the burnt-out cars that marked out verge from bog, I felt full of the joyful conviction that I would succeed in my mission: to pass the REPS course that would make me a farmer, if only on paper. The most important thing I had found out since becoming caretaker of my late uncle's flock of fifty-seven ewes and herd of fourteen cattle was that the state agricultural agency Teagasc, for a modest annual fee, would suffer to answer the enquiries of a Big House ingénue. It was Teagasc who advised me that twenty hours' instruction on the maintenance of hedgerows, farm safety, fertilizer usage and drainage schemes was all that stood between me, my certificate, and the monthly paycheque, issued in Brussels, for entering the Rural Environment Protection Scheme. But while I was confident that I could pass the course, I had to acknowledge that much of a sheep was still a mystery to me, and quite what suckler cows were for, or, more to the point, how they generated any income in their steady mooch from mart to abattoir with only the occasional calf squeezed out every other year, remained an unsolvable riddle.

My REPS advisors, Vincent Salter and Sean Finn, were huddled in the porch smoking as I dashed from the car in the torrential rain.

Inside, I got myself a chair and budged up next to the only other woman present, Mary. A poster for Relate and a typed advertisement for free-range geese were pinned to the noticeboard behind the door. The gas heaters high on the walls gave out a steady heat that soon had steam rising from my modestly high-heeled leather boots. 'You'd have been better off in Wellingtons,' advised the man sitting behind me, and I couldn't disagree.

There were about thirty men in the hall, mostly in their fifties, some older, including one man who looked to be in his early eighties, with white hair stained nicotine yellow, accompanied by his teenage grandson or great-grandson. Saying hello to the people around me, I sensed myself being discreetly but firmly placed when I gave my surname. In 1936 my great-grandfather, Col. Charles Davis Guinness, shot what was probably the last corncrake seen on Glendhu mountain, above Glencullen. One of the men told me that his father used to beat for him, alongside many other neighbours from the valley.

That night, and over the following six weeks of the course, I would learn that REPS provides a financial incentive to create a pastoral world of ecologists' and poets' dreaming. Under a five-year plan drawn up in consultation with the farmer, stocking densities are kept low, down to one cow or – marvellously – 6.66 sheep per hectare, and fertilizer usage is minimized. Two out of a list of fourteen optional measures must be undertaken within the first two years of the plan; these include the planting of broadleaf trees, the maintenance and repair of dry-stone walls, permitting public access to architectural sites, and the creation of new wildlife habitats. Supplementary payments can be earned through the establishment of native apple orchards and – most lucratively of all, at €1,300 for 2.5 hectares – the sowing of bird seed. ('Would it not make more sense to be paid feed them by the Department?' one participant quipped.) The scale of payments, which trails off at 40 hectares, is designed to make REPS attractive to part-time, dry livestock or mixed tillage farmers, not the beef barons of Meath or the dairy kings of north Cork.

Farm buildings must be painted in the vernacular colours authorized by the Department of Agriculture (rust-red, dark green and grey), and screened from the surrounding countryside by stands of trees, with native oaks, whitebeam and ashes preferred to the planter's beeches that still glow along the autumnal avenues of refurbished country house hotels. Nothing to do with history, I am assured; where a whitebeam might support 5,000 species of flora and fauna, a beech is considered sterile with a mere 500. National pride is catered for by the extra subsidies provided for keeping pedigree breeding stock of Kerry cattle, Connemara ponies and Galway sheep. There is special provision too for harvesting hay meadows from the centre out in the Shannon callows where the last corncrakes hide.

The farmers around Glenasmole mostly graze sheep on commonage on top of Glendhu and Kippure, and some have small suckler herds in the lower fields. Grazing rights have been passed down through families and measured in callops – a callop being the amount of land it takes to graze the animal most usually stocked on any particular section of commonage, whether it be sheep, cow, horse or goat. In the townland of Castlekelly, the callop needed to graze an upland ewe translates into 1.039 hectares of heath. This year, when for the first time the payment a farmer receives from Brussels will no longer take account of what he has produced on the farm, this practised knowledge of the terrain and what it can support will finally become obsolete; satellite photography will determine the number of hectares farmed. The satellite eye requires each field and each farmer to have a file of documents: land deeds, ewe subsidies, area aid applications and the like. But agricultural practices up here have been informally documented for much of the twentieth century. In places where verbal agreements between one generation and the next have stood in lieu of wills, and where the Big House ledgers that allocated grazing rights on the commonage have been lost via the sale of estates, the poorest hill farmers risk losing thousands of euros in the transition from payments based on headage to payments based on hectares. In the absence of written documentation, these farmers may be unable to demonstrate that they have inherited the right to farm a given number of callops. Under REPS, meanwhile, the number of livestock on the commonage is to be reduced, in theory allowing the heather and frauchauns to reclaim the hillsides – at least, as one man pointed out, until weekend walkers and their dogs make new paths across the slopes. 'Sure some Sundays you'd be out and there are cars stretched all along the top road and the dogs just let off the leash with no regard for ewes about to yain or anything. And then there are the kids on scrambling bikes …'

I commiserated with him about it all – all the noisy encroachment of a city in search of peace and quiet in a landscape proudly considered empty – but realized too that the proximity of urban jobs is what has kept this valley populated and halfway prosperous without yet selling out too many fields for planning permission. There wasn't a full-time farmer in the room, Mary assured me: 'No one could be now with the way it's going, not on this scale, not up here.' By the end of the year, it is expected that 50,000 Irish farms will be in REPS, with holdings averaging 30 hectares, most of them farmed part-time. The average payment of €7,000 will fail to provide a living wage, given that the profit margins on lambs and suckler cattle are barely sufficient to cover the costs of their keep, particularly on so small a scale.

After two hours of a PowerPoint presentation on nutrient management, tea came as a welcome relief. The men milled round in the hall while Mary and I gravitated instinctively towards the kitchen, where I filled teapots from the Baby Burco and lobbed what I hoped were unobtrusive questions: 'Mary, you couldn't tell me what "pine in the sheep" is by any chance? And "u-grade lambs", what does that mean?' Outside, explosive crumbs of Kimberley and Goldgrain biscuits punctuated the laughter of sturdy men chafing each other about their different ways.

On the way home across the Featherbed, a car was blazing on the roadside despite the rain, and further on three cars packed with teenagers were parked facing out over the glen, headlights on, wipers going, little to see bar the wet and the bog and the blurred lights of Tallaght beyond. Up above, the mast on Kippure flashed its new strobe lights onto the low cloud. I thought about how my account of the evening would have amused my late uncle, Charles; how he would have set down *The Times* crossword, got up from his armchair in the drawing room to hunt out a photograph of a Massey shooting party up at Cruagh and read out the names of the participants penned in on the back, looking for the name of my classmate's father among the beaters. Or he might have searched out the Colonel's game diaries and found with a gleeful giggle the few days when the tallies of snipe, widgeon, woodcock and grouse shot by Father Behan and the gamekeeper, Stubbs, outnumbered his own grandfather's poorer bag. But Charles's greatest amusement, masking a supportive concern, would have been reserved for the efforts I was making now, returning home at 10.30 on a Tuesday night, to turn a semi-feudal, neglected and impoverished estate into the very latest in EU-subsidized, under-productive, Capability Brown-style *fermes ornées*.

2

Down in the pen, the ram looks like Tony Soprano, which Colin and I think is a good thing, but he also reminds me of the model sheep/footstool they used to have in the Bunratty Woollen Mills, which might be bad. We bought a Texel because the flock, according to Joe, was 'getting too pure-bred'. 'Let's hope there's a bit of a spring in him,' he says, while punching a tag through the ram's left ear. At €600 hammer price at Blessington mart, it had better be well sprung. Over breakfast that morning we'd already had a confusing conversation about his possible prowess, with Joe announcing that of the rams he'd seen he'd picked the best: 'Some of them had no length in them at all, they need a bit of length, but your fella would be a good two foot or so long, so he should be fine.'

Joe has been buying and looking after what I still think of as my uncle's sheep, in addition to his own, for a shocking number of years. In late November, after my REPS course outing to a beef farm in Meath, I had come back home all gung-ho. 'Joe,' I started carefully, 'you know the way you're meant now to have a farm safety statement for insurance and to check over all the machinery and make sure it's all working right? Well, I thought perhaps we should draw one up together, if you had the time.' 'Yes, Selina, if you think it's needed,' he agreed. I opened up the form I'd been given and started going through the categories. Halfway through page one, I saw we had a problem: I'd written 'N/A' next to most queries relating to farm machinery, and now found myself writing 'N/A' across the whole section on power sockets. I put down my pen. 'Joe, if there's no electricity in the yard, how do you manage in the winter?' With a twinkle, he replied, 'Well, it's not used for much bar dipping and the day is long enough for the work that's in it.' We completed the rest of the form very quickly.

Joe used to work in forestry, but he started off his working life with plough horses, which he would round up as colts and then break in for a farmer up at Mont Pelier. 'You see there's an awful expense in this machinery, and in the fertilizer and sprays they use now,' he tells me as we're loading timber from a fallen oak. 'Whereas when you had the horses, didn't they manure the ground as they went along, and you always had a colt to sell in the spring.' I nod in agreement, thinking about how the world turns back to the same place, and glance up for a minute, before he starts the chainsaw again.

On clear days it looks as if you could step out from the bottom of the lawn and reach the Pigeon House in a few short strides, but today the trees of St Thomas stretch down through Marlay Park and end in obscurity. When a visitor complimented Mary Davis on the view from her new house, built by her father as a wedding present, she is reported to have replied, 'I have grown heartily sick of it.' That was in 1859, when she married a Castleknock solicitor, Thomas Hosea Guinness, and moved two hundred yards up the hill from the house she grew up in. I imagine her looking out over Dublin Bay, watching the passenger ships coming in and out of the North Wall and receiving letters from a brother, or later her son, telling of their adventures or sicknesses or the plain tedium of working in the imperial services in Persia or China. But the field that she would have looked out on, with its slim lime tree, would not have been empty as it was now, saving Joe and me. When I came to live in the house as a child, Muriel Jackson, who worked for my grandmother for over thirty years, used to tell me of going down to watch 'the men' playing football on long summer evenings, matches with thirty or more who worked here or down at St Thomas for Aunt May in the 1940s and early '50s. She spoke with such wistful regret for lost conviviality that I realized the strange household of my grandmother, her eldest son, the cook Kathleen Fox, Muriel, and my eleven-year-old self represented a skeleton crew on the *Mary Celeste*, listening for the echoes of more propitious times.

What made the pitch playable was the hard work of the previous generations who drained the land. One night up in Glenasmole, Sean, Mary's husband, explained to me that the green pastures I so admired as the outcome of Ireland's natural fecundity were simply a delicate skin concealing a robust dermis of engineering works. Probably running underneath our fields, he told me, certainly under his, were little stone channels about twelve feet down, laid at five-foot intervals and bedded in gravel that drained rainwater away into the perimeter ditches. 'If you cut back the brambles and clear the sides you should be able to see thin streams trickling out in a storm.' He went on to talk about the land he used to rent for grazing at Stocking Lane, sold last year for a housing estate of 1,500 units. 'If you go down there now, you'll see water everywhere, and it wasn't wet when I had it. They've broken up the old drains and have yet to lay the new, so the whole place is flooded.'

I think about the men who dug these deep gullies spanning the fields and how they laid the stones – flat, sides and cap – to create the small channels. How the gravel they laboriously pitched in on top would have been dug from the river bed, fetched by donkey and cart up the slope, piled out, pitched in, then the earth packed back in on top, over and over again. I wonder what they were paid. I don't know whether this work was carried out for John Jones, the farmer whose house, described in 1839 as being of 'tolerably good repair', provided the foundations for Mary Davis's new residence. Perhaps the heavy labour began earlier for the family of itinerant bookseller turned millionaire financier Luke White, who bought land here and in Killakee from Speaker Connolly in the mid-eighteenth century; but that too seems late for land that cost good money. Maybe it was on the orders of Peter Talbot de Bulloch, into whose hands much of the townland passed during the reign of Henry VIII when it was confiscated from its previous owners, the Fitzgeralds, on their conviction for high treason. But if it was worth as much then as was reported, most likely the fields had already been drained for the Kilmainham Priory of St John at Jerusalem, which held the lands from the late 1100s.*

When Mary Davis was a child, she would have watched workers pass through this field on their way to the mills powered by the River Glin. The women walking down to Mr Hughes's silk factory and the men heading for Mr Doolan's flour mill down at Kilmashogue Bridge would have made use of the old drive that is now a gentle hollow winding for a mile or more along what we now call the stream. In the 1840s there were thirteen mills on the Owendoher River and the River Glin employing between 20 and 120 people each, making paper, silk, wool, and flour. One, run by Moses Verney in the 1760s, made paper foil to prevent gold and silver lace from tarnishing. I fancy the foil was used in the main for keeping ecclesiastical fineries bright at the altar, but there might also have been a small domestic market for it within the parish of Whitechurch, for the parish was prosperous. The 1841 census records that only 2.9 per cent of its population lived in 'category one' housing (one-room cabins), compared with 28.8 per cent for Co. Dublin as a whole; and the number of good farm- and townhouses was nearly twice the county average. Despite this relative

---

*For much of this local information I am indebted to Ernie Shepherd, *Behind the Scenes: The Story of Whitechurch District in South County Dublin* (Dublin: Whitechurch Publications, 1983), pp. 5–9.

prosperity, the same source reveals that over the four years to 1841 the parish population dropped by 20 per cent, to 2,354 inhabitants. A cholera cess of one penny levied in the early 1830s hints at one possible explanation. It is clear, in any case, that by the early 1860s, when Mary's husband, Thomas Hosea, decided to put in a boating pond on the River Glin and lay out its banks as a Victorian water garden, many of the mills on this river had gone. When she was growing up, Mary Davis's prospect would have been crowded and busy in the foreground, with carts travelling along the old avenue to the mills. By the time she was a married woman, the unlit city must have seemed to loom closer as the fields and river emptied of this industry and the estate became one of the main local employers: beaters, gardeners, a gamekeeper, men to clear the silt from the traps in the river and to maintain the boat-ponds. Servicing the recreational pastimes of gentlemen amounted to its own small and prototypically modern leisure industry.

3

Early spring brings an odd problem: an orange helicopter has appeared in the lower lawn where the ewes due to lamb later this month are grazing, and I don't know who owns it or why it's there. A friend suggests clamping it, but is short on suggestions as to how this might be achieved. I call a new neighbour, who has a helicopter of his own berthed next to his house. 'It belongs to a relative of mine,' he states matter-of-factly of the intruding craft, 'he had to land there yesterday afternoon.' It transpires his nephew lives in Rathfarnham and berths his helicopter in west Dublin; after landing yesterday, he cadged a lift home with another of our neighbours, who assured him I wouldn't mind if he left the craft there overnight. I'm not entirely convinced by the story I'm told of an emergency landing in sudden mists (which escaped me while I was weeding), and I suspect traffic on the M50 was the more immediate cause. After some discussion, we agree his relative might call up to the house for a brief chat when he comes to collect his chopper. I am surprised, when I open the door, by the nephew's youth: he looks to be in his early thirties. 'Do you mind me asking what line of business you're in?' I inquire, as neutrally as possible. 'Property,' he replies, 'but I'm training to be a flying instructor.'

Shortly after starting my REPS course, I heard Shane Kenny on the *News at One* interview a developer about the future of the Dublin housing market. 'I think it's a disgrace that young people should have to commute from Gorey and as far away as Longford town when there's plenty of land around Dublin that could be rezoned for housing. From the M50 you can see whole fields across south Dublin that are just lying derelict.' Later, I cruised the stretch of motorway between Leopardstown and Firhouse, and, passing St Columba's College, slowed down to look up the slopes of Kilmashogue. The broad green expanse of Marymount was illuminated in the winter sunlight, its pasture lying fallow in preparation for spring. A dark speck hovering above the landscape suddenly swooped down towards the traffic: one of the kestrels nesting in the blue cedars that crosshatch the long, white stone wall between our field and the townland of Aidencarrick above it.

In a sense the developer is right to say the fields are derelict. On my REPS plan, most of the hedgerows are listed as 'escaped'; I am required to fill the gaps with sheep wire and spindly new hawthorn whips rather than attempt to cut the hedgerows back to their original lines. Gorse trims our view of Dublin Bay with a gaudy braid and blackberries are plentiful on the long briars that sometimes ensnare our sheep. Deer and grey squirrels have ring-barked some of the oldest trees along the stream so that we lose more with every storm. For the six years my grandmother managed the farm during the Second World War, it turned a good profit with a herd of four hundred ewes. Now we are down to fewer than sixty.

Under REPS, this state of natural dereliction can generate a modest income in ways a developer would be slow to comprehend. If I fence off the gorse bushes at the end of the field and abandon 'any agronomic activity', allowing the pimpernels, harebells and stitchworts to grow back along the sheep tracks and the grass to grow long enough for hares to hide their leverets, I'll be creating a new habitat in accordance with Measure 4A. Another option (4C) would be to create a 'nature corridor', which means leaving a 2.5-metre margin out from the perimeter of each field when spraying with fertilizer or pesticides so the weeds can grow and provide cover and food for wildlife. The way Vincent and Sean see it, this farm's long-standing inefficiency means that, bar the odd unsightly pallet stuck in a gap, there are few changes to be made to ensure we accord with 'environmentally friendly farming practice'. The balance between wildlife and our paltry amount of stock seems to be just about right for a time when the European Union has decided it is no longer feasible to continue linking subsidies to agricultural production amid a landscape of butter mountains and milk lakes.

REPS is not the only agricultural policy to encourage a decrease in agricultural production. This year, the quietest revolution in Ireland's history is underway as reforms to the EU's Common Agricultural Policy finally take effect. Under the Single Farm Payment Scheme, the subsidies that farmers used to be paid for producing livestock and tillage crops will be replaced by a cheque at the end of each calendar year whose value will not be linked to current farm output. The reforms, devised by the former EU agricultural commissioner Franz Fischler, are rooted in the idea that 'decoupling' payments from actual production will diminish the stockpiling of commodities like sugar and dairy produce whose prices were kept artificially high through subvention for the last forty years. This change has allowed the EU to argue during world trade talks that these payments will support farmers rather than produce, and hence will not contravene trade agreements with the United States. Without subsidies, it is predicted that true market values for agricultural produce will finally be established within the EU, ending decades of waste and the practice of dumping Europe's excess produce on poorer markets. However, both Sustain ('the alliance for better food and farming') and Oxfam have greeted these claims with scepticism. They point out that by the Commission's own assessments, gluts of grain and dairy produce will continue to be a feature of European agriculture for many years yet, partly because the many rounds of negotiation among member states mean that the cuts in subvention monies have turned out to be far less radical than originally promised by Fischler. These NGOs also predict that the EU will simply become more adept at hiding the export subsidies that allow European farmers to undercut producers from poor countries. Their reports make Fischler's reforms seem less concerned with ensuring the stability of Europe's rural civilizations than with the smoke and mirrors of a Victorian conjuror, making excess commodities vanish with a quick wave of the fiscal wand.

At the national level, these conjuring tricks take on a Gothic character: farmers will now be paid for the ghosts of those sheep and cattle that grazed the land at the dawn of this millennium. Each member state was allowed to choose the method by which a farmer's entitlements would be allocated, and Ireland was one of the few to opt for the full severance of payment from production. As might be expected, Ireland selected the 'historic model' to implement these changes: farmers are assessed retrospectively on the subsidies claimed and number of hectares farmed during the years 2000–2003 (known as 'the reference period').

Whereas inefficiency in our fields has produced a haven for wildlife that chimes well with REPS, my uncle's scant regard for correspondence with the Department of Agriculture during these years may weaken our position when it comes to reckoning our Single Farm Payment. Spidery biro figures on the backs of unopened envelopes indicate that a bare minimum of ewe and slaughter premiums were claimed, while the accounts of how each field was used don't seem to have been transcribed from scribbled notes made in conversation with Joe onto the required application forms. This past year I've felt like an archaeologist of sorts, piecing together the jottings I've found tucked into battered ledgers or in drawers filled with string and paper bags in the hope of assembling a record of what was actually farmed during 'the reference period'.

With almost 50 per cent of Irish farms less than twenty hectares in size, and 41 per cent of farmers over the age of fifty-five, there are concerns for the many, like my late uncle Charles, who never quite managed to keep up with the paperwork during the subsidies era. Few realized at the time that their future farm income would depend on the level of their activities during those four crucial years. Teagasc hopes that the poorer 50 per cent of Irish farmers will avail of REPS and choose to scale back their enterprises further, putting some of their land into forestry, and keeping a bare minimum of livestock, if any at all. Under the Single Farm Payment Scheme, the area farmed can be reduced by half without affecting the payment. For the many in dry-stock cattle and sheep production, the opportunity to abandon activities where profits were minimal or non-existent is welcome. Although farmers must continue to engage in 'agricultural activities', this no longer necessarily means rearing livestock or growing crops: it is defined simply as 'maintaining the land in good agricultural order.' This condition suggests it will still be necessary to keep some four-footed lawnmowers to graze the pastures clean, even though the new regime makes keeping a small herd seem like an expensive hobby for the future.

If all this looks like a good deal, it should be noted that the payments take no account of inflation; and most agricultural advisors believe the single-payment scheme will be abandoned in 2013, when it is euphemistically 'due for review'. What will succeed it is as yet unclear, but out of each farmer's payment, a clawback of between 3 and 5 per cent is being set aside for 'alternative rural development'. Reading the *Irish Farmers Journal*, it becomes clear there is little consensus on how this reserve should be spent – whether it should be reinvested in agriculture, or perhaps used to provide start-up loans to off-farm local enterprises that might benefit the whole rural community. The latter view accords with the implicit argument running through both REPS and the Single Farm Payment Scheme that at least half of Ireland's farms are simply not viable in the mid- to long-term future, and that other sources of employment, such as rural tourism, will need to be found. Over 80,000 Irish farmers currently do not rely on farming for their main income and it is anticipated that over 6 per cent per annum will give up entirely.

Combine the Single Farm Payment Scheme with REPS, then, and you seem to have a phased-in retirement scheme for more than half of Ireland's farmers. Outside the areas of interest to property developers, the price of agricultural land is likely to fall as the older generation retire to garden the hedgerows or to watch goldfinches feed on the new patches of wilderness seeded in place of corn or pasture. The *Irish Farmers Journal* has calculated that, in order to gain a €28,000 profit from sheep farming (including REPS payments), a farmer will have to own a minimum flock of 850 ewes producing 1.4 lambs per ewe at €70 a lamb, yielding a €20 net margin. The consensus emerging is that under the new market rules beef farms are unlikely to attain good profits unless they comprise upwards of 2,000 acres of good pasture.

These figures suggest that over the next two decades the Irish landscape will come to resemble a patched and darned blanket more than the kitsch patchwork quilt of lore. Interspersed between cattle ranches and large tillage farms planted with GMO crops to reduce the escalating costs of pesticides and fertilizers will be a greater number of small forestry plantations, mainly of conifers, and pockets of straggling fields grazed by sparse herds, perhaps of native breeds, or exotics for which premium prices can be attained at farmers' markets. The last slide on that first REPS evening in Glenasmole displayed a stark message for all in the room:

♦Look at all your options
♦Less could be more
♦Don't farm for the sake of it

4

The return to nature supported by REPS and indirectly by the Single Farm Payment Scheme may be greeted with some joy by the leisured urban classes who, like my ancestors, look to rivers not for mills but for recreation, whether as boating ponds or the spawning grounds for trout. Rural diversification might result in the proliferation of small food companies whose home-cured bacon and organic sausages, ordered online, will arrive vacuum-packed with the post in time for breakfast. It might mean planting willow saplings to be harvested after five years and turned into wood pellets to burn for industrial heating. Mary White, a Green Party member of Carlow County Council, has suggested that the beet growers of the county, recently made redundant, should cultivate rape and other brassicas to supply the vegetable oils which new research suggests are a sustainable alternative to fossil fuels for the tiny numbers of cars yet adapted to run on them; and the small producers of farmhouse cheeses, hedgerow jams and upper crust B&Bs heralded each weekend by the *Irish Times* magazine as the new rural pioneers may be ideally suited to the changing patterns of subsidies. But many of these markets have barely been tested and require the enterprise skills, training and financing that few of Ireland's smaller-scale farmers possess, or, given their age profile, are likely ever to possess.

With the decline of manufacturing, class has become defined by habits of consumption: a hearty peasant stew cooked to Hugo Arnold's recipe offers not just gastronomic pleasure, but something akin to transubstantiation for a middle class that has become evangelical in its worship of nutrition. Meanwhile, the hearty if hapless proletariat and peasants on *You Are What You Eat* have their turds picked over by Dr Gillian McKeith to diagnose not just the physical but the moral ills of eating the white bread that serves as communion wafers across these islands. CAP reform, too, ultimately comes down to shite. The Nitrates Directive, adopted by the Commission in 1991 but not yet implemented in Ireland, holds governments responsible for the pollution of watercourses and inland waterways by silage effluent and runoff from other farm fertilizers. It seems at first sight surprising that of all the Commission's agricultural reforms, this piece of legislation controlling water pollutants should be the most keenly contested by the Irish Farmers' Association and the

Department of Agriculture. For recreational users of the countryside the penalties demanded by Brussels for Ireland's non-compliance with this measure are expensive reminders of the wider shame we should feel over the abuse of our natural resources. But the reason for Ireland's resistance gradually becomes clearer as we are asked to take out our calculators in the REPS classes.

The directive sets a limit of 170kg of nitrogen per hectare. This doesn't just cover the spreading of artificial fertilizers or slurry; it also includes the shit produced by each animal in the field. Let's take Joe's example of old-fashioned agricultural efficiency: the plough horse that manures the soil as it tills each furrow. Each horse will produce upwards of 50kg per annum of nitrogen in its own dung, which sets a stocking limit of three horses and a lowland ewe (at 13kg per annum) to graze each hectare. More critical are the figures for dairy cattle, which produce 85kg of nitrogen per annum: this allows for only two cows per hectare. The implications are not hard to see. A profitable dairy farmer with a herd of 500 cows, mostly housed indoors, will under the current directive now need upwards of 250 hectares of land to meet these requirements regardless of the grass quality or how much extra feed they are given. The Netherlands has managed to negotiate a higher limit for its nitrogen production, due to its reliance on intensive farming, but so far the Irish government has been unable to win a similar concession and negotiations are ongoing without any prospect of a deal in sight. Without the derogation, the larger farmers will be unable to expand their herds without considerably expanding their farms.

If the directive is implemented here as it is currently drawn, a new market is expected to open up which will bring the small REPS farms and the larger cattle ranches into a symbiotic co-existence. Commercial farmers who strive to continue their intensive dairy or beef farming without purchasing more land will be forced to buy up spare nitrogen quota from part-time farmers, who, in accordance with the slim stocking levels allowed by REPS, will be grazing barely half the number of animals allowed by the directive. Put simply, those who don't farm up to the 170kg limit will be in a position to sell their unused shite allowance to over-producers. This is analogous to the provisions of the Kyoto Agreement, which will require Ireland to fuel its continued economic expansion by buying spare carbon quota from less prosperous nations.

After doing these sums, and thinking about it on my way home, it dawns on me that the logic of Europe's consumer society is revealed in all its scatological glory within the Nitrates Directive. Under its requirements we witness what Freud might term a 'return of the repressed' as the anal origins of money are revealed in the exchange of euros for the license to shit freely. Long before Freud, it was Jonathan Swift who saw the indispensable logic of repletion and excretion in the liberal economy and who, in Part IV of *Gulliver's Travels*, satirized the bourgeois shame in its denial. Just as Joe's plough-horse would have me learn the true value of production, so Gulliver is taught the lesson of his own beastliness by rational horses in the land of the Houyhnhnms. His revulsion at the filthy habits of those hairy quadrupeds, the Yahoos, kept by the Houyhnhnms as servants, who climb to the tops of trees and pelt him with excrement when he first arrives, is insufficient to protect him from the slow realization that he and his fellow Europeans are of the same kind. In daily conversations with his master, Gulliver seeks to explain how human civilization differs from his host's in its politics, law and economy, and in time he comes to explain too the basis of its trading empire:

England was computed to produce three Times the Quantity of Food, more than its Inhabitants are able to consume, as well as Liquors extracted from Grain, or pressed out of the fruit of certain trees, which made excellent drink, and the same proportion in every other convenience of life. But, in order to feed the Luxury and Intemperance of the Males, and the vanity of the Females, we sent away the greatest Part of our necessary Things to other Countries, from whence in Return we brought the Materials of Diseases, Folly, and Vice to spend among ourselves.

To the gentle horse, Gulliver's account of his country's inability to share surplus produce among its citizens, rather than dumping the 'greatest part' on foreign countries, is incomprehensible, and positions Gulliver firmly among the Yahoos.

For Freud and Erich Fromm, capitalism shows human society to be arrested at the infantile stage of anal erotism, fascinated by the symbolic meaning that attaches to its own shit as gift, property, weapon or play. In his essay 'The Excremental Vision', Norman O. Brown observes that Swift understood that the elaborate system of bourgeois manners in the eighteenth century merely served to repress this association, thus allowing the circulation of commodities to continue without association with the natural and human waste left in its wake. Gulliver's great insight from his observation of the Yahoos is that society can never hope to disguise the excremental origins of capitalism's grubby interest in hoarding or throwing or boasting about money. When the traveller returns to civil society, he is forced to block his nose against the stench of denial within the polite confines of his family home, his only relief from hypocrisy afforded by close conversation with his odorous gardener.

Gulliver, who is a trained physician, notices during his stay abroad that the Yahoos have discovered a particularly nasty but effective cure for their own ailments. Whenever one of them falls ill,

a Mixture of their own Dung and Urine [is] forcibly put down the Yahoo's throat. This I have since often known to have been taken with Success: And do here freely recommend it to my Countrymen, for the public Good, as an admirable Specifick against all Disease produced by Repletion.

The Nitrates Directive is undoubtedly a Yahoo cure for the ills of European agricultural repletion which the Irish farm organizations are finding difficult to swallow but will have to in the end. In contrast, it is unlikely that the developers who view these fields as simply the next meal for their gargantuan appetites will ever submit to such a purgative. Their prosperity depends upon denying the logic that endless consumption inevitably entails waste. The process of being forced to confess publicly at the Flood Tribunal to every symbolic turd passed in a brown envelope might have served as a form of colonic irrigation for the most affluent members of Irish society, but it is one that seems to have served little lasting effect on 'the publick good'.

Perhaps, however, there are a growing number of Gullivers in Ireland today who share his *nostalgie de la boue*. Shoppers in the farmers' markets dream not just about how their purchases will taste, but about the good which unindustrialized modes of production will bring to them and to society. The pork sold at my local farmers' market, which is touted as coming from 'happy Tamworth pigs', is not just tastier: it is seen as a more moral purchase than the intensively reared and processed Danish chop sitting on the supermarket shelf. But the ethical superiority felt in purchasing from the small agrarian producer should not blind us to the fact that being able to taste the difference is intrinsic to our bourgeois identities, and serves also to put distance between our 'tasteful' lives and the 'tasteless' pursuits of the white pan eaters whose livelihoods have traditionally depended upon areas of processing and manufacture no longer considered viable in Western Europe. With half of Ireland's farmers likely to cease agricultural production, a few instead becoming guardians and protectors of the remaining outposts of rural heritage squeezed between expanding cattle ranches and tillage farms, our sense of an autochthonous national identity – which for so long has relied upon the stability of the rural landscape – will have to adapt rapidly.

As the weather turned colder in January, a neighbour asked me whether I had any sloping fields that might be good for tobogganing should it snow. When I confirmed I did, and asked him whether this was one of his own winter pursuits, he tutted briskly. 'You know it takes only one stupid fecker to hurtle off, smack his head on a rock and paralyse himself for there to be a claim against you, and the insurance won't cover you unless you've signs everywhere warning everyone that they are stupid fecking eejits at their own risk.' 'Well, you can't stop someone from tobogganing down a hill if that's what they want to do,' I protested, remembering the exhilaration of the snowy Glencullen slopes when I was a kid. 'No, you can't,' he admitted, 'but what you can do is take out your slurry tanker the night before and give the field a good coating. That'll stop most of them.'

5

Out in the car park, or more accurately on the basketball court that serves as one on REPS nights, Sean says to me, 'Do you remember the first night when you came up here and you didn't have a clue where you were coming to at all?' There's a warm quiet in the valley and voices float down from the top road. Sean glances up. We can see the interior light of a car and another pair of headlights. 'You usually go up that way, don't you?' he asks. 'Better go down by Billy's Bridge at Oldbawn tonight. You never know, probably teenagers, but they can be wild.' I linger a bit, reluctant to head for home now that the course is over. I realize that I had been vaguely hoping for an announcement on this last night that a refresher course was planned for later in the year, or, even better, a practical course in sheep-shearing and dipping. As I drive away, glimpsing the reservoir between the trees, I remember that Glenasmole is where Oisín stooped to help his aged friends from the Fianna roll away a stone, and, falling from his horse, instantly grew old. And I think of a poem by Fergus Allen, which ends like this:

> Glenasmole now has its solitaries, flitting
> Between the alders, senses tuned to receive
> Warnings and conjurations that rarely come –
> Lonely, if that's how you see them, or defenders
> Of the last bridgehead, as they themselves might put it.

(Summer 2005)

The poor old horse

JOHN BANVILLE

Maurice Blanchot invites us to perform a thought experiment. Imagine, he muses, the last writer, the very last, 'with whom would disappear, without anyone noticing it, the little mystery of writing'. What would be the result of this demise? A great silence would fall, certainly, but behind the silence something would be detected, the approach of a new sound.

Nothing serious, nothing loud; scarcely a murmur, which will add nothing to the great tumult of cities from which we think we suffer. Its only characteristic: it is incessant. Once heard, it cannot stop being heard, and since one never truly hears it, since it escapes all understanding, it also escapes all distraction, it is all the more present when we turn away from it: the echo, in advance, of what has not been said and will never be said.

The murmur of this 'unknown and meaningless language … capable of destroying all the others' insinuates itself into every moment and level of our lives. 'It is beneath everything we say, behind each familiar thought, submerging, engulfing, although imperceptible, all the honest words of man; it is the third part of each dialogue, the echo confronting each monologue.'

For Blanchot, 'a writer is one who imposes silence on this speech, and a literary work is … a rich resting place of silence, a firm defence and a high wall against this eloquent immensity that addresses us by turning us away from ourselves'. The writer is the dictator, 'the man of *dictare*, of imperious repetition … the providential man, called into being to obliterate the fog of ambiguity of phantom language with his commands and iron decisions'. It is the dictator who enters, 'more than anyone else, into a relationship of intimacy with the initial rumour. It is at that price alone that he can silence it …'*

Among the dictators of silence, few in recent times have made so loud a noise in the world as Michel Houellebecq. The inevitable comparison is with Salman Rushdie, for Houellebecq too has provoked the wrath of the Islamic world. In 2002 he was brought to court in France by a group of powerful Muslim institutions, including the National Federation of French Muslims and the World Islamic League, who accused him, under an obscure protocol of French law, of racial insults and incitement to religious hatred, after an interview in the magazine *Lire* in which he declared Islam to be a dangerous and stupid religion.

Houellebecq's court appearance provoked shock, outrage, and laughter, in equal proportions. He dismissed the charges brought against him by pointing out that he had not criticized Muslims, only their religion, which he had a right to do in a free society. Asked if he realized that his remarks could have contravened the French Penal Code, he replied that he did not, since he had never read the Code. 'It is excessively long,' he remarked, 'and I suspect that there are many boring passages.' All this would seem mere comedy, another lively entry in the annals of France's excitable literary life, if we had not the example of Rushdie and the fatwa, and if the French media and many French intellectuals had not at best kept silent and at worst sided with Houellebecq's accusers.

The reception accorded Houellebecq's work in some influential quarters is equally disturbing, and puzzling. The French literary world, still dominated by the surviving would-be Jacobins of May 1968, has largely dismissed his novels. A number of anglophone reviewers have been no more kind – the *New York Times* found *Atomised* 'a deeply repugnant read', the London *Sunday Times* described it as 'pretentious, banal, badly written and boring', and

---

*Maurice Blanchot, 'Death of the Last Writer', in *The Book to Come*, translated by Charlotte Mandel, Stanford University Press, 2003.

the *Times* said that Houellebecq was no more a novelist of ideas than the comedian Benny Hill. Such passionate vituperation is hard to understand. Have these critics, if critics they are, not read Sade, or Céline, or Georges Bataille – have they not read Swift?

Although Houellebecq insists, as any artist will, that it is not he but his work that is of consequence, a little biographical background is necessary in his case, given the public and controversial nature of that case. He was born Michel Thomas, on the French-ruled island of Réunion, in the Indian Ocean, in 1958. His father was a mountain guide, his mother an anaesthetist. The couple seem to have been less than ideal parents. When Michel was still a young child his mother left his father for a Muslim man, and converted to Islam; of course, many critics see here the seed of the adult Houellebecq's animosity to Islam. Then, at the age of six, Michel was abandoned to the care of his grandmother, whose name, Houellebecq, he adopted when he first began to publish. Granny Houellebecq was a Stalinist, and those same critics detect in this a cause for Houellebecq's animosity toward ideologues of the left. How simple and determined it must be, the life of the critic!

In France, Houellebecq trained as an agricultural engineer, but went to work as an administrator in the computer department of the French National Assembly. He suffered from depression, and spent some time in psychiatric clinics. He was married, divorced, and married again, in 1999, when with his wife he moved to Ireland, and now lives on Bere Island in Bantry Bay. His writings include a biography of the American writer of macabre tales, H.P. Lovecraft – titled, suggestively, *Contre le monde, contre la vie* – and several volumes of poetry. His novels to date are *Extension du domain de la lutte*, 1994, in English *Whatever*; *Les Particules elémentaires*, 1999, in English *Atomised*; *Lanzarote*, 2000; and *Plateforme*, 2001, in English *Platform*.*

No sooner does it seem that the traditional novel is safely dead at last than someone comes along and flogs the poor old horse into life

***Les Particules Elementaires* was translated as *The Elementary Particles* in the US edition. Paul Hammond translated *Whatever*, Frank Wynne the three subsequent novels.

again. Michel Houellebecq wields a vigorous whip. In form, his novels are entirely straightforward, and very readable; they would have done a brisk turnover in a Victorian lending-library, after a few editorial suppressions. They tell of 'ordinary' people going about their 'ordinary' lives. True, these are lives of noisy desperation, hindered by psychoses, prey to boredom and accidie, and permeated from top to bottom by sex. In other words, just like the home-life of our own dear selves. Houellebecq's tone varies between jaded bitterness and disgusted denunciation; the narrative voice in all the books seems furious at itself for having begun to speak at all and, having begun, for being compelled to go on to the end. But Houellebecq knows, as Beckett knows, that the murmur must be kept at bay, that the silence, our silence, must be preserved. Yet Houellebecq is darker even than Beckett, and would never allow himself, or us, those lyric transports which flickeringly illuminate the Beckettian night.

It would be interesting to know how Houellebecq's first novel gained its English title. Irresistibly, one imagines a telephone exchange between English publisher and French author as to how the rather grand and revolutionary-sounding *Extension du domain de la lutte* might be translated, terminating in an electronic shrug and a murmured, 'Whatever …'. For all the iconoclastic belligerence of his persona, Houellebecq presents himself as firmly within the tradition of Gallic *désenchantement* – if one can speak of someone being disenchanted who shows so little sign of having been enchanted in the first place – with baleful Sartrean stare and negligently dangling Camusian cigarette permanently in place.

Yet Houellebecq possesses one quality in which the Left Bank existentialists of the 1940s and '50s were notably lacking, that is, humour. Houellebecq's fiction is horribly funny. Often the joke is achieved by a po-faced conjunction of the grandiloquent and the thumpingly mundane. The first page of *Whatever* is headed by a tag from Romans XIII – *The night is far spent, the day is at hand: let us therefore cast off the works of darkness, and let us put on the armour of light* – the radiant promise of which is immediately extinguished by the opening paragraph:

Friday evening I was invited to a party at a colleague from work's house. There were thirty-odd of us, all middle management aged between twenty-five and forty. At a certain moment some stupid bitch started removing her clothes. She took off her T-shirt, then her bra, then her skirt, and as she did she pulled the most incredible faces. She twirled around in her skimpy panties for a few seconds more and then, not knowing what else to do, began getting dressed again. She's a girl, what's more, who doesn't sleep with anyone. Which only underlines the absurdity of her behaviour.

This is a remarkably representative statement of Houellebecq's themes and effects, culled from the drab world of office drudges, with its weary salaciousness, its misogyny, its surly awareness of the futility of all its stratagems of transcendence and escape. Indeed, *Whatever* is all of Houellebecq *in nuce*. It states repeatedly, in baldest terms, the essentials of his dour aesthetic:

There are some authors who employ their talent in the delicate description of varying states of soul, character traits, etc. I shall not be counted among these. All that accumulation of realistic detail, with clearly differentiated characters hogging the limelight, has always seemed pure bullshit to me, I'm sorry to say.

The pages that follow constitute a novel; I mean, a succession of anecdotes in which I am the hero. This autobiographical choice isn't one, really: in any case I have no other way out. If I don't write about what I've seen I will suffer just the same – and perhaps a bit more so. But only a bit, I insist on this. Writing brings scant relief. It retraces, it delimits. It lends a touch of coherence, the idea of a kind of realism. One stumbles around in a cruel fog, but there is the odd pointer. Chaos is no more than a few feet away.

The novel form is not conceived for depicting indifference or nothingness; a flatter, more terse and dreary discourse would need to be invented.

But I don't understand, basically, how people manage to go on living. I get the impression everybody must be unhappy; we live in such a simple world, you understand. There's a system based on domination, money and fear – a somewhat masculine system, let's call it Mars; there's a feminine system based on seduction and sex, Venus let's say. And that's it. Is it really possible to live and to believe that there's nothing else?

Despite the opening disclaimers as to the deliberate absence of 'realistic detail' and 'clearly differentiated characters', the novel's protagonist – hero is really too large a word – is a convincing and even compelling, even appealing, creation, in all his shambling incompetence and emotional disarray. He is a Meursault without the energy or interest to commit a murder, even a pointless one – 'It's not that I feel tremendously low; it's rather that the world around me appears high.' He is a computer technician who in his spare time writes peculiar little stories about animals, such as *Dialogues Between a Cow and a Filly*, 'a meditation on ethics, you might say', a couple of paragraphs of which are quoted. 'The God presented in this short story was not, one observes, a merciful God.'

Whatever pays its sly and sardonic tributes to the great French tradition. In the opening pages the protagonist has forgotten where he parked his car and finds himself wandering in search of it through the Rue Marcel-Sembat, the Rue Marcel-Dassault ... 'there were a lot of Marcels about', while in the book's central section he falls seriously ill in Rouen, the birthplace that Flaubert detested. Indeed, while it could hardly be described as Proustian, the book, all dreamy drift and sour recollection, does have something of the minutely observed inconsequentiality of Flaubert's masterpiece, *L'Education sentimentale*.

The writer Houellebecq most resembles, however, is Simenon – not the Maigret Simenon, but the Simeon of the *romans durs*, as he called them, such as *Dirty Snow* or *Monsieur Monde Vanishes*, masterpieces of tight-lipped existential desperation.

There is one aspect in which *Whatever* differs from the three novels that followed it, and that is the relative absence of sex. Sex, 'the only game left to adults' [*Platform*], is a commodity – one deliberately chooses the word – in which the other books are soaked. In *Atomised*, the main character Michel's half-brother Bruno devotes his life to the pursuit of women, or at least of what women can provide – in fact, Houellebecq and Benny Hill would probably see eye to ogling eye – while at the heart of *Platform* is a detailed and, it must be said, numbingly tedious account of the setting up and running of a sex-tourism venture in Thailand. *Lanzarote*, a brief, fictionalized account of a package holiday on that eponymous isle, interspersed with gnomic photographs of the island's rock formations taken by Houellebecq himself, is little more than the tale of a young man getting lucky with two lesbians on a beach – 'Barbara's excitement continued to mount … I myself found myself close to coming in Pam's mouth'.

It is hard to know how seriously Houellebecq intends us to take all this. Certainly he expends a great deal of writerly energy on his erotic scenes, yet for all the unblinking explicitness of the descriptions, the sex itself is curiously old-fashioned. Women are treasured, but mainly as receptacles for men and their desires. Rivers of semen gush through these pages – 'small clouds floated like spatters of sperm between the pines' [*Atomised*] – a great deal of it disappearing down the throats of women. Houellebecq's females never seem to menstruate, or go to the lavatory, and are ready at all times, day or night, in private or in public, to perform such acts as may be required of them by men; nor do they evince the slightest fear of or interest in getting pregnant, of which, in any case, there is not the faintest danger, in Houellebecq's world. True, the women enjoy the sex as much as the men do, but in a free, undemanding and uncomplicated way that few women, or men, would recognize from their own experience. Sometimes Michel has a thought for AIDS, but his partners merrily brush aside any such qualms.

Yet all these couplings, all these threesomes and foursomes, take place in a curiously innocent, almost Edenic glow. In a horrible world, these melancholy concumbences are the only reliable source of authenticity and affectless delight.

A source of permanent, accessible pleasure, our genitals exist. The god who created our misfortune, who made us short-lived, vain and cruel, has also provided this form of meagre compensation. If we couldn't have sex from time to time, what would life be? [*Platform*]

*

Atomised is Houellebecq's masterpiece so far. What might be its premise is re-stated in a passage from the book that followed it, *Platform*:

> It is wrong to pretend that human beings are unique, that they carry within them an irreplaceable individuality; as far as I was concerned, at any rate, I could not distinguish any trace of such an individuality. As often as not it is futile to wear yourself out trying to distinguish individual destinies and personalities. When all's said and done, the idea of the uniqueness of the individual is nothing more than pompous absurdity. We remember our own lives, Schopenhauer wrote somewhere, a little better than a novel we once read. That's about right: a little, no more.

The hero of *Atomised* – in this case the word is not too large – is Michel Djerzinski, a molecular biologist, who at the end of the book, having given up his position at the Galway Centre for Genetic Research in Ireland (!), retires to a cottage on the Sky Road in Clifden – 'There's something very special about this country' – to complete, between the years 2000 and 2009, his magnum opus, an eighty-page distillation of a life's work devoted to the proposition 'that humanity must disappear, that humanity would give way to a new species which was asexual and immortal, a species which had outgrown individuality, individuation and progress'. After Djerzinski has gone 'into the sea', his successor, Hubczejak – a private play, one suspects, on another hard-to-pronounce name beginning with H – makes a synthesis of his work and presents it to an at first disbelieving world. Dzerzinski's conviction is that

> any genetic code, however complex, could be noted in a standard, structurally stable form, isolated from any mutations. This meant that every cell contained within it the possibility of being perfectly copied. Every animal species, however highly evolved, could be transformed into a similar species, reproduced by cloning and therefore immortal.

At the close of the book the twenty-first century is half done and humanity as we know it has all but disappeared, its place taken by a new species of Djerzinskian immortals. 'There remain some humans of the old species, particularly in areas long dominated by religious doctrine. Their reproductive levels fall year on year, however, and at present their extinction seems inevitable.' It is a strangely compelling, strangely moving conceit, this peaceful making way by the old order for a new. The book's reigning spirit is Auguste Comte (1798–1857), follower of Saint-Simon and founder of the religion of Positivism, the rules of which he laid down in his *Système de Politique Positive*. Supremely silly as Comte's philosophy of altruism is – the Positivist religionist must, among numerous other devotional duties, pray three times a day to his mother, wife and daughter, and wear a waistcoat buttoned down the back so that it can be put on and taken off only with the help of others – it had a worldwide influence, not least in France.

What are we to make of the Comtean aspects of Houellebecq's work? For all the darkness of his vision, gleams of light now and then break through – 'In the absence of love, nothing can be sanctified' [*Platform*] – but what a peculiar light it is, as it seeks to illuminate these arid landscapes where the only solace for us dying humans is the sad game of sex. Djerzinski's 'great leap', according to Hubczejak, is 'the fact that he was able ... to restore the possibility of love', while Djerzinski himself in one of his final works, *Meditations on Interweaving* – inspired, not incidentally, by the Book of Kells – ponders the central motive force of our lives in rhapsodic tones worthy of D.H. Lawrence at his most ecstatic or, indeed, of *The Sound of Music* at its most saccharine:

The lover hears his lover's voice over mountains and oceans; over mountains and oceans a mother hears the cry of her child. Love binds, and it binds for ever. Good binds, while evil unravels. Separation is another word for evil; it is also another word for deceit. All that exists is a magnificent interweaving, vast and reciprocal.

Yet *Atomised* is genuinely affecting in its vision of the end of the 'brave and unfortunate species' that we human beings were and our replacement by the brave-new-worlders made possible by Djerzinski's 'risky interpretations of the postulates of quantum mechanics'. Houellebecq, if we are to take him at his word, and not think ourselves mocked by his fanciful flights, achieves a profound insight into the nature of our collective death-wish, as well as our wistful hope for something to survive, even if that something is not ourselves. The omniscient narrator, dedicating his book 'to humanity', meditates on what is past and passing and to come:

History exists, it is elemental, it dominates, its rule is inexorable. But outside the strict confines of history, the ultimate ambition of this book is to salute the brave and unfortunate species which created us. This vile, unhappy race, barely different from the apes, had such noble aspirations. Tortured, contradictory, individualistic, quarrelsome, it was capable of extraordinary violence, but nonetheless never quite abandoned a belief in love. This species which, for the first time in history, was able to envisage the possibility of its passing and which, some years later, proved capable of bringing it about. As the last members of this species are extinguished, we think it just to render this last tribute to humanity, a homage which itself will one day disappear, buried beneath the sands of time.

And yet, after the death of the last man, what a swelling murmur would come back, what a gabble, of all the things left unsaid at our passing. And who would there be, among the immortals, to impose the necessary silence?

(Winter 2004–5)

Letter from Ground Zero

PATRICK McGRATH

On the first of October, descending into Newark on American Airlines flight 93, the plane almost empty, I saw the Manhattan skyline with my own eyes for the first time since the attacks of September 11. The strange new flatness at the tip of the island made it seem modest. New York is many things, but modest has never been one of them, nor has injured, broken, or enfeebled, but that's how it looked from the air that afternoon. Normally, returning to this most exhilarating of cities carries with it a sharp keen savour of anticipation. The excitement was muted this time, compounded as it was with grief, and loss; and as flight 93 landed without incident I was also feeling a distinct unease. My home in New York is just a few hundred yards from Ground Zero.

The Holland Tunnel was closed and the cab had to come in by way of Jersey City. Flags were everywhere, taped to windows, fluttering from vehicles, hanging down the sides of buildings. At a stoplight near the Lincoln Tunnel a uniformed firefighter went from car to car with a huge battered boot, collecting for the families of men lost from the local firehouse. He didn't have time for all the proffered donations before the light changed. It was a glorious afternoon, the light soft and clear, the leaves turning, and it's been like this almost every day since. We're having one of the best autumns anyone can remember.

Unsure if I could get back into my apartment, that night I stayed with friends. We had supper at the kitchen table. I heard stories, the first of the multitude of stories I would hear in the days to come, and I realized that almost everyone I knew in New York, by the fact of their presence here on September 11, was in one way or another a witness to an event of immense historical gravity: such is the layout of the city, and such was the height of the towers, that a large number of people actually saw the planes go in, and the towers come down. One friend of mine described the first plane being *swallowed* by the north tower; he was five blocks away, taking his daughter to school. Another, who was also close to the trade center that morning, told me the plane went in as though it were going through kleenex. One of my dinner companions was actually on the ground floor of the north tower at the time, and fled with the rest as a huge black cloud came sweeping through the shopping concourse; she said there was no panic.

But what was it they had witnessed? The opening salvo of an apocalyptic war, whose course would dominate the rest of our lives, or perhaps *end* our lives? The question remains unanswerable. They went off to bed, my witnesses to history, but I was restless, and far from ready for sleep. I was relieved to be back, the apprehension I'd felt earlier completely dissipated. At midnight I went downtown.

Crossing Canal Street I had to show identification before the cop at the barrier would let the cab through. Then we were in Tribeca. For almost all of the twenty years I've been in New York I've lived in Tribeca, a wedge-shaped neighbourhood of massive nineteenth-century warehouses flanked by Broadway to the east and the Hudson River to the west. In the 1980s big raw lofts could be had for next to nothing down here, and artists and poets stalked the desolate potholed streets by night. Ten years later the area became fashionable, developers fixed up the big raw lofts, and now they sell for a million dollars plus.

Chambers Street, where my wife and I live these days, abuts the financial district, which encompasses the twin towers site, and here the character of the neighbourhood changes. Warehouses give way to stores and apartment buildings, and by day the streets are thronged. City Hall is close by, also the courts, also Wall Street. I got out of the cab when we reached the police barriers two blocks north of Chambers.

The smell was not nearly as bad as it had been in the first days apparently, when New Yorkers were nauseated if the wind blew from the south. That night I smelled an acrid, smoky odour, not unpleasant, by no means a stench, which has grown milder in the days since. As for the source of that acrid odour, I had been aware of it for the last few minutes I'd been riding in the cab. It looked as if a movie was being shot five or six blocks away, for the night was lit with powerful artificial light, a pale, milky blue in colour, and framed by high buildings on either side of the street, which boxed in the light and gave the impression of a vast stage set. Smoke was billowing up through this weird light, and I could see cranes moving about. A group of men emerged from out of the smoke, exhausted men in hard hats and covered in dust and ash. There was a new sound too, a steady distant rumbling and clanking and rattling, the sound of giant bulldozers with massive shovels scooping up debris and pouring it into trucks, which then carted it away to barges moored on the Hudson nearby. The barges take it across the harbour to Staten Island, where, at a landfill called Fresh Kills, it is sifted and inspected, piece by piece, for evidence, and for body parts.

I walked two blocks east to Broadway. Across from City Hall men from the telephone company were digging up the street. A sanitation truck went by, yellow lights blinking, spraying the street to keep down the dust. More barriers, NYPD trestles, painted blue, stencilled, familiar from a thousand street closures of one kind or another. Cops manned the barriers and chatted amiably with the few sightseers and residents still up and about at this time of night. A stone's throw from the Brooklyn Bridge I had to cross over to the east side of Broadway. All that had once been so familiar was now strange, and it was not always easy to know what I was looking at. Streets I had walked down many times, with high buildings on either side – what were those buildings called? Which ones had survived? Which came down? Suddenly, I saw the side of a building torn open and its innards spilling out, sheared off, twisted, *tortured*, and starkly illuminated by that weird light; and in that instant I was viscerally awoken to the unbelievable violence of the event. When the towers came down, corkscrewing as they collapsed on themselves, they spewed out steel girders, which tore open the walls of adjacent structures.

A block or two further down, at Liberty Street, I stood behind a barrier among a small silent crowd and stared at the remains of the south tower, fretted sections of what had once been the northeast corner of the building thrusting up from the rubble at skewed angles like the tombstones in the nearby graveyard of St Paul's Church. The gothic detailing of their aluminium-faced columns possesses a grim aptness, now that the tower is in ruins.

That night there were still many flyers attached to walls, windows, and fences, each with the particulars of someone missing, someone not seen since 9.11.01, perhaps a photograph, and a phone number to call, or a website to visit. The mayor had them quietly removed a few days later, when the search for survivors was officially called off.

A little later I retraced my steps and walked west toward the Hudson. The West Side Highway is closed to ordinary traffic and I was able to wander out into the middle of its eight lanes as they come sweeping down the side of Manhattan to its most southerly point at Battery Park. At Chambers Street a pedestrian bridge crosses the highway, linking the city to Stuyvesant High School and the Hudson River Park on the far side. The bridge is a handsome structure of iron girders painted white, with a horizontal span and a curved arch overhead. At night it is lit like a half moon tipped on its flat side, and shines like a beacon, demarcating the tip of the island and the skyscrapers crowded there. The night sky overhead, with the river and the harbour off to the right, and the Statue of Liberty out in the bay, and the lights of the Jersey shore beyond – and to the left the financial district with its cluster of skyscrapers – was once the backdrop of the twin towers. This was where they were best viewed, where they most dramatically asserted their authority, constructed, as they were, on a scale far greater than anything around them; this was their frame, and now it was empty.

And that's when it properly hits you, like a hard-swung shovel to the back of the head, the awful comprehension of what we've lost here. It's the empty sky over the West Side Highway.

For a month now I have been trying to get used to the empty sky. The weather has not been helpful to those who like their reality a touch misty, a touch muffled and obscure, like a Henry James sentence from the late period. At this time of the year a fierce Atlantic light bathes every building, and every face on the street, with an intense stark clarity. The sky, day after day, is a sheer unclouded blue. It is an exhilarating quality of light if all is well with the world; but it's not, so better by far to go out at night. But the Tribeca night now flickers with the circling lights of emergency vehicles, and hums with heavy generators. From the ruins comes the steady rumble of demolition and clearance. The Tribeca night no longer belongs to its one-time denizens, late-night drinkers, walkers of dogs, and sleek urbanites spilling out of marvellous bistros like Odeon and Zinc. Now it belongs to steamfitters, truck drivers, firefighters, cops; the good guys in hard hats who come tramping up out of the smoking horror, or buzz round the streets in motorized buggies, or bring in the trucks from Long Island, from upstate, and New Jersey, to cart off the rubble to barges bound for Fresh Kills.

That first night I went to Tom's, one of my old haunts, Tom being a soft-voiced Kerry man with a quiet humour beneath which he sustains a steely authority quite terrifying to those who misbehave. The bar has a large plate-glass window facing onto the street, but this night it was darker than usual, and the regulars were clustered conspiratorially up at one end. I thought not of London in the Blitz but rather of Graham Greene's Vienna of *The Third Man*. A shadowy, maudlin place it seemed, and I soon discovered that my own mood of the previous days was mirrored here. It is a persisting grief. It has characteristics of depression. It disrupts concentration and leaches the joy from projects and aspirations that gave zest to life before September 11. It messes up our sleep, and we startle at sudden loud noises. Nobody I know has escaped it. Some are seeing their therapists every day now, or taking strong medication, or floundering in marital discord, or alienating their friends. Drinking and smoking are popular. Some have gone into survivalist mode. One man I know has stocked up on 140 lbs of dog food; otherwise, he says, his dogs will eat him while he's asleep. Everybody's wobbly – why? Inasmuch as a city is no more than the sum of its residents, and each resident identifies with his city – particularly a city with as distinctive a personality as New York – then each one of us was attacked that morning, and we hurt as we would at any unprovoked assault, never mind an assault as deliberate, and destructive, and evil as this one was. And five thousand of us were killed!

Nor have our souls been eased in the days since; rather, grief is now compounded with dread. For the narrative has continued to unfold. The country is at war. Commandos have already been on the ground in Afghanistan. We are under bioterrorist attack, and as of yesterday eight people had been diagnosed with inhalation anthrax. Three of them have died. It comes in the mail, or so we thought; today we learn that a New York woman who did not handle mail professionally is fighting for her life, and the source of the anthrax deep in her lungs is unknown. The government told us yesterday that another terrorist attack is anticipated in the next few days, and we should be at a heightened state of alert; but alert to what? We are told no more than that.

Episodes of peripheral insanity have erupted, weird bits of evil apparently stimulated by the attacks, as for example the deaths aboard a Greyhound bus in Tennessee, when a knife-wielding Croatian slashed the driver's throat and the bus careered across two lanes of oncoming traffic, then flipped over, killing six. There is a man called Zacarias Moussaiou, now in custody, who enlisted in a Minnesota flying school and aroused suspicion when he expressed a desire to learn to fly large commercial jets but showed no interest in taking off or landing. The days prior to the attacks now seem idyllic in retrospect, and many of us feel a sharp sense of nostalgia for that more innocent time.

There have been small boosts to the spirit. Three weeks after we were allowed back into our home on Chambers Street, more streets were reopened around Ground Zero. Once more I set out to circumnavigate the ruins. Coming down Broadway, close to Wall Street, I came upon a store that oddly I had never noticed before. It is called The New York Stocking Exchange. It sold stockings of a provocative variety and little wispy bits of attractive ladies' underwear. Now its treasures were coated by a thick gray layer of dust and ash. Behind a metal grille the plate glass of the store window had cracked, and large shards of glass lay among the disordered display. A limbless, headless mannikin's torso clad in a skimpy red teddy dangled from a string, turning gently in the breeze. The legs of mannikins thrown down by the blast lay in thick ash, still sheathed in fishnet. And there was a large sign that read: 20% OFF ALL BRAS AND GIRDLES. It reminded me of something I'd seen some nights before, another curious juxtaposition of eros and death. Coming home late, I noticed four men leaning against a concrete barrier at the edge of the sidewalk. They were gazing into the bar of a respectable Mexican restaurant whose doors were flung open to the street. Loud music was pouring out. As I passed the bar I glanced in, and saw a pale blonde woman in a long black dress dancing, by herself, with abandon, for the benefit of the watching men. It was surreal, it was sexy, and it seemed to be fuelled by the strange energies emanating from the smoking ruins six blocks south.

Ground Zero has now shrunk to the extent that a pedestrian can stay within two or three blocks of the ruins on all but the west side of the site, so that as you thread your way along narrow streets that once lay obscured in the shadow of the great towers, new perspectives of the devastation are suddenly apparent. That gothic remnant of the south tower, five stories high, is now visible in its entirety from the stub end of Greenwich Street, just off Rector. Nearby, the morning I was last down there, a team of labourers loaded black garbage bags of rubble onto a flatbed truck. Each bag seemed to hold nothing bigger than a melon, but the weight of it taxed even the most muscular of the men. Beyond the wall section, from high pipes, water poured ceaselessly into the ruins, where subterranean fires still burn; and smoke lazily drifted up among the tilting cranes, into a cloudless October sky.

All the buildings close to Ground Zero that are still standing are draped from top to bottom in a kind of industrial curtain, some an orangey-red colour, others dark grey. They look like projects by Christo. It is to shield the workers below from falling glass. And the ground is still so hot that a pair of workboots lasts only a few days. The soles literally burn out.

Battery Park City is open again, though strange in its emptiness, the absence of the usual convoys of strollers and nannies, joggers and rollerbladers. The apartment buildings in this affluent new development at the bottom of the island suffered extensive damage when the towers came down, and a number of moving vans are in evidence as tenants, perhaps with small children and worried about air quality, head out for the suburbs. There is an esplanade along the Hudson here, and very peaceful it is on a fresh autumn day; many of the workers from Ground Zero eat their lunch here, gazing out across the river to the large construction projects clearly visible on the Jersey shore, these in stark contrast to the grisly work going forward on the Manhattan side.

The esplanade at its north end gives onto a boat basin, now empty of vessels, and the Hoboken ferry terminal, and here you see where the American Express Building took a glancing blow from material spewing out of the collapsing towers. It looks as if the claw of a lion the size of a football stadium had swiped in its rage at the corner of the building, and torn away a ragged strip of skin; windows fell out where the lion breathed on them, and now they're patched with plywood.

Then you see the Winter Garden below, and remember that people sheltering there were killed that day. It is a soaring glass atrium, once a beautiful structure, a thing of light and grace, but it is now fouled with dust and ash. There is devastation within. It was the home of a number of very tall palm trees, a bookstore, cafés and restaurants – a civilized public space where I once heard a full symphony orchestra accompany a Chaplin movie. It makes you cry to see it polluted and filthy and ruined, and for what? But depressing as it is to come upon such wreckage, with the shrinking of the parameters of Ground Zero we no longer seem to be living on the edge of a demolition site-cum-cemetery, a place which one worker told me 'reeked of death, literally, metaphorically, and metaphysically'. We are once more living in lower Manhattan, which contains a demolition site but is not entirely dominated by it, as it had been before.

It does you good to get out of the city. We took a day trip to Cold Spring, a village on the Hudson an hour north by train. The river was glorious on this clear fall day, the dense foliage on its steep banks rich in shades of red and gold. Returning in the late afternoon, we came into Grand Central Station at rush hour. Fighting through the crowded main concourse to the subway I relished the waves of New Yorkers streaming by us, frowning, bustling, hardworking people intent on getting home. It was hard not to feel a sort of Whitmanesque elation at the sheer diversity and energy of all this turbulent rushing preoccupied humanity; nor was it difficult to imagine a bomb exploding here, with all the ensuing horror and mayhem. Such thoughts are never far from anyone's mind, these days.

For we are living in a state of dread. By the time this is published everything might have changed, and if so, it will certainly be for the worse. The best we can hope for is to continue to live in dread. Another 'monstrous dose of reality', as Susan Sontag called it, may at any time overwhelm the fragile structures of everyday life. All projections of the future are tentative, provisional, now. There are still a million tons of rubble to be removed from the disaster area, and the work is expected to take a year. The argument about what should be done with the site will probably grow more heated. The city will haggle with the federal government about the size of the handout New York requires for rebuilding and recovery, its first request for $54 billion having been met with some scepticism by the Bush administration. And if nothing monstrous happens, lower Manhattan will remain a magnet to visitors, and to the street vendors who sell them flags, pins, posters, postcards, scarves, baseball caps, anything at all that has the twin towers or the stars-and-stripes on it. (I saw one man with the burning towers tattooed on his biceps.) Local businesses, particularly the restaurants which draw people into this neighborhood, will struggle, for a while, to survive. But gradually the dread will ease, it will turn to apprehension, and then, one day, we will awake to find that it has faded away altogether. If nothing monstrous happens in the meantime.

31 October 2001

(Winter 2001–2)

On translating Joseph Roth

MICHAEL HOFMANN

I was first offered a Joseph Roth novel to translate in 1988. The book was *Right and Left*. Roth's previous translator, John Hoare, I think had died. I had been reading Roth for some years, reviewed some of the books – *Weights and Measures*, *Job*, *Hotel Savoy*, *The Spider's Web*, *Zipper and his Father* – and written an introduction for a paperback edition of one: *Flight Without End*. A bit of Zipper had even made its way into a poem I wrote in the mid eighties: 'Once, I left a bit of Joseph Roth bleeding on your desk' (the pun on 'Roth', red, and 'bleeding'). I had done some translations, and thought of it as something I would do from time to time, but I had no ambitions for myself as a translator.

I should perhaps mention that I was born in Germany, of German parents, came to England at the age of four, and was brought up in a German-speaking household; after my parents returned to Germany and left me in an English boarding-school, I spent the holidays there, and read German easily and relatively uncomplainingly. My German is familial and somewhat literary: that of a child who's read Thomas Mann, as I've sometimes described it. There are things in German I find difficult or distasteful – contemporary slang, bureaucratic language, technical terms of all sorts – but it is not a language I've ever had to learn.

Perhaps this sounds like an ideal background for a translator, until I remind you that translating, in a bilingual family, was not something that ever happened. That reflex was missing. We spoke in whatever language we were speaking in – generally, at my parents' insistence, German – and if we got tired or angry, or there was a better word in English, then we used that. The natural language for all of us was macaronics of one consistency or another. Translation was not a naturally occurring activity, and was in fact, probably, the last thing such a background equipped one for. I have subsequently acquired the reflex, and it's a tedious thing: generally now when I read German, I translate it to myself as I go along. But it's not something I ever used to do, and I presumably won't ever have the messianic zeal of the basically monoglot translator, someone who habitually and by necessity moves things out of the relative darkness of other languages into the light of his own, where he can truly possess them.

Something came between me and the translation of *Right and Left* – namely, another Roth title. The publisher got wind of the fact that the Italian director Ermanno Olmi had made a film of *The Legend of the Holy Drinker* – Roth's last work, from 1939 – assumed that this was another novel, and got me to do it first, so that they could have the 'movie tie-in' and Rutger Hauer (in the title role, a natural following his work with Guinness) moodily gracing the cover. What he had neglected to find out – the estimable Jeremy Lewis, then working for Chatto & Windus – was that *The Legend of the Holy Drinker* was a long story or a short novella, not more than twelve or thirteen thousand words, way below anything of publishable length in English. (It has long been one of my grouses against publishing in England that short books – and hence short literary forms – are thought to be impossible: the public is allowed to exercise a tyranny based on 'value for money' analogous to the theatre audience's 'right to laugh'. In either case creative freedom is stunted. Well, not many dead.) In the event, a large type-size was chosen, the layout left space wherever possible, I was obliged to throw in a Translator's Note at no extra cost, and, weighing in at an unlikely forty-nine pages, the book was published in 1989. A little later, a Sunday paper editor, not having troubled to see that I had translated it, asked me if I would like to review it. I confessed my part in the book, offered my acceptance anyway, and was of course not allowed to write about it. All this strikes me as pretty much par for the course; the history of the translation and publication of foreign books can probably best be seen as a series of well-intentioned blunders.

All my previous engagement with Roth's work seems to have left me unprepared for its variety, and, in this instance – it's a strange word to use – its plumminess. I took no decisions of principle – I rarely do, it's usually the province of uninformed editors, saying they want a book (which they are not in a position to read) to turn out in such and such a way – but found myself moving in unexpectedly arch, ironic and polysyllabic territory. In my 'Note' I even, unusually, tried to explain myself:

It is customary – and usually correct – to praise Roth's style for its simplicity. But Roth is not monosyllabic and not Hemingway. He is a thoughtful, quirky and refined writer. Simplicity in English is apt to be taken for rawness, simple-mindedness or blandness, and Roth is very far from being any of these. Nor would he have allowed simplicity to obstruct him in what he was saying. Therefore, after little hesitation, I have decided to plump for a style that gives expression to Roth's ironic capacity, flexibility and qualities of thought. In English, this means using French and Latin words, and this I have very occasionally done, conscious all the time that Roth would have deplored such a practice (and even more the condition of the language that necessitates it), but thinking that in the end he too would have had to adopt it.

In fact, fourteen years and seven Roths later, I'm not so sure he would have deplored it; my sense of him then was perhaps overly influenced by his early plainness and brightness of language, and I think I felt guilty at following my own predilections of vocabulary. The fact is that Roth's hero Andreas Kartak – a Polish ex-miner, murderer, gaolbird and vagrant wino and 'illegal' – is a man possessed of a medieval sense of honour and Absurdist punctilio. He and his associates – other vagrants, whores, shop assistants and casual labourers (oh, and 'the celebrated footballer, Kanjak') – express themselves with exquisite courtesy and genteelness; they are as solicitous and forbearing as a bunch of knights. (I wonder whether Beckett might not have known the book.) I fell, therefore, into courtois parlance, and, partly because of that, partly because of the Parisian setting (Andreas sleeps under a different bridge every night), into a lot of French: confrère, bagatelle, quartier, patronne, foulard. The originals, in most cases, were German words. When Andreas has some good fortune and comes into some money, he 'decided unhesitatingly to follow some good, yes, some noble prompting, and for once not go to the Tari-Bari, but instead, newspaper in hand, to seek out some classier establishment, where he would order a roll and some coffee – perhaps inspirited with a jigger of rum'. Here, the original was French, 'mit Rum arrosiert' (i.e. 'arrosé rhum'), but I went for the very high-toned 'inspirited', tempered, or perhaps diluted, by the 'jigger'.

I had the feeling I had to stay on the move, as it were, take German into French, French into Latin. The translating itself became vagrant and courtly. There is, I think, often something to be said for not adopting the obvious 'equivalent'. The translation asserts itself, throws over the traces, refuses simple obedience. Later on, when I came to translate Roth's *Rebellion*, for instance, the first sentence came out as: 'The 24th Military Hospital was a cluster of shacks on the edge of the city.' There is a perfectly good English word, 'barracks' – that was the German – but I didn't want it. I imagine something of the second-hand status of the word would somehow leak through into the English. 'One is always nearer', Thom Gunn says, 'by not keeping still.' For me, there has to be some fun, something erratic, something discretionary – otherwise someone else might as well be doing it, if not (the translator's nightmare) a machine. These moments of departure, surely utterly harmless for the most part, are enough to set one's chilly pedantic blood racing.

There is one in *The Legend of the Holy Drinker* that still worries me. Andreas, as I say, is a drunk. On the second page, he receives an astonishing offer: 'The vagrant took a step back, and for a moment it looked as if he might fall over, but he managed to stay on his feet, if with a little local difficulty.' Those last words – I can't remember whose they are, but a very famous tag from British history: Palmerston, Gladstone, Churchill, Eden? – still alarm me. How did I dare? I'm pretty sure I wouldn't do it now. It was opportunism, a spree, something not – obviously – in the original, but available in

English, a signal, hence, of what I once called 'the strange bi-author-ship of translation'. If translation is often best likened to performance, this is the actor or violinist winking at the hall, or something like the phrase 'larking with the mails' in 'The Whitsun Weddings'.

Up to the late eighties, my translations had been one-offs, hit-and-run exercises. Because of the circumstances in Roth's case, where I was given a second book to do ahead of the first, Roth was always going to be a serial engagement – though, of course, I could never have guessed I would end up doing eight books and counting. This must have improved my morale and deepened my identifica-tion and my interest in the role; to stick to the performance metaphor, it was like learning that one's engagement had been extended, or that one was going to tour a production. *Right and Left*, published ten years before *The Legend of the Holy Drinker*, comes out of Roth's *Neue Sachlichkeit* period: brisk, satirical, contemporary. Its par-ticular interest for me was the circumstance that its central figure, Paul Bernheim, was sent to Oxford by his nouveau riche anglophile father. This has a certain piquancy for the translator, as it was to have for me later as well, when I translated Kafka's *Amerika* / *The Man Who Disappeared*. The translation has the rare opportunity to be more echt than the original! In the case of Kafka, whose America is of course deeply unecht (the word exists in German, though not in English), that meant eschewing all Americanisms, no twang, no ele-vators. But with Roth I could indulge myself in the mimicry of upper-caste Oxonian.

It begins with the preposterous self-identification with England of a group of citizens in a landlocked little burg in Mitteleuropa: 'For a time it looked as though there was a little Anglo-Saxon enclave growing up in the town, perhaps ultimately seeking its absorption into the British Empire. In this town, with its thoroughly Continental character, where there was never any hint of fog, they had to eat, drink and be clothed as though they were on the roaring sea-coasts of England.' Some of the pleasure of this for me lay in writing veiled self-mocking autobiography: I was once like this town, a thoroughly Continental (always a semi-poisonous word in English) little boy, who from the age of four did indeed suffer his own anglicization. Once at Oxford, Bernheim, like many of Roth's characters, writes wonderfully inadequate letters home: 'The tone of these letters of Paul's was strictly conventional. Sporting expressions and bewilderingly alien terms for rowing and sailing boats alternated with the names of distinguished families, while the short, monosyllabic names of his friends, "Bob", "Ted" and "Pete", went off like bangers in the text.' The fact that this passage would remind me ruefully of what letters I wrote home from Winchester is probably a source of purely personal – invisible – gratification, but it does count in the way that the translator has to find in himself all the various gestures and tones of his original, and these I found particularly easy and congenial. The actual letter, when it comes, goes like this:

Well, old chap, the time's come! Cavalry, dragoons with any luck. Telegraphed the old man right away. Two years' grace, by then my riding should be up to snuff for the Wild West. Bought a horse over here, call him Kentucky, licks my face, as much character as a tomcat. Medic was a brick. But then I was the fittest fellow there, some feat, all the rest were pen-pushers, one labourer. Poor specimens. Still, all taken. As though there was a war on. Then spent two days in London, touring the dives. Saw the female sex again, after the monkish life in college. Thought of the old catechist, what a terrific chap he was. He alive still? Well, old boy, another year, and I'll be home for a fortnight. Got to go out now, practise for next week. Big day! Fencing tournament, with ball to follow. Completely forgotten how to dance, will have to learn again from basics. You see, all go. Oh well, cheerio!

The combination of telegraphic urgency, exiguous content and utter self-complacency was irresistible to me: you can practically hear the twittish monocle. This is, if you like, translation as revenge.

Not much of the book is set in England – that's just a bonus – but the rest is so swift and vivid and incisive, it doesn't much matter. Plots and characters and settings veer impulsively. There seems to me to be so much drudgery involved in translation that staying interested is a problem for the translator. In particular, most descriptive passages seem to exist purely for the benefit of the writer; to the reader, they transact little or nothing. How much preferable, then, are short, fast-moving books like Roth's. To someone coming from poetry as I do, flashes of intensity, local beauties, balance, surprise, memorableness, concision are all especially cherished values, and Roth, who took a lot of his prose style from Heine, has them in wonderful abundance. I used to talk about him with Joseph Brodsky, who said there is a poem on every page of Joseph Roth. Equally, the epic qualities like structure and form matter less, and the fact that Roth's novels burn up their material with ill-concealed impatience doesn't matter at all: I'm impatient as well! I don't care, for instance, that *Right and Left* was supposed to be about a pair of brothers, one on the right, one on the left, but that Roth lost patience with them, and introduces instead ('In stepped Nikolai Brandeis') the enigmatic figure of Brandeis, a kind of ex machina character from the East – that East that is sardonically described as beginning at Katowice, and extending as far as Rabindranath Tagore – or that at the end of the book, as of many or even most of Roth's novels, character and author simply walk away.

To advocates of, as it were, the 'well-made novel' – analogous to the 'well-made play' – these habits and these books are unsatisfactory (although exceptions can safely be made for *The Radetzky March* and *Weights and Measures*, perhaps for *The String of Pearls*). But, taking my lead from Randall Jarrell, who described a novel as so and so many thousand words of narrative prose 'with something wrong with it', I can't say I find the 'imperfections' or 'indiscipline' of these books all that troublesome. One can either read them 'lyrically', like Brodsky, for the beauty and interest of individual sentences, scenes and tropes; or else in their totality. My image of Roth's oeuvre is of a sort of Rubik's cube: each plane – each novel – may contain stray or surplus material, but one can take them together and recombine them in one's mind to make an incredibly rich whole. The 'fault', if it is a fault, is that Roth's 'fable' – Edwin Muir's term – is too complex and contradictory to be written in any single book, not even *The Radetzky March*. In his life and his person and his opinions, Roth was multitudinous and unresolved. Instances of this can be produced practically ad infinitum: he was 'red Roth', he was a monarchist and Habsburg apologist; he was a pacifist, he was an Austrian officer; he was a Jew, he was a Catholic; he loved women and enjoyed their love, he was a misogynist and feared their destructive power; he was a novelist, he was the premier journalist of his period; he was an alcoholic, he was a disciplined and immensely productive writer; he was fatherless, he was father-obsessed and circulated seventeen versions of his own paternity; he was 'a hotel patriot'; he was 'a Frenchman from the East'; and so on. Nor is it necessarily the case that he was in transit from one set of beliefs to another; rather, he held them all in unresolved suspension. (As I say, a lot of the novels and stories end with departure – one may well wonder whether anyone ever arrived. Roth himself, when he died, had in his possession an invitation from American PEN.) Hence, perhaps, the conviction and insight of this brilliant catalogue that is one of my favourite parts of *Right and Left*:

To escape it [emptiness], he surrounded himself with friends. They were people who sponged off him, shadows that had emerged from the fog of the time, and were formed from it. All of them moved in the vague, indefinite and constantly shifting terrain between art and gambling. They were connected with the theatre, with fine art, with literature, but they didn't write, didn't paint and didn't act. One started a magazine that lasted for a week. Another took an advance for a newspaper article he would never write. A third set up a theatre company for young performers, and was arrested after the opening night. A fourth let out his rooms to a gambling club, could no longer stay at home, and gambled away the rent he was paid in other gaming clubs. A fifth, who had studied medicine, performed abortions, but in the interests of discretion only in the circle of his friends, from whom he could earn no fees. A sixth organised spiritualist meetings, and was denounced by one of his own mediums. A seventh spied simultaneously for the state police and for foreign embassies, cheated them all and was afraid of retribution from them all. An eighth fitted up Russian emigrants with false passports and genuine residence permits. A ninth passed false information from secret nationalist organisations to the radical newspapers, which a tenth bought before it could be printed, and was rewarded for doing so by moneyed conservatives.

This glorious, hilarious and utterly logical list would probably resist incorporation into most narratives – it reminds me of Kafka's terrific story 'Eleven Sons' – but one could find others like it in any book of Roth's.

There followed – for me – a gap of seven years during which I diverted myself in other ways. Chatto was bought up, stopped publishing translations; Roth fell out of print. Across the Atlantic, things were much the same. Of course I regretted this, but by now I had been made to understand that, as far as publishers were concerned, translations like mine were basically a short-lived and mistaken undertaking. During the eighties and nineties the very idea of a 'classic' book suffered grievous and irreversible harm. I had no expectation of ever translating Joseph Roth – or much of anything – again. Then, by coincidence – I am not enough of an optimist to read trend or providence in it – Robert Weil at St. Martin's and then Norton, and Neil Belton at Granta separately but simultaneously took up Joseph Roth. I translated *The String of Pearls* (*The Tale of the 1002nd Night* in the US), *Rebellion*, the non-fiction book *The Wandering Jews*, *The Collected Shorter Fiction*, a selection of journalistic pieces about Berlin (to be called *What I Saw* in the US), and a *Radetzky March* for the UK. For most of the past four years I have had a Joseph Roth book in the works. It has, if not professionalized me, then at least given me routine and focus as a translator.

Roth remains a deeply impressive writer to me, working in a period – the twenties and thirties – that was at the very least a Silver Age of German letters (in the lee or the shadow of Kafka and Brecht and Musil and Thomas Mann, there were such figures as Heinrich Mann, Odon von Horvath, Alfred Döblin, Ernst Weiss, Wolfgang Koeppen, Marieluise Fleisser, the two Zweigs and several others). Within and among these writers there is a lively dialogue between left and right, east and west, traditional and Modernist-Expressionist, collective and individual. I don't think subsequent generations have had much to teach them.

I am continually surprised by Roth. When I translated *The Wandering Jews*, it was his cleverness; in *The String of Pearls* the lightness of this Viennese confection (especially given that it was published in 1939); in the *Collected Shorter Fiction* the sheer variety, so that the seventeen different pieces seemed to require as many different keys to open them. He is still unknown to me, and probably unknowable. I realized this when a *New York Times* journalist rang me to collect information for a profile of Roth (which never was written, or at least never appeared). What would he have been like in a room? – a fair question. I had absolutely no idea. I have never heard his voice; I don't think a film or recording of him exists. In the few photographs his face is either averted or else impermeably frontal – perhaps the most helpful shot of him I saw was the cover of the US *Collected Stories*, where the photograph was printed in mirror image, so that one has the sense of seeing him as he would have seen himself. He was short, ugly, well turned out (except when very drunk), formal, thin when young then with a drinker's pouchiness and puffiness, of indeterminate hair-colour – a little blond moustache, a kiss curl like Bill Haley's – prematurely aged. He collected pocket knives and watches, and liked to tinker with them. He is only two long generations away, and I have known people only a decade or so younger, but meeting Roth is quite unimaginable to me. He espoused such irretrievably historic things as the Dual Monarchy and the pre- and anti-Zionist distribution of Jews throughout Europe. Partly because of that, it's as though at some point his life went into reverse, into the nineteenth century. He died when he was as old as I am now, not quite forty-five.

In the case of other authors I have translated – Wolfgang Koeppen, my father Gert Hofmann, one or two contemporaries like Zoe Jenny and Peter Jungk and Wim Wenders – I understood that what drew me to them was tonal and vocal. Their books were audible to me in a way that was familiar to me from poetry, my own and others'. Even this doesn't hold for Joseph Roth, whose books (with

occasional exceptions, like the short story 'April' or the novel frag-
ment 'Strawberries') are written, rather than sounding. Translation
involves vanity and delusion. The translator puts on a mask (otherwise known as the author), and admires his features in the mirror. I
reread my translations endlessly, both before publication – at that
wonderful stage when the drudgery is done, and each little tinkering
change animates and improves the text – but also after. It probably
sounds foolish, but on the other hand, if I didn't and if I didn't want
to, then what right should I have to expect anyone else to buy them
and read them? It's my version of a guarantee, of after-sales care. I do
it, I have to say, more often with the voice-based translations –
Koeppen and my father and the rest of them – than with Roth.
Perhaps it's that the former provide a better mirror; perhaps Roth
gives me less licence; perhaps, try as I may, I can't find myself
responsible for something so briskly and personally encyclopaedic:

Night is full of feeling and surprise, out of the blue, longings come to us,
when the distant whistle of a locomotive catches in the window, when
a cat slinks along the pavement opposite, hungry for love, and disappears into a basement window where the tom waits. There is a big
starry sky above us, too remote to be kind, too beautiful not to harbour
a God. There are the little things close at hand and there is a remote
eternity, and some relation between them that escapes our understanding. Maybe we would understand it, if love were to visit us; love relates
the stars and the slinking cat, the lonesome whistle and the vastness of
the stars.

('The Blind Mirror')

Our autumn consisted of molten gold and molten silver, of wind,
swarms of ravens and mild frosts. Autumn lasted almost as long as winter. In August, the leaves turned yellow, in the first days of September
already they lay on the ground. No one bothered to sweep them up. It
wasn't until I came to Western Europe that I saw people sweeping up
the autumn into a proper dungheap. No wind blew on our clear autumn
days. The sun was still very hot, and already very slant and very yellow.
It went down in a red west, and rose every morning from a bed of silver
and mist. It took a long time for the sky to become a deep blue, but then
it stayed like that for the whole of the short day.

('Strawberries')

Most people, who only know corals from seeing them in shop windows and displays, would be surprised to learn how many different varieties of them there are. For a start, they can be polished or not; they can be trimmed in a straight line or rounded off; there are thorny and stick-like corals that look like barbed wire; corals that gleam with a yellowish, almost a whitish red, like the rims of tea-rose petals; pinkish-yellow, pink, brick-red, beet-red, cinnabar-red corals, and finally there are those corals that look like hard, round drops of blood. There are rounds and half-rounds; corals like little barrels and little cylinders; there are straight, crooked and even hunchbacked corals. They come as stars, spears, hooks and blossoms. For corals are the noblest plants in the oceanic underworld; they are like roses for the capricious goddesses of the sea, as inexhaustible in their variety as the caprices of the goddesses.

('The Leviathan')

These passages – there are thousands more where they came from! – show what a harmonious writer Roth is, though without any of the defensiveness and pedantic limitations of harmony. Each sentence is instinct with mind and sensuality, with colour and form, with rhetoric and reality. They are technically beautiful – if not perfect – but it's not technical prose, it's never merely decorative. It's too supple, too imaginative, too important: 'not to harbour a god', 'sweeping up the autumn into a proper dungheap,' 'stars, spears, hooks and blossoms'. It's closer perhaps to Zbigniew Herbert than it is to most other writings. Humour, whimsy, surprise, are always in the wings. Balance is subtly shifted to accommodate unexpected content. A little of the character and the predicament are dissolved in the telling: the virginal Fini, the rascally speaker of 'Strawberries', the innocent deist Nissen Piczenik. In truth, I don't think I can claim much credit for them, but they are beatific sentences, and habit-forming.

(Autumn 2002)

Sabbath

KATHLEEN JAMIE

On the headland, as though looking out to sea, were many cairns built of stones. They came into view as you walked up through the wicket gate toward the cliff top, and you'd think them the recent work of tourists with time on their hands, but when you got close, you could see they were whiskered with green lichen. You might fancy them the petrified remains of people who'd spent too long sitting in contemplation. The headland was covered with them, some shaped like old-fashioned beehives, others like houses of cards, with uprights and horizontals. With those, you could bend and look at the sea as though through a letterbox.

I found a place well back from the cliff edge, out of the wind, and sat down. To the south a headland jutted out into the sea, and round its end gannets kept coming in threes or fours, heading north, all but invisible until they tilted into the sunlight, and then their white wings gleamed. The horizon was interrupted only by the Flannen Isles, where, according to the ballad, the lighthouse keepers had so simply, so mysteriously, disappeared.

It was still early. I sat on a damp rock, took my notebook from my inner pocket, made earnest notes: *south – sky thin line of rosy pink, straightened blue-pink, blue-greys. Flannen Isles, horizon fine slate-grey line. [unreadable] 3 gannets.* I made notes, but the reason I'd come to the end of the road to walk along the cliffs is because language fails me there. If we work always in words, sometimes we need to recuperate in a place where language doesn't join up, where we're thrown back on a few elementary nouns. Sea. Bird. Sky.

Besides, it was the Sabbath, the day of rest. A sign at the wicket

307

gate that gave onto the coastal walk read 'Please, keep dogs on leads', and 'Please, avoid disturbing the Sabbath.'

It was summer's end – I had a few days to clear my head. The summer had been hard going, with one family crisis after another. There was our grandmother, whom we call Nana, slipping into dependency, and mother, who was adjusting to life after having been paralyzed by a major stroke, and my scared heroic dad doing his best; there were the needs of small children to be met, and then my daughter had missed her first ever day at school because she was in hospital having a head-wound stitched; but the summer had passed, and already, like migrant birds, my university students were arriving, waiting for the teaching term to begin, expecting to be taught how to engage with the world in language.

Keeping the sea to my left hand I walked northwards, the way the gannets had indicated. The cliff-top land dipped into damp troughs and then rose onto promontories where bedrock broke through the thin earth. There were pools of peaty water between rocks, and foraging parties of golden plover. You might call it a wild place, what with the Atlantic to one hand and peat-bog to the other, but in each saddle between the headlands was evidence of some human intervention, an enclosure or a wall. In one I saw the undulations of old lazy-beds. Cruel misnomer: looking down from above, they resembled beds right enough, like sleepers blanketed in peat, but they spoke of hard graft, of carting creels of kelp from the shore to fertilize the thin soil, to extract a hard living from the land.

I walked up on to the next headland, and there, in the next bay, was a sea-stack, a hundred foot or so high. It didn't stand out proud, commanding the ocean, but shrank almost shyly at the back of a dark forbidding concavity of cliff. I dared forward to look down at the water and could see it wasn't a true stack, not truly free-standing, but joined to the cliff behind it by an untidy rocky causeway. Nonetheless, the fulmars loved it. They rested in its ledges, or tipped off the rough pinnacle to glide effortlessly about.

There seemed to be something on its summit. Not a person,

surely, but perhaps another of those odd cairns. I lifted the binoculars, turned the focus wheel until I had in view an impossible little building, no more than a cell. There was a doorway of sorts, but the lintel had long slewed sideways and the whole edifice was leaning at a crazy angle. Whatever it was, hermitage or lookout post, it had the aura of something very old, possibly prehistoric, and it was falling into the sea. A saint or sentry creeping out of that tiny doorway, eyes full of light and ears full of surf, would have to be careful – one false step and he'd pitch clean over the edge and plummet down through the indifferent fulmars into the water below.

But there was something appealing about it. To live alone in a stone cell on a sea-stack, the fulmars for neighbours, the Atlantic breakers and the crying wind; so what if it was slewing to one side? To reach it, you would have to climb. You'd need ropes and harnesses, and you'd have to carry your provisions in a creel on your back. With the glasses, I tried to pick out a route. Perhaps as second, following a trusted leader on a very tight rope, I could try to feel my way up. It would smell of guano and mineral. At that moment I could almost remember, from my youth, the intimate feel of rock.

Twenty years ago I had a boyfriend called Peter, a rock climber thrilled with the stretch and fluidity of his body. He's a senior physiotherapist now, charged with restoring broken bodies to function, if not to grace. I called him when my mother was in rehab leaning to walk again after her stroke, for an honest opinion of her prospects, and I thought about him again now as I looked through the glasses at this stack. I recall him shouting down at me once, when I was struck with fear halfway up some rock-face:

'Remember! It's your skeleton that holds the position, not the muscles. You can let the muscles relax.'

'I can't do this!' I'd wailed.

'You are doing it,' he replied.

I put the binoculars away to move on. I'd find out what it was, this strange inaccessible cell. The mood I was in, it would suit me just fine. I'd look it up in Stornoway Library. I'd look it up in estate agents' windows.

*

The week before I'd come to Lewis, I'd spent a day with my sister in our parents' home town in the west. We'd come to see our grandmother. Every other weekend, someone drives over to see our grandmother. She is either in her own tiny flat, with its gas-fire and armchair and plaster dolphins leaping on the mantelpiece, or, as today, in the ward of the hospital she's frequently admitted to. There had been a phone call: someone telling me they were even now breaking the door down, lifting Nana from the floor where she'd lain all night, carrying her to the ambulance, taking her again into hospital.

None of the family lives in that town these days. Our parents left when they were young and first married, and now that our mother is herself suddenly disabled, and our father charged with her care, and we children already approaching middle age with infants and bread-winning responsibilities of our own, Nana's situation is a constant anxiety.

We had come together, my sister and me, with appointments to see social workers and doctors. In windowless offices we'd signed long forms and discussed doctors' opinions and money. Nana had been a cleaner much of her life, and a single parent: not wealthy. We'd been given a list of care-homes for the elderly in that town, and then we went to have a difficult conversation with Nana herself.

She was sitting in a green high-backed chair in a hospital day-room, one old lady among the rest, dressed, like the others, in a blouse and cardigan and loose trousers. With great attention to detail, she told us what had been served for lunch. We, her two granddaughters, sat before her. My sister held her hand and at last we put the case that had been building over the preceding few years. Around us were other old women, and old men sitting on chairs identical to our Nana's. There were tables with magazines, a TV that was always switched on. Sunlight glinted off the cars parked outside. Now and then snatches of other conversations reached us, cheery banter pitched loud enough for the hard of hearing. I longed to be back outdoors. As we entered my sister had said, 'When she sees us both together, she'll think something's wrong. She'll think mum's had another stroke or something.' And I, never skilled at small talk, thought of news to tell her, tried to dredge up incidents from family life. I rehearsed the story of my daughter's gashed head, and the stitches.

We were surrounded by the very old. The woman in the next chair was asleep, her chin reaching her chest. Next along was a woman who was awake. She wore a blue knitted cardigan, or rather, because her shoulders and breasts sloped at odd angles, a blue cardigan had been arranged round her. Though we were talking to our own grandmother, too loudly for such a delicate conversation, I could see out of the corner of my eye a tiny persistent movement, as you might see a spider in a corner of a window. A little table was pulled up in front of the woman in blue, and on it stood a carton of orange juice. The old woman was struggling to get the end of the straw into the tiny foil-covered hole. The bony hand, the feeble, stabbing straw, the carton, which at any moment would go skiting off the table onto the floor – all became intolerable, so I went and asked if I could help. 'Thank you my dear,' she said, 'thank you.'

The gannets had come to Dalmore, which is a surfers' bay, but no surfers were out this Lord's day. White waves surged between twin headlands, and the gannets, not feeding, not breeding, not going any place, were turning and lifting on the winds. Among the dunes at the top of Dalmore bay is the cemetery. It is enclosed in stone walls and defences had been built to prevent the sea from disturbing the graves. Of course, you'd be more likely to approach the cemetery from the landward side: there is a thin island road that ends at its gate. The headstones stand in neat rows; plots yet to be occupied were marked with numbered metal labels. Presumably there are people who have wandered from this parish all over the world, but who know their number, who carry in their heads an image of this burial ground at the end of the thin road, at the bay.

From the cemetery, I followed the road inland. The township's houses were shut up for the Sabbath. Even the dogs were quiet, and only one house betrayed life, and that only by condensation on its windows, the breathing within. I walked self-consciously, noting wire fences, disused cars, peat-stacks, wondering if to be moving at all, making a display of oneself through the stillness of the afternoon, was to disturb the Sabbath. Sheep were bleating, though. Penned in the in-fields, ewes with fat lambs bleated and bleated. Perhaps they knew it would soon be time for the lambs to be taken away.

A friend said to me – we were talking about our stage in life, when we suddenly discover that *we* are the grown-ups, with children and parents, and even grandparents to tend to, not to mention our pupils or patients or clients or employers – that we spend so much time dealing with it all, there is scarcely time to *feel*. I walked up the silent road, wondering if I couldn't reconcile myself again to the idea of the Sabbath, to the day of dreary silence and mutton broth I'd known as a child, if we couldn't close the shops and still the traffic and institute a modern, churchless day of contemplation and rest, and if it would help at all.

The little hostel was surprisingly busy. It's one of a cluster of half-a-dozen blackhouses some distance above a rocky shore. They're pretend blackhouses, reconstructed for tourists, with curved thatched roofs, thick stone walls, and tiny windows. A pretend blackhouse, because there is no peat fire in the middle of the floor. There are Calor gas stoves, and electricity, and people round the table from Spain and Germany, Australia and England. There were youngsters who'd just finished college and were about to look for their first job, and, almost old enough to be their parents, the jaded and weary, like myself and the Australian chemistry teacher who'd taken a year's leave and had been living out of a car for months.

'Quite right too,' I said. 'Do it while you can. Carpe diem and all that.'

'Are you Scottish?' she said. We were sitting at the gable in the last of the light.

'Not from here. From the other side of the country.'

'Holiday?'

'Few days to clear my head before the term starts.'

'You are so lucky. I had to come right round the world for this.'

There was a young man called Tom, who had straggly blond hair and a bike with a trailer. He must have been superbly fit, because after I'd made his acquaintance I saw him everywhere, for the next few days, from Mealister to Stornoway, beating along the single track-roads, grinning, in love with the world.

'What did you do today?' I asked him. He was repairing a tyre.

'Went to church! I don't, usually. Just wanted to know what it was about, you know?'

'And what was it about?'

'I don't know. It was in Gaelic. A twenty-minute sermon and I couldn't understand a word. You should have heard the sweetie-rustling! But – that psalm-singing was like nothing I'd ever heard before, not even like some of my African tapes, amazing.'

Then he asked: 'What about yourself? What did you do?'

'Me? I just wandered along the cliffs.'

'Cool.'

It had never entered my head, this Sunday, to go to church.

I'd called all the old people's homes on the list the social worker had given us, and for the next few days the postman had pushed through my letter box leaflets and brochures, pictures of dining rooms and bedrooms, always empty. One showed an entrance hall. The carpet was tartan, the walls were papered in a different, clashing tartan. Dolls dressed in black velvet stood like sleepwalkers on one sideboard, on another was a tank of hapless tropical fish. A huge clock, like a sunburst, ticked away the minutes of the days. It looked like the ante-chamber to hell, but when I phoned I heard much cheerful laughter in the background. I'd to ask, 'Do you have a waiting list, and how long ...'

'Well,' the woman had said, 'when someone demits ...'

Demit – I'd to look it up. A Scots word, it means 'relinquish'.

'A few days to clear my head,' I'd said, and it was true. But where to go? To the end of the road, I told myself, and the notion pleased me. So I hired a car. I'd been to one road-end, and walked up to the strange cairns and the cell atop the stack, but there were a couple more days and there were more island roads. I thought, Why not go to them too? Go to all the ends of all the roads, and see what's there.

So, when the Sabbath was over and washing flapped on the lines, I followed a road over peat-moor, where the peat banks were freshly cut and shone as brown as polished leather in the sun. I passed a blighted pine plantation, and a man working at his croft with a scythe. I passed newly-built, un-let business units. There were knapweed and yellow coltsfoot in the ditches, not a cloud in the sky. At times the road turned inland, across peat-bog, between lochans, and at times it followed the shore, offering sudden vistas of yellow beaches and low distant dark purple promontories. There were a few other vehicles on the single-track road, mostly vans: working lads travelling at speed. I tucked into a passing place to allow a huge empty livestock lorry, doubtless come for lambs, to inch by. It was a hot day, such vast light. Tethered in sea-lochs were fish farms and mussel farms. I drove down to a jetty and left the car to listen for a minute to a stack of lobster creels, which was twittering with starlings as they picked scraps.

Inland the hills rose stony and pale and unshadowed, as in Greece or Italy. At Uig, I pulled into a passing place to let an approaching vehicle go by. It wasn't a lorry come for lambs, but a black hearse. Within its stately windows the coffin shone, brass handles gleaming in sunlight. The two undertakers lifted their hands in acknowledgement as they passed. There would be a walled burial ground, perhaps at the end of a bay, at the end of a road.

Feeling as though I had strayed into a film, I carried on, past the houses of Ishiving. Where the road ended, there was a five-bar gate, with a sign hung on it: 'common grazing'.

I parked and wandered down to the shore. Half buried in the green turf were the ruins of an ancient convent. Someone had knocked together a cross out of driftwood, and hung a sign on it: '*Tigh na cailleach dubh*': The place of the black (veiled) women. I walked within its walls, wondering what it would be like to be a nun, black-veiled and in retreat from the world. Out in the bay the sea was glassy blue, bar where waves broke to white over a hidden reef. A lobster boat moved slowly between two islands. From the corner of my eye, though, I noticed a quick dark movement about the seaweed of the tidal rocks. It was a mink, interloper and arch-predator, enemy of sea-birds.

Back on the track again, a young man was striding toward me, with blood on his tweeds. Not blood, I thought, I'm becoming over-wrought. It must be mud, he's a farm lad, a crofter.

'Is it always like this here?' I said of the clear skies.

'I *wish*,' he said.

Three other men were processing down from the hill, one dragging the carcass of a stag over the rough ground, then a man with a gun in a case, then a third man, hauling another stag. They made slow progress, and looked for a moment like a framed print you might find on the wall of a country pub. There was the sudden noise of an engine, and the bloodstained man brought a pick-up truck to meet the shooting party as they gained the road. Together they heaved the dead animals into the back, so only a rack of antlers stuck up over the side. Then the truck moved off along the thin road between hill and shore.

Later in the afternoon, driving back along the same road, I pulled over to let pass a convoy of several cars coming home from the burial ground, each driven by a man in a black tie. If this was a film, it needed editing.

In Stornoway's big supermarket, I thought: Maybe it's a language problem. Maybe the world would make more sense if you could think about it in a different language. Once, some years ago, I'd met an angry young Gael who said he was fed up with people treating his islands like a sort of Eden, people who came to 'escape' but refused to learn Gaelic. I could learn Gaelic. Right here, I could learn the Gaelic for tea and coffee, cat food and tinned vegetables, from the signs hung over the aisles where the people push their trolleys.

Gaelic for cornucopia. I could learn place names from the dual-language road signs, and the OS map. One language breathing down the neck of the other. The painted sign on the five-bar gate at the road end was in English, 'common grazing' it said. But the sign beside the ruins of the convent, that had read '*Tigh na cailleach dubh*'. When, at An Gearranan/Garenin, I'd passed two men in blue overalls conversing over a gate, they spoke in Gaelic, but gave me the time of day in English. When their collie trotted after me it was called back, and apologies offered me, in English. The librarian in Stornoway/Steornabhagh was an Englishman, a Geordie, I think. He brought me old maps and gazetteers to look at. I was hoping to find out about that wild building on the sea-stack. Someone had taken a red biro to the old maps, scored out the anglicized names and re-substituted the Gaelic. In the window of the newsagents, a few doors along the street, were two little black and white printed notices each announcing a funeral. They were in English. The language of the service, and the graveside murmurings, I don't know. The language of the school children scaling down the hill from the Nicolson Institute, girls in black skirts, a boy calling to his mates as he skateboarded along, that was English. The people standing outside the newsagents, waiting for the English papers to come in off the plane, were speaking together in Gaelic. I could learn Gaelic, learn every language under the sun, but I don't know if it would help.

A time to live, a time to die, a time to speak, a time to refrain from speaking. Yesterday, other than a couple of civil greetings to strangers, I'd spoken to no one, which was fine by me. Today, two or three shops had notices in their windows, saying they'd be observing a minute's silence because it was September 11th, the anniversary of all those deaths. Minutes of silence, of remembrance. A momentary Sabbath. I'd watched the Twin Towers on TV as I knelt on the floor of a guesthouse in the Lake District. I'd been booked to give a poetry reading that night, at Grasmere, home of Wordsworth. Did I want to cancel? they asked. I said no. It's poetry's job, isn't it, to keep making sense of the world in language, to keep the negotiation going? We can't relinquish that. A surprising number of people came to hear the poetry, considering. 'Minute's silence!' a friend had snarled. Did they not know, the silence-keepers, how many children had died even that morning in Angola, in Sudan, just because they have no clean water? Was there to be a minute's silence for them? A minute's silence for each, and the world would be hushed forever.

Perhaps, though, if we join up all these minutes we are beginning secularly to observe, we could string them together in a new kind of Sabbath; where there are no men in black blighting our lives with their notions of sin, no chaining up the children's swings for the Lord's day. I mean a contemplative time, a time reserved to reflect. Perhaps we would feel less imperilled.

I called home, standing with my mobile phone on a street that smelled of peat-smoke. Everything was okay. Nothing had gone wrong. My daughter said, 'Hello Mummy, I can't find my homework.'

'How's your head?' I asked

'Oh, it's fine.'

My husband said, 'Elaine called. She seemed a bit upset.' So I called Elaine, who told me what had happened. Her colleague at work had turned up as usual, then, after an hour, made some excuse to leave. He had then driven to a certain spot in a beautiful part of the country, among mountains and lochs, the kind of place one might go to think things through in peace. There he had killed himself. As she told me about this man's solitary drive, it brought to mind the images of my own, the five-bar gate, the vaulting sky, the islands set in a turquoise sea, the mink worrying among the rocks.

Everything will fall into the sea, so far as I could tell, looking at the archaeologists' reports in Stornoway Library. Does this matter? A team of archaeologists had walked and mapped all the features on that part of the coast, and with their expert eye, and by dint of asking local people, had measured and defined and assessed every human intervention in that landscape: illicit stills, sheep-fanks, standing stones. Their anxiety was coastal erosion, things were in danger of slipping away forever. The report itself had been poorly bound; pages slithered out and fell on the library floor.

There was mention of the little building on the stack, it had been labelled and numbered. The report said the little building was prehistoric, and in imminent danger of collapse, but I still don't know what it was. No one had dared climb up to it.

I'd called Peter, the rock-climber and physiotherapist, and asked his opinion on my mother's chances of walking again. He was about to enter his forty-third year, which he was doing with some trepidation, because at that age his own father had died.

'And we're trying to find a home for our grandmother,' I was saying. 'Och, it's awful.'

'Why is it awful?'

Not for the first time, I failed to find an answer to Pete's brusque Yorkshire questions.

'Granny's at that stage in life, you're in yours,' he said. 'It's not awful.'

'I can't do it!' I wailed, half in jest.

'You *are* doing it,' he replied.

Another day, another road end. I'd envied Tom his bike, so hired one of my own, then went cycling out of Stornoway on a grey, unsettled morning. I cycled around traffic islands with palm shrubs, mistook a turn and pedalled past the hospital and through a council scheme before finding the coast road north. I rode under a grey sky that threatened rain, relishing the movement of my body, its own small continuing strength. It wouldn't last forever, that was the truth of it, but today I could cycle along a road, to see where it led.

There were low, rendered houses, a pharmacy, a big serious church, and then I was alone with moor to my left side, to the right the waters of the Minch and the distant mainland mountains. When the road neared its end it descended in a great hill to the huge beach at Tolsta. Black-back gulls and kittiwakes formed two distinct parties at the shoreline, all facing into the wind. A drizzle had set in, and then it turned to real rain. At an empty car park beside a lily-filled lochan the metalled road became a track, which in turn became a churned up peaty path leading onto the moor. But: there was a bridge. In the middle of the peat-bog was a grand single-span Victorian bridge. I leaned the bike on the parapet and watched the water coursing below. The bridge – they call it the 'bridge to nowhere' – was one of Lord Leverhulme's grand schemes. Landlord of Lewis in the 1880s, he'd thought up many a plan for the island: a railway, a kelp industry, a castle at Stornoway now boarded and disused. At the bridge to nowhere, I turned back.

I'd missed, of course, the minute's silence – I'd been free-wheeling downhill at the time, bawling old Rod Stewart songs aloud to myself. Instead I stopped in the tiny garden that encloses the Tolsta war memorial. The bronze plaque lists too many names for this small place; the same surnames recur over and again. The memorial, in the shape of an open book, also remembers the many soldiers who were returning to Lewis from the Great War, only to be drowned when their ship, the *Iolaire*, struck rock outside Stornoway harbour, which is a difficult one to make sense of. There are memorials, too, to the 'heroes of the land struggle': men who'd made it home and demanded not railways or bridges or castles, but land. 'All the crofts of Upper Bac lie on land so seized.'

We would soon have to arrange, my sister and I, to sell our grandmother's tiny tenement flat to pay for her care in her last years. The back-kitchen would have to be relinquished, the armchair and plaster dolphins taken away.

At the end of the road there is a burial ground, enclosed by a stone wall. But we know that. There are other roads, which may end variously. There might be a five-bar gate, with a hand-painted sign opening onto common grazing. It may end at a well-known beauty spot. Possibly, a pick-up truck is waiting, or even a bridge to nowhere, or an old folks' home with tartan carpets, or a strange wild building on top of a sea-stack, demitting stone by stone into the waves far below. The road may end in Sabbath silence and wind, or nothing at all.

I left the memorial, got back on the bike and headed into town, ready to travel home. The students would be arriving at the university, expecting to learn how to deal with this mortal life in language, how to sculpt something beautiful out of silence. I really don't think I can help. Perhaps I'll take to speaking in riddles, like an oracle in a lonely cell. When they get stuck or overwhelmed, I'll intone: 'Let the muscles relax, the skeleton's doing the work.' 'Using no words, describe your ideal Sabbath.' 'Remember, the end of the road is also its beginning.' 'You *are* doing it,' I'll say.

'Your own room' my sister was saying. 'Some of your own furniture.'

    'Company when you want it ...' I added.

    'How's your mother?'

    'She's doing okay.'

    ' ... peace and quiet when you don't.'

    Our grandmother was looking at us, one to the other. Neither her grandchildren nor her great-grandchildren have inherited her hazel eyes, more's the pity, or that long hawkish nose. She was beginning to nod in agreement.

    'Meals all cooked, ay? No washing up.'

    'Someone to keep an eye on you ...'

    'You wouldn't have to worry ...'

    My sister and I glanced at each other, and spoke both at once. 'Move in myself,' I muttered. She said, 'Where do I sign?'

The school bus passed, and when its noise abated all I could hear was wind in the electric wires. A man in blue overalls was closing his gate, a collie at his feet. He watched solemnly as I cycled by.

(Autumn 2004)

A hundred acres, a few ditches, some mist

VONA GROARKE

After my father died, my mother became the husband of his land. Lofty and unassailable as the aspic jelly she made one Christmas (much admired and subsequently dumped), her decision to manage the farm had all the grandeur of implausibility. Before his death, she had kept herself away from the mucky imperatives and persistently unquiet animals of the surrounding fields; I never saw her set a foot on the land that was actually worked. Her domain was the house and garden: the lawns into which sheep would occasionally break; the flowers they shattered or ate; the floors muddied by our forgetful boots; the talk over dinner of foxes and fluke; the rows of drench and tablets in the pantry; the sleep disturbed by rooks and lambing ewes. She was mindful of the fence, which was never quite as discriminating as she would have wished. It began wooden and finished as steel: in between, it was barbed, electrified and chicken-wired. But it never kept the farmlands properly at bay, or the house sufficiently discreet.

Occasionally, there would be a breach of her acknowledged domain, usually in the lambing season, when my father would bring an orphan or rejected lamb back to the kitchen. Once, he put one in the bottom oven of the Rayburn, and not even her strongest motherly instincts could overcome her conviction that the taste of wool and birth would sully every dish for months after.

She had been born and raised on Amsterdam Avenue in Manhattan; the fields of Lissoy must have been a let-down. There was nothing you could call height to which to aspire, and not even she could make a populous grid of the network of ditches and fields that passed for home. She had seen pigs at the market in Ballyhaunis when she was twelve, on her first morning in Ireland. She had heard the noise of them and had thought there was a massacre going on beneath her window. She thought of the Mafia and was terrified. The sight of the pink mass with the shiny ears and knowing eyes that threatened retribution did nothing to calm her or to win her tender advocacy for the farm animals of Ireland.

She thought she liked Nature, and had books on trees and wildflowers with whole passages underlined, that never underwent the test of comparison in the field. She had more books on roses, and had planted some under the kitchen window, but the sheep who pruned them for her one May evening also did for her horticultural desires. What was manageable appealed to her, and she must have thought the farm would be just that when she undertook to keep it on under her own clean hand. I'd say she might have wanted to sell it, and move to a bungalow in a town, there to grow roses and wake to traffic, but maybe she'd been in Ireland long enough to heed the claim of an ancestral farm passed down. She had three sons and three daughters and she might have seen herself as keeper of their farmed inheritance. Or maybe she thought she should work her assets instead of turning them to dangerously liquid cash.

Whatever the reason, my mother turned farmer in September 1977. She knew it would be a challenge, but she was confident that labour and necessity combined would surely master the dull resistance of a hundred acres in a midlands farm, and that the enterprise would thrive. Something of the American combination of doggedness and innocence stuck with her all her life. I can't believe it did her any favours.

While my father had been a part-time farmer, my mother was never a one for halves. She undertook a three-year programme of reform, largely based on research in the kind of magazines that featured news on levies and ads for the latest liver fluke pills. The red pen was out with gusto and whole paragraphs, whole pages, were underlined: big decisions were made. The first was a changeover from the cutting of hay to the making of silage, a prosaic ritual that involved molasses and old tyres, and did away entirely with the picturesque of fork-bearing men doubling as sun-gods in meadows gold with a pre-industrial glow. Now it was a tractor and, god help us, a slatted house, complete with slurry tanks and their attendant pong. Somehow the lilac never got over it. She was only branding an old-fashioned farm with the heat of the nineteen-seventies, but there was a frenzy to it that fairly singed the corners off my pastoral idyll.

Her next agricultural masterplan was to clear her fields of stones. We should have known. The silage-making machines cut lower than our fields were used to, and were more sensitive to hard objects that might shoot up and deprive the operator of an eye. I happen to be small, never before (or since) considered very much of an advantage, but apparently my proximity to the ground made me the ideal candidate for the work in hand. For what seems now to have been years, I spent my weekends home from boarding school parallel to the interrupted growth of the midlands soil.

We picked stones for hours and hours. I had a crowbar and gloves and, by midday, a general ache. We made piles with the pickings, straightened up, compared our yields. We moved on to another patch, and began again. I favoured the erection of numerous small stacks over my brother's larger statements. That way, I thought, I looked busier. There was a radio for company, and my mother's encouragement when she'd step out to survey our mounting harvest. We slept at night. We got into no trouble. The stones moved from one place to another. The machine operator enjoyed the use of both his eyes for another year. The soil may have crept into some fresh hollows, and yes, there may have been a cumulative square foot or two of new grass the following year.

Unamusing as this work was, it was bloody good training for a poet. Or at least for the poet in me. It taught me that even my homeplace was at a far remove from the romantic. Had I ever wanted to believe (and I did) that this farm, these fields were somehow lodged in a steady continuum of myth or poetic tradition, my aching back and dirt-encrusted nails would have screamed me back to a nastier, unswathed reality.

At the farthest end of the farm, reached by passing through two fairy forts that accentuated the sense of spatial warp, was a line of strong beech trees. I took my school poetry anthology there once, pre Inter Cert, and learned the whole of 'Ode to a Nightingale' with my backside mossy on a fallen trunk, ankle-high in cowslips and my own idea of a burgeoning vocation. Goldsmith's Parsonage was two fields away. From here, he made it to Trinity College to serve dinner to more fortunate counterparts. From here, eventually (his mother's small hopes and smaller income exhausted), to Scotland and to London where he heard too much of the disappointed consonants of home. He imagined a homeplace and set it down slant-wise, littered with landmarks and far more people than had ever left a mark on that townland. There's still a right of way through the bottom of the farm that would take you from the ruined Parsonage to his father's ruined church at Kilkenny West. Not much of an odyssey, god knows, not even if you count the bottomless lake or a trek through the copse of scorched birch trees that has always been, to my mind, the aftermath of a skirmish in some brutal, unspecified war.

That way went south: never a very auspicious way to go. The real road at his door, and at mine, runs east to west. My mother called it (without so much as a hint of irony) 'the main Glassan-to-Belfast road'. She may have been geographically correct, but the whole point of that road was to take you to Dublin, past Uisneach, if you truly knew where you were for. In the midlands, north and south are not political distinctions. A journey in either direction is likely to bring you nowhere: at best it could be a deviation, at worst a dead end. True journeys must be either with or against the sun: only in this path does anything visibly change. And if it wasn't change you were after, why then you could stay at home. Goldsmith must have known the truth of it when he drove his Fiddleback nag from Cork back up to his mother's exasperated door. My mother must have known the opposite when she shuffled the Irish shuffle backwards from Manhattan to Ballyhaunis to Lissoy. There simply was no going back from there. Which perhaps explains her strange obsession with having the earth turned up around her, as though there were nowhere else to go but down, no world elsewhere but this one, exposed and bluntly modernized.

My father's family, to which she subscribed through marriage in October 1947, were middle-class Catholics who bought up under favourable Land Acts and learned to keep horses and be Justices of the Peace. My father and I used to walk the farm at home to the silvery rhythm of Thomas Hood's 'I remember, I remember, the house where I was born, the little window where the sun came peeping in each morn.' It's the perfect metre for swinging a stick. Even now when I encounter the kind of language that has breath being borne away (and you'd be surprised at just how often one still does), the image that comes immediately to mind is windswept thistledown, scattered from his stick.

My father's style of agricultural practice involved minimum intervention. He let grass grow and he cut it as hay. He let sheep and cattle fatten, and he sold them on and bought younger versions. My contact with the land, through him, was superficial. I walked the fields with him, picked blackberries, and in summer helped with the hay. I confess I believed that fairies lived in the hollow trunk beside the pump. In hindsight, I see that that was a necessary and approved-of fiction. I was not supposed to have a utilitarian relationship with the land. Much as my mother's complete disregard of it was considered neither shocking nor shameful, my willingness to turn our farm into a Victorian fantasy landscape was the product of an education and an attitude my father could afford to indulge.

Now and again, I helped herd cattle from one farm to another a few miles away. My job was to block the gateways and crossroads which might have provided recalcitrant cattle with a chance to make a run for it. I'd guard the gap until the animals were through, then run ahead to the next gap, where I would flap my arms a lot and make big noises to magnify the threat of my ten-year-old self. I was doing my damnedest to act the part of a labouring swain. If my mother had only made me a pinafore, I'd have been the perfect embellishment to a psychic landscape that owed more, I see now, to

Polanski's *Tess* than to either Goldsmith's verse or the realities of any particular time and place.

As the youngest of six and a girl to boot, I got off lightly enough when it came to farm work while my father was alive. My agricultural engagements tended to be either decorative or playful: larking around with crab apples, bringing armfuls of lilac from the yard down to the house – that sort of thing. What useful tasks I did actually perform – feeding lambs with baby bottles; picking thistles out of fields of grass; opening and closing gates when bid – allowed me maximum opportunity for a romantic interpretation of our farm and what it stood for. When I first read Wordsworth, I made myself recognize the version of my homeplace that I had magicked out of the crude materials of a hundred acres, a few ditches and some mist. I had myself convinced that 'Lycidas' too was set in the fields between Tang and Tubberclair, and no amount of nationalist history could prise me from that belief.

It was the crowbar that finally accomplished that, and the cramp in my spine after six hours of picking stones as part of my mother's land-clearance plans. I was always much too poetic a child to enjoy what caused me physical discomfort. Back then, I wasn't thinking of an *ars poetica* – even pronouncing such a term would have gotten me sent to my bed – but if someone had asked me about the place of poetry in this rural life of mine, I would have known enough to position it pre-1977 when the lilac was fragrant and lavish, and the stones slumped undisturbed. After this, I forgot to look for poetry in the midst of crepuscular mists. I'd looked in more unlikely places than that, and hadn't found it. Which made me think that poetry was a little more than a pretty landscape in which I could position myself like a hired prop. I wasn't sure I liked that landscape any more, and began to think in some vague way that it might just be possible to lever poetry out of the cosy camouflage I had stuck on it, and to throw it elsewhere and maybe follow it later.

So it dawned on me that maybe poetry didn't always arrive fully formed and determinedly melancholy, but was something that could be rough and awkward, mean and full of unlovely, unfragrant things.

(I'm sure I would have realized this anyway with more, and wider, reading, but then maybe I wouldn't have bothered with that reading had I not begun to move poetry away in my mind from the sweetness of my earlier, rustic years to the proposed deliverance from all things back-breaking and sullenly agricultural.) Once I figured this much out, it wasn't such a big deal to begin to think that if it didn't always come smoothed with usage and polished with respect, then it could be written imperfectly to begin with: it could be made, unmade, written, crossed-out, written again. It could be fragile, implausible, unhelpful, unconsolatory, difficult, fraught or terrific. It could be made by people I might meet. It could even be made, to some degree, by me.

My father had written some sunny undergraduate verse (the kind that rhymed 'college' with 'knowledge'), but a life of legal casework and the duties of farming (however part-time) and six educable children had left small room for anything other than Thomas Hood and a few amusing quotes from Goldsmith. Likewise my mother, who had read the poems of Yeats (I know because I have her edition, underscored with the same robust red pen) but managed somehow to get along without much reference to them. There were no other poetry books in our house. Poetry wasn't something we held in very high regard. But then, who does? I can think of no Irish poet who talks of growing up in a family where poetry mattered a whit. I wasn't unusual, amn't unusual: my coming to it was as tricky and devious a process as it surely ought to be. Like every other poet, I discovered my subjects and my voice almost by stealth: by reading; by noticing what I was supposed to be writing; and by learning by writing that, and then eventually, not quite that.

Kavanagh was a help, despite himself. I recognized in his early work something of the same process that had made me look up from the rather less fatalistic stones of Westmeath. Of course, he was more sophisticated than I was, and had a wider and more generous nature. As a man, he had been closer to the land; had leaned in a little farther and stayed with it for longer, and been better placed to observe its coarse demands. He also had fewer choices (not all to do with poetry), and he was brave enough to choose the same road east, even though he had to walk the most of it. But Kavanagh is only one of many Irish poets who have written of the untidy relationship with the land that has often been the lot of the sons of Irish farmers. Sons who were educated out of their family farms, which then became wellsprings of imagery and vocabulary for them in their subsequent careers. Why would it not? There aren't many poets who work as farmers, and I haven't come across too many farmers who write poems, though I've read plenty of poems about the grey area between the two. And they're all, that I can think of, written by men.

I don't know why so few Irish women poets have written about their relationship with the land. Maybe they too have been educated out of it, but more thoroughly and with greater and harsher success. Maybe they were never educated into it, or given the leisure for a proper contemplation of their place in the pastoral tradition. Or possibly, their relationship with the land was as thin as my own, and they, like my mother, looked with favour on a landscape of interiors because they were never required to prove themselves the masters of the land. Maybe knowing that they wouldn't inherit it knocked the corners off their wish to join in spiritual or poetic communion with their brothers' future property. I don't know, and I'm inclined to resist any simple answers, especially from people who wouldn't know a cowpat if it was thrown at them during a panel discussion.

Of course, I know of the argument that the land itself has been written by male poets over centuries into the role of a passive female. And if the land is female and the poet is male, then maybe the female poet is obliged to light out on her own for new territory, where she will sing a new song that will have to sound a good bit different from the plaintive wail of the Shan Van Vocht or from Caitlín Ní Houlihan calling the prices at Ballymahon mart. If you live in New York that's probably not too much of a challenge, but I suppose it gets harder if what you want to write about is being a woman bringing her cattle for sale in Ballymahon mart. Likewise, if you want to write poems about the female orgasm or Class A drugs, you're unlikely to have to brush the chips of too many Irish poets, male or female, off your shoulder before you begin. But maybe, if you live in Ballymacargy and haven't been to too many raves down there, you might not know where exactly to begin or how you would put it down in a poem that lived up to its name and also to its fiery subject matter. In other words, the song might be a little too new for the words you know. It's never easy to keep one eye on tradition while fixing the other firmly on originality: it even sounds like it would give you cramp, especially when they're asking you if it's your tradition anyway, or one that's borrowed or, worse still, one that's been forced on you. And who's to say what 'original' means? (My kitten, I'm sure, would be an original poet: it gets harder to tell with people who insist on using words I know in a pattern I recognize.)

Think of Millet's painting *The Gleaners*: it shows a group of women at work, stooping in laboured positions over a harvested field. They look exhausted, but intent: put upon, but remarkably dignified. (Hospitals love this picture, especially maternity units – I've spent time in two, and yep, it's been there in both. I suppose if I had to work my full shifts with women in labour, the idea of silent suffering would seem like a joy to me too.) At the risk of over-theorizing what now seems a fairly unrevolutionary work of art, can I suggest that its gender politics would not be unrecognizable to the reader of the Irish pastoral poem? The artist has observed the women at work; he has watched them bend and buckle – he can see the strain of it, the suffering in their posture at the end of what has surely been a long and exhausting day. In thus observing, Millet made a political gesture which his contemporaries resisted and labelled 'socialist'. But is there not also a paternalistic gesture of kindness in evidence there? The women depicted are neither graceful nor beautiful, yet their labour is bathed in a golden, pre-lapsarian glow that projects solemnity and significance on them, and amplifies their moment and their lives.

By painting the women in a light traditionally preserved for more conventional heroic figures, Millet asks us to translate the three women from particular into symbolic figures. But viewing it now, almost 150 years after it was painted, we don't necessarily see the picture from Millet's point of view. Although he never was one for painting *en plein air*, we're as like to find ourselves standing some distance behind his imagined position, including his presence in our view, judging the picture as a set of images refracted through one man's talent and ideology in one time and place.

Like Millet's shadow akimbo in some imagined tillage-field, I am also me in the here and now, as beset by defining viewpoints as any artist may be. Town-dweller, reluctant and talentless gardener of a thumbnail patch of mossy grass, here I am, making much of a rural childhood that is not quite, I daresay, without its own Freudian pickings. I admit that my initial vision is probably simplistic, and therefore both reductivist and reduced. My second vision of the same place turned unlovely and punishing is no doubt an inverted version of the first, streamed through the eye of adolescence and a very great loss. Neither vision, I suppose, would be recognized by anyone else who knew that place at that time. (Not that this would matter. When has poetry ever trundled along the narrow gauge of literal truth?)

The pastoral plays with a dialogue between prettiness and suffering. It tends towards extremes and likes to idealize, usually with a particular end in sight. Goldsmith certainly had a point to make when he wrote 'The Deserted Village', and it wasn't all to do with charming old codgers and manly sporting displays. It's the kind of poem that can form the backbone of anthologies of both pastoral and political poetry. In fact, the amount of crossover between such anthologies is striking. Not that the pastoral vision, or its products, are obliged to be inherently political (though it will often lean towards a general hankering after the times before these invariably rotten ones), but its politics tend to be of the paternalistic sort, the sort that finds ready solutions to identified ills, that is comfortable with its own knowingness and gently delighted with its ability to notice and transcribe. Nor is the pastoral inimical to the lyric. While Goldsmith may not have written himself into the beguiling community of Lissoy, nor Millet have painted himself into that field of stooping women, the pastoral poetry of the twentieth century did often deign to notice the poet's own mucky boots, or to pluck a strand of golden straw from the poet's fashionably rustic duds. The tradition, it seems, is flexible and capable of powerful swerves, but what it still has not managed to get around is the fact that it has been serviced and steered by male poets mostly, and has rarely (if ever?) felt the masterful hand of an Irish woman poet.

What that leaves us with are blind spots in the Irish pastoral tradition. So what? I'm sure readers everywhere can identify blind spots of astronomical proportions in their own particular poetic galaxies. And poetry tends to like blind spots; it so often burrows where it really oughtn't to, or delves past decency and approbation. To recommend subject matter is a foolhardy thing to do. Equally, the suggestion that any particular group of people ought to be writing (more) poems – 'you know, dear, it would do you so much good' – could net you anything from a stiff rebuke to a full-blown sock in the kisser. There are no prescriptions for poetry, no magazines that you can underline in red that will point you towards elysian pastures and a better bank balance for all. And in case you're wondering: no, my mother's farming career was not an unqualified success. She rented out the farm, planted no more rose bushes, and was planning her move to a house in the town right up to when she died.

(Winter 2001–2)

Ballistics

TIM ROBINSON

Flat in long grass, I watch the bomber coming in low over the palm trees. As its bomb doors gape open I tilt my bren gun up and fire into the dark of its belly ... Battle is the shift and crisscross of death-lines in the hand of space; one is supposed to read them, lurk in their interstices, then run between or under or magnificently over-leap them, to claim a vantage and reconfigure them. However, I had no bullets in my gun to bring the plane down in flames, and who-ever was in it had no bomb to smear me around the walls of a crater; the episode was a practice-run, a moment in a military exer-cise that swept over me in a mind-splitting roar and otherwise left me for long hours to contemplate ants crawling up grass stems. But it was a thrill, even if I had to smile at myself wrestling with my bren gun, which toppled over at the crucial moment; I was invinci-ble, a solo hero, like the man in a war film I saw once who lobbed a stick of dynamite into the path of the fighter diving to strafe him, causing the plane to disintegrate satisfactorily in a whirl of black smoke.

Ballistic space, the space imposed by weapons of death-at-a-dis-tance, with its fields of fire, possible and actual trajectories, its terrains denied and zones of security and danger, is a playground mankind exults in. Show a male child a gun, the sociobiologists say, and he climbs back up the spiral staircase of the genes to the African savannahs, where a million generations were spent killing animals with throwing-sticks; that was the age of the world in which the qualities of manliness were born, and ours is the age in which they have entered into a suicide pact with technology.

Not so, womankind. During the war my parents were living near a target of the Luftwaffe. When sirens howled in the night and Daddy went out in his bomb-proof ARP hat, my mother used to crouch beneath a great stone slab in the larder with us two children gathered under her (it was the most dangerous place in the house, but how was she to know?) and try to assure us that the forces thundering around us were all protective: 'Was that one of ours, Mummy?' we would crow whenever a bang shook the house, and she would wail, 'Yes! That was one of ours!'

As it happened, no bombs fell in our suburb and we children never saw the ugliness of war. Some mornings we were delighted to find trees and bushes hung with ribbons of aluminium foil, the chaff dropped by German bombers to confuse radar signals. Once when we had stolen away, unknown to our parents, to dig out spent bullets from a sandpit used by the Home Guard for target practice, we stirred up a puddle with some yellowish oily stuff in it, which suddenly exploded into a delightful momentary fountain. When Flying Fortresses began to be talked of by the adults, my imagination was fired and I made many drawings of winged castles that rose in battlements rimmed by cannon. The family moved to Ilkley in Yorkshire shortly after VJ Day, and in subsequent years one of the ways in which I came to know the Moor was as a network of routes for crossing it under sniper fire: crawling through stands of bracken, worming along little watercourses, sprinting from the shelter of one boulder to the next. At that age my zest for life required an enemy to enliven the action; the War was in the past and I had missed it.

When I did find myself in a sort of war, as a National Serviceman in the RAF towards the end of the Malayan 'Emergency', I was inexcusably (so it seems to me now) unconcerned with its moral and political dimensions. The hothouse of adolescence, which had protected me from the tedium of my latter years in school, the savagery of Basic Training and the ice of a nine-month radar course in huts on the Wiltshire Downs, seemed to expand in Malaya to enclose a whole fervent world. The towers of cumulus pulsing with lightning all round the evening horizon, the exquisite girls who grouped themselves like bouquets and garlands of flowers in the streets or on the beach, the abyssal silences between gong strokes in the Buddhist temple I haunted, the lurid backstreet nightlife to which fellow-conscripts less inhibited than I were keen to introduce me, all existed in the same perfumed atmosphere as my own rampant blooms of knowledge, desire, religion and poetry.

The malign aesthetics of weaponry took root in this tropical garden too. After some months spent puzzling into defective radar sets in the quiet of the servicing bay, I was banished to work on aircraft on the dispersal strip, where wing surfaces grew too hot to touch in the afternoons and one's shoulderblades made dents in the tarmac when one lay under the fuselage of a fighter. This was supposed to be punishment for arguing with the sergeant, who regarded me as lazy and insubordinate (whereas I was merely incompetent and distrait); but in fact I preferred the ferocious sunlight on the strip, the vigorous camaraderie, even the stinging blast from jets manoeuvring on the ground, to the torpid slacking of the bay. My letters home were rhapsodies:

… a much better life, spacious and turbulent with noise and movement, and full of hard angular facts, sun, wind and blue sky; a welcome relief from intellectual questionings. The expanse of sky is immense. Inland, mountains show far away over lines of dark green palm forests, and towards the sea runs the long air-strip, past the line of Canberras gleaming in the sun, past the control-tower, ending right on the beach. The sea shows through a last screen of curving palms, and immediately opposite rises Penang Island – paradise island – sunlit and forested hills behind the busy harbour, white houses showing around the top of Mount Pleasant (its actual name). One towering white cumulus cloud is invariably anchored there, trebling the height of the island, like a fantastic whorl of cream on a small cake. In the early morning the island's hills are banded with layers of mist and the guardian cloud rises majestically through white sheets of stratus. The first jet-engine wakes and breaks the ice of the morning silence, and a Venom roars along the runway to blast its way into the air, rising slowly against the mass of the island, banking and climbing over the shoulders of its hills to disappear into a sky no longer a blue ceiling but a palace of invisible corridors and stairs. All day there is a coming and going: groups of Venoms and Canberras perform endless evolutions and circuits above, Valettas and Dakotas, Hastings, Hermes and Argonauts arrive majestically, occasional odd specimens drop in and everyone stops work to argue their names – Beaufighters, Provosts, Doves, Pembrokes, Pioneers, Austers, wind-tossed Tiger Moths, immense Lincolns creeping down the sky and almost overshadowing the hangar, Bristol Freighters and Vampires.

The Canberra is one of the most beautiful man-made things I have seen. Eight of them stand in line here, crouched with their noses low, every contour taut and purposeful, rounded poised motionless bulk giving an appearance of weight and power almost belied by the slim long engines. They move down to the end of the runway in solemn whispering procession, and turn into position one by one. Each pauses for a few moments letting the engines rise to full power, then releases the brakes to slide slowly forward and accelerate steadily, until first the nose and then the wing-wheels leave the ground as it streaks past our dispersal-strip. At that climactic moment the engines are battering the air with a rich bellying thunder, a gamut of sound from a thin speed-whisper to great dark waves of din shuddering the ground and gripping the buildings with giant hands, undertones of savagery and war. The power and the menace die to distant thunder and grumble over the horizon, the still clouds reaffirm silence, the heat nails sound to the earth. Then the Canberra returns, power sublimated into speed, swooping silently towards us and breaking into a great climbing turn sliding easily over the sky as the shriek hits us like a wave breaking on the shore. What a bomber, to climb more steeply and manoeuvre more adroitly, fly faster and higher than any fighter! One sees why they carry no guns!

What more could the heart desire – a finer ballet in a more romantic setting? ...

But what was it about, this savage parade? The elusive Chin Peng lurked somewhere in Malaya or over the border in Thailand; we were not told why his terrorist bands had to be exterminated or what they were fighting for, nor did we ask. Only once did I see the planes taking off in anger, as it were:

Worked all Saturday from 5.30 a.m. to 5.30 p.m., all for some terrorists causing trouble down south. I remember loading rockets by yellow moonlight before dawn, and the Canberras and Venoms taking off at first light (Canberras climbing implacably, black against the green-grey eastern sky, each trailing two long wavering streamers of vapour). And at midday bombs, and in the afternoon, when we were tired and our eyes beginning to feel gritty and there was an awful clarity of light under the metallic heat of the sun, we were battering open boxes and hauling out the long heavy chains of ammunition for the cannon; beautiful things to handle, each bullet about 8' long with bright brass and black enamel, richly glittering weighty ropes of them. Snatching meals while the planes were out on each strike, hurrying to meet them when they came in and rectify any snags and unload and reload etc. And what a day for the poor bandits. They ambushed an Aussy patrol in the morning and killed three, and lost two men in the ensuing battle, and then our strikes were mounted in an immediate follow-up (these are the only times their positions are known for bombing, when they meet a patrol like that). So they were chivvied through the jungle with bombs bursting and rockets shrieking and Venoms diving with their automatic cannon pumping bullets at the treetops, and finally (in theory) into the arms of encircling patrols. All five of them, no doubt.

In general we knew, or thought we knew, that such sorties did no good and no harm, that these thousands of missiles would fall into the forest and be buried in leafmould. It was said that the rockets the Venoms carried were too crude to hit a target, but that the noise they made in smashing through trees was effective in demoralizing the enemy. Perhaps we accepted such opinions as palliatives to our consciences; certainly we felt no ill-will towards the jungle shades. The reasons for the Emergency, its dark roots forking and reforking down through the Independence Movement and the resistance under Japanese occupation, into the long Imperial past, were sometimes discussed in the circle of expatriates and local intellectuals I came to frequent, but I never joined in, aware of my ignorance and obsessed by internal debate as I was. Often I visited the temple of Ayer Itam on the island, heard the gongs, 'so slow that every stroke seemed the last, a draining of the blood out of the world', contemplated the house-high nut-brown Teaching Buddha sitting with raised hand behind threads of incense rising from joss-sticks. Once I brought one of those 'hard angular facts' learned on the strip to him, but 'he just sat there and, as always, said nothing ...'

... He might have told me the reason for this: On Thursday the Venoms went on rocket practice. Early in the morning a tractor towed onto the strip a train of low trolleys stacked with rockets – heavy cylinders about 6' across and 1'6" long, of concrete (for practice purposes) backed by a metal tube about 4' long crudely finned at the tail. These were loaded onto the fighters, two or four under each wing, close by the fuselage. The planes trouped off, and came back at odd times of the day. A few came back at lunchtime when I was standing by. One of them for some reason had not fired its rockets. I went out to ask the pilot of the plane next to it how the wireless had behaved. As I approached him there was an explosion and a great rushing noise like a continued explosion from the other plane and a rocket cut a groove across the tarmac, hit a lump at the edge and I watched its trajectory high over the palm trees some 150 yards away. Behind the plane a man was lying on his back where he had been thrown from working on the rockets under the wing; his forearm stood up in the air oddly. Someone was running and shrieking 'Ambulance!' and someone else was crouched whimpering; everyone was running and calling; then they stopped, and someone brought a sheet of canvas, because he was dead ...

In reading through these diary-like letters (carefully dated and preserved in order by my mother and now, after her death, returned to me as if finally deemed undeliverable) I notice certain tactful omissions and elisions, and I wonder why I worried her with this episode, which I had to follow up with assurances that such accidents happened extremely rarely and that I was in no danger. However, two subjective details of the event did remain unmentioned, and have often resurfaced in my thoughts. First, while all that commotion was taking place – and it was over in a few moments – I was following the rocket's flight with my eye. Though aware of the sudden vortex of distress off to one side of me, and the death at its still centre, I was fixated on the great leap and distant fall of the inert lump of concrete and metal, as if testimony to every detail of its parabolic arc would be required of me. And secondly, and hardly more than a second later, finding myself face to face with the young pilot officer I was about to salute, who had just ⁻tepped out of the cockpit and still wore the gaunt marks of his oxy-mask, I asked him about the wireless, as if it were of prime importance to hold to the procedures of normality. He looked at me astonished, then said politely that the wireless was in order. He might even have been grateful; a crevasse in time had opened before us, I had stepped across, he had followed, and it had closed again behind us. In fact we had all got across it in one way or another, except for the lad who died.

(Winter 2000–1)

Notes on contributors

JOHN BANVILLE's novels include *Birchwood*, *Kepler*, *The Book of Evidence*, *The Untouchable*, and *The Sea*, which won the 2005 Man Booker Prize. 'The Poor Old Horse' is from *Dublin Review* 17 (Winter 2004–5).

ANGELA BOURKE is Professor in the Department of Irish Language and Literature at University College Dublin. Her books include *The Burning of Bridget Cleary* and a biography of Maeve Brennan. 'Adventures with Old Things' is from *Dublin Review* 4 (Autumn 2001).

CIARAN CARSON's collections of poems include *First Language*, which won the 1993 T.S. Eliot Prize. He is also the author of versions of Dante's *Inferno* and *The Táin*, and of prose works including *The Star Factory*, *Last Night's Fun* and *Fishing for Amber*. 'This Is What Libraries Are For' is from *Dublin Review* 4 (Autumn 2001).

AMIT CHAUDHURI's novels include *Afternoon Raag*, *Freedom Song* and *A New World*, which won the Los Angeles Times Book Prize in 2000. 'The Shadow Line' is from *Dublin Review* 16 (Autumn 2004).

CATRIONA CROWE is Senior Archivist at the National Archives of Ireland. 'The View from Street Level' is from *Dublin Review* 24 (Autumn 2006).

BRIAN DILLON is the author of *In the Dark Room*, which won the Irish Book Award for non-fiction in 2006. 'Lost Time Accidents' is from *Dublin Review* 19 (Summer 2005).

ANNE ENRIGHT's books include *The Portable Virgin*, a collection of stories, and *What Are You Like?*, which won the Royal Society of Authors Encore Prize for best second novel in 2000. 'Five, Four, Three, Two, One' is from *Dublin Review* 1 (Winter 2000–1) and subsequently appeared in *Making Babies*.

Notes on contributors

ROY FOSTER is Carroll Professor of Irish History at Hertford College, Oxford. His books include *Modern Ireland 1600–1972* and a two-volume biography of W.B. Yeats. 'The Red and the Green' is from *Dublin Review* 24 (Autumn 2006).

VONA GROARKE is the author of four collections of poems: *Shale*, *Other People's Houses*, *Fiction* and *Juniper Street*. 'A Hundred Acres, a Few Ditches, Some Mist' is from *Dublin Review* 5 (Winter 2001–2).

SELINA GUINNESS edited *The New Irish Poets*, an anthology. 'These Derelict Fields' is from *Dublin Review* 19 (Summer 2005).

SEAMUS HEANEY's collections of poems include *Death of a Naturalist*, *North*, *Seeing Things* and *District and Circle*. His essays were gathered most recently in *Finders Keepers: Selected Prose 1971–2001*. He was awarded the Nobel Prize for Literature in 1995. 'Sixth Sense, Seventh Heaven' is from *Dublin Review* 8 (Autumn 2002).

MICHAEL HOFMANN is the author of four collections of poems. His criticism was gathered in *Behind the Lines*. He has translated numerous works of prose and poetry from the German, by writers including Franz Kafka, Herta Müller and Ernst Jünger. 'On Translating Joseph Roth' is from *Dublin Review* 8 (Autumn 2002).

ANN MARIE HOURIHANE is the author of *She Moves through the Boom*. She is a columnist with the *Irish Times*. '"She's live, she's modern …"' is from *Dublin Review* 6 (Spring 2002).

KATHLEEN JAMIE's books of poems include *The Tree House*, which won the Forward Prize for best collection in 2004. She is also the author of *Among Muslims*, a travel book. 'Sabbath' is from *Dublin Review* 16 (Autumn 2004) and subsequently appeared in Jamie's essay collection *Findings*; it is republished here by kind permission of the publisher, Sort Of Books.

MOLLY MCCLOSKEY is the author of two collections of short stories and of *Protection*, a novel. 'If a Guy Doesn't Think This Is Fun …' is from *Dublin Review* 16 (Autumn 2004).

PATRICK MCGRATH's works include two collections of short stories and the novels *The Grotesque*, *Spider* and *Asylum*. 'Letter from Ground Zero' is from *Dublin Review* 5 (Winter 2001–2).

DEREK MAHON's collections of poems include *Night-Crossing*, *The Hunt by Night* and *The Hudson Letter*. He was awarded the David Cohen Prize for Literature in 2007. 'Yeats and the Lights of Dublin' is from *Dublin Review* 8 (Autumn 2002).

CHRISTINA HUNT MAHONY is the author of *Contemporary Irish Literature*, a critical survey. 'Crossing the Delaware' is from *Dublin Review* 14 (Spring 2004).

LIA MILLS is the author of two novels and of *In Your Face*, a chronicle of illness and recovery. 'Boarders' is from *Dublin Review* 21 (Winter 2005–6).

ANDREW O'HAGAN is the author of three novels, including *Personality*, which won the 2003 James Tait Black Memorial Prize, and of *The Missing*, a work of non-fiction. 'A Dublin Journal' is from *Dublin Review* 10 (Spring 2003).

GLENN PATTERSON's novels include *Burning Your Own*, which won the Betty Trask Award, *Fat Lad* and *Number 5*. 'Writing Against the Writing on the Wall' is from *Dublin Review* 14 (Spring 2004).

TIM ROBINSON's books include the two-volume *Stones of Aran* and *Connemara: Listening to the Wind*, which won the Irish Book Award for non-fiction in 2007. 'Ballistics' is from *Dublin Review* 1 (Winter 2000–1) and subsequently appeared in Robinson's essay collection *My Time in Space*; it is republished here by kind permission of the publisher, Lilliput Press.

IAN SANSOM's books include *Ring Road*, a novel, and *The Truth About Babies*. 'Shalom à la crème' is from *Dublin Review* 26 (Spring 2007).

GEORGE SZIRTES's collections of poems include *Metro* and *Reel*, which won the T.S. Eliot Prize in 2004. He has translated works by László Krasznahorkai, Sándor Márai and other Hungarian novelists and poets. 'Fables of Home' is from *Dublin Review* 5 (Winter 2001–2).

COLM TÓIBÍN is the author of novels including *The Blackwater Lightship* and *The Master*, which won the International IMPAC Dublin Literary Award and the Los Angeles Times Book Prize; travel books; and *Love in a Dark Time*, a collection of essays. 'Barcelona, 1975' is from *Dublin Review* 18 (Spring 2005).

MAURICE WALSH's book on foreign correspondents and the Irish revolution is to be published in 2008. 'Good Works for the Locals' is from *Dublin Review* 17 (Winter 2004–5).

Subscriptions, back issues, selected content and a complete index:

www.thedublinreview.com